COLORWAYS

WATERCOLOR FLOWERS

TIPS, TECHNIQUES, AND STEP-BY-STEP LESSONS FOR LEARNING TO PAINT WHIMSICAL ARTWORK IN VIBRANT WATERCOLOR

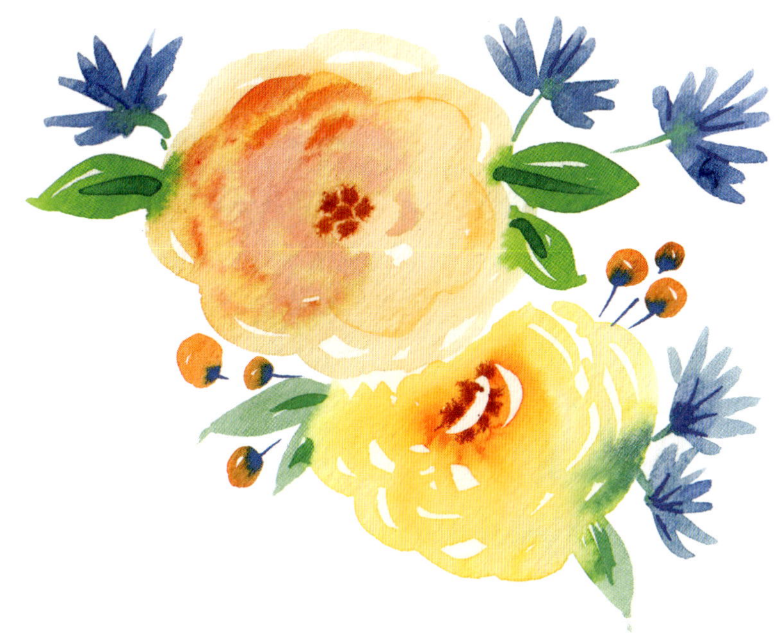

BLEY HACK

Quarto Knows
Inspiring | Educating | Creating | Entertaining

Brimming with creative inspiration, how-to projects, and useful information to enrich your everyday life, Quarto Knows is a favorite destination for those pursuing their interests and passions. Visit our site and dig deeper with our books into your area of interest: Quarto Creates, Quarto Cooks, Quarto Homes, Quarto Lives, Quarto Drives, Quarto Explores, Quarto Gifts, or Quarto Kids.

First published in 2018 by Walter Foster Publishing, an imprint of The Quarto Group.
26391 Crown Valley Parkway, Suite 220, Mission Viejo, CA 92691, USA.
T (949) 380-7510 **F** (949) 380-7575 **www.QuartoKnows.com**

Walter Foster Publishing titles are also available at discount for retail, wholesale, promotional, and bulk purchase. For details, contact the Special Sales Manager by email at specialsales@quarto.com or by mail at The Quarto Group, Attn: Special Sales Manager, 100 Cummings Center, Suite 265D, Beverly, MA 01915, USA.

ISBN: 978-1-63322-612-8

Digital edition published in 2018
eISBN: 978-1-63322-613-5

Page layout: Melissa Gerber

Printed in China
10 9 8 7 6 5 4 3

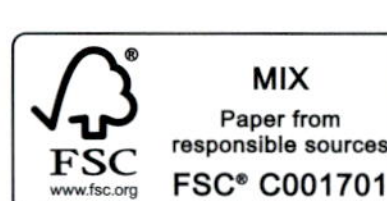

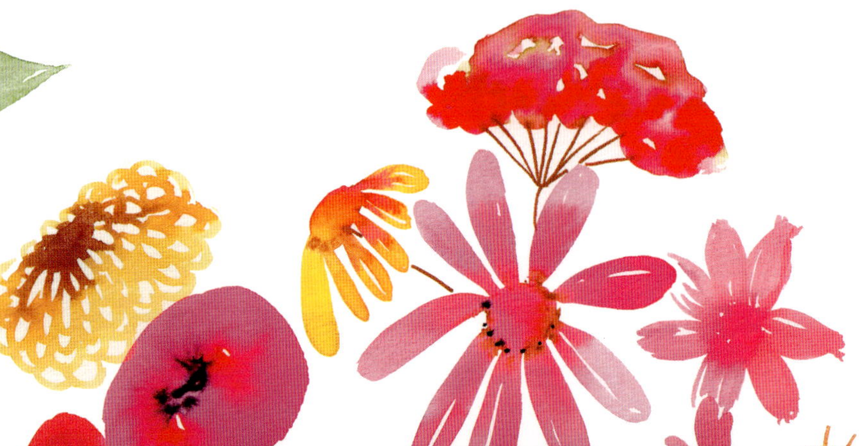

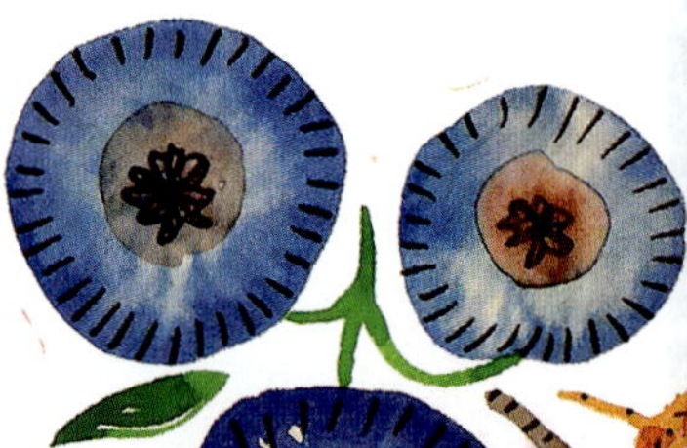

TABLE of CONTENTS

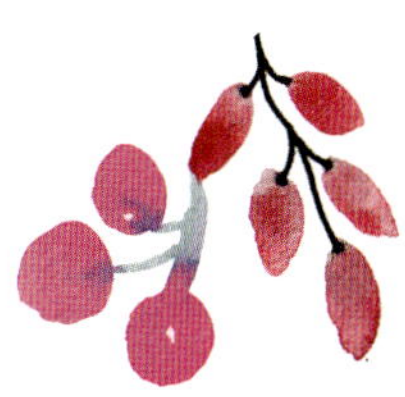

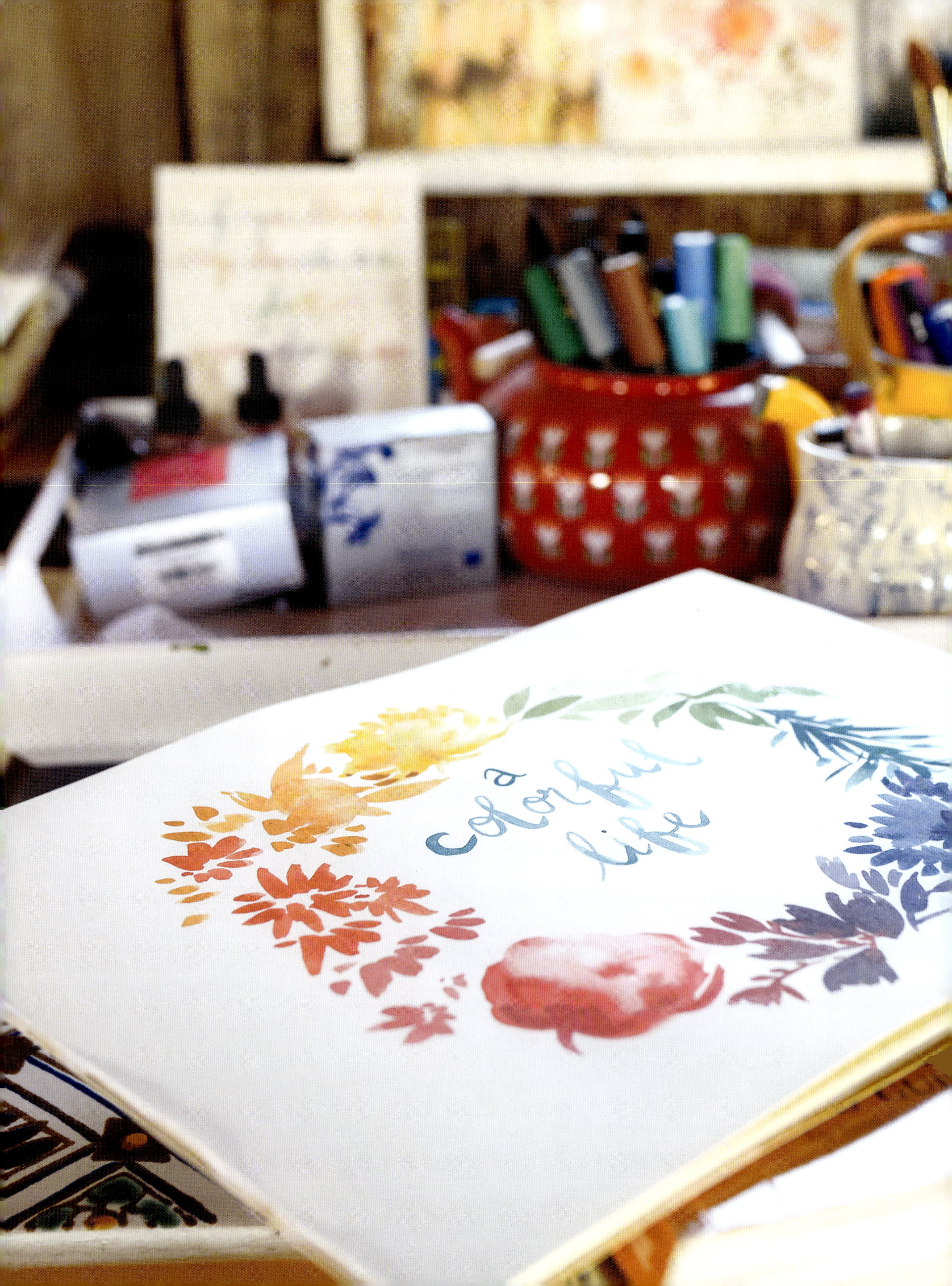
a colorful life

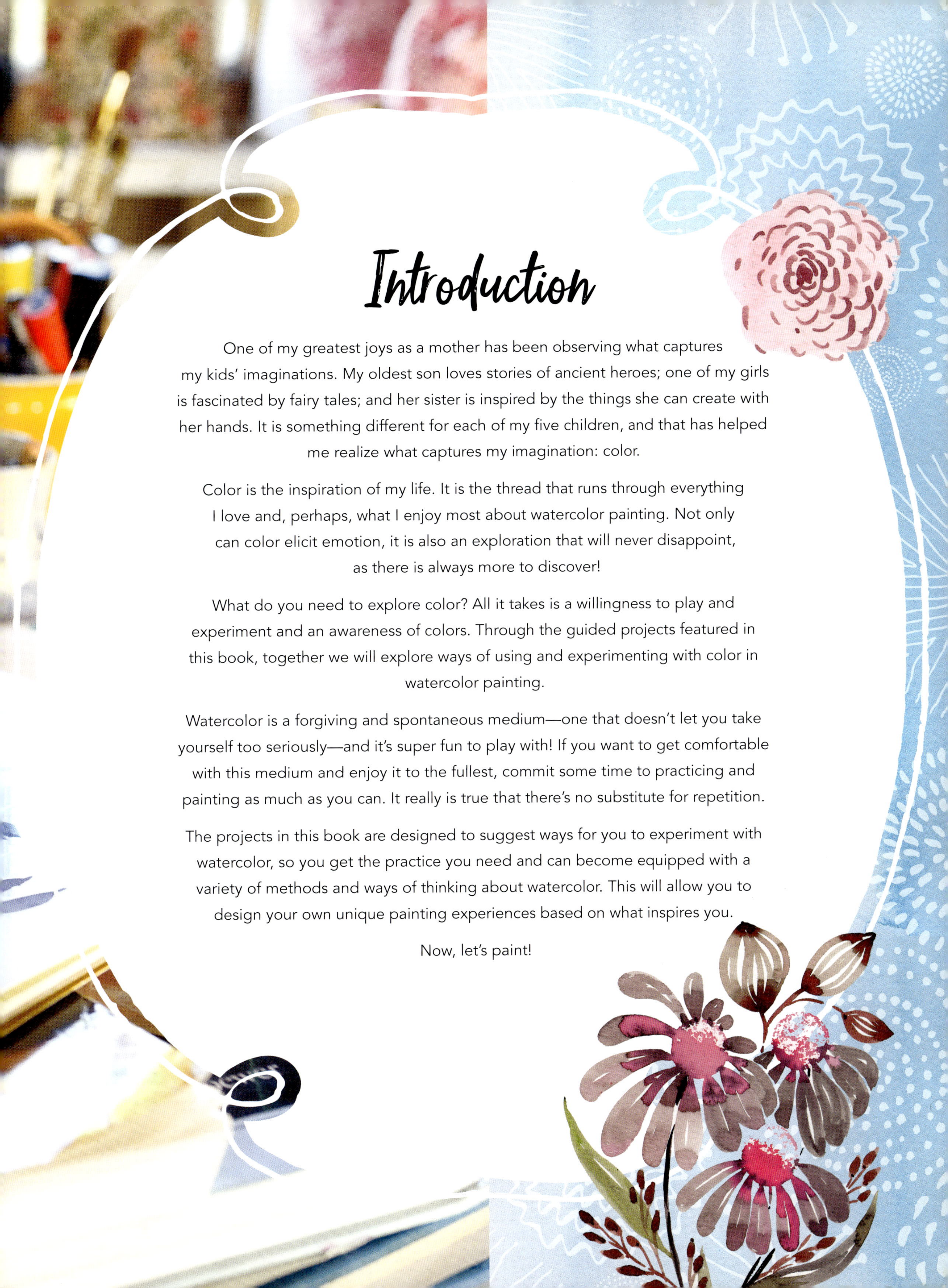

Introduction

One of my greatest joys as a mother has been observing what captures my kids' imaginations. My oldest son loves stories of ancient heroes; one of my girls is fascinated by fairy tales; and her sister is inspired by the things she can create with her hands. It is something different for each of my five children, and that has helped me realize what captures my imagination: color.

Color is the inspiration of my life. It is the thread that runs through everything I love and, perhaps, what I enjoy most about watercolor painting. Not only can color elicit emotion, it is also an exploration that will never disappoint, as there is always more to discover!

What do you need to explore color? All it takes is a willingness to play and experiment and an awareness of colors. Through the guided projects featured in this book, together we will explore ways of using and experimenting with color in watercolor painting.

Watercolor is a forgiving and spontaneous medium—one that doesn't let you take yourself too seriously—and it's super fun to play with! If you want to get comfortable with this medium and enjoy it to the fullest, commit some time to practicing and painting as much as you can. It really is true that there's no substitute for repetition.

The projects in this book are designed to suggest ways for you to experiment with watercolor, so you get the practice you need and can become equipped with a variety of methods and ways of thinking about watercolor. This will allow you to design your own unique painting experiences based on what inspires you.

Now, let's paint!

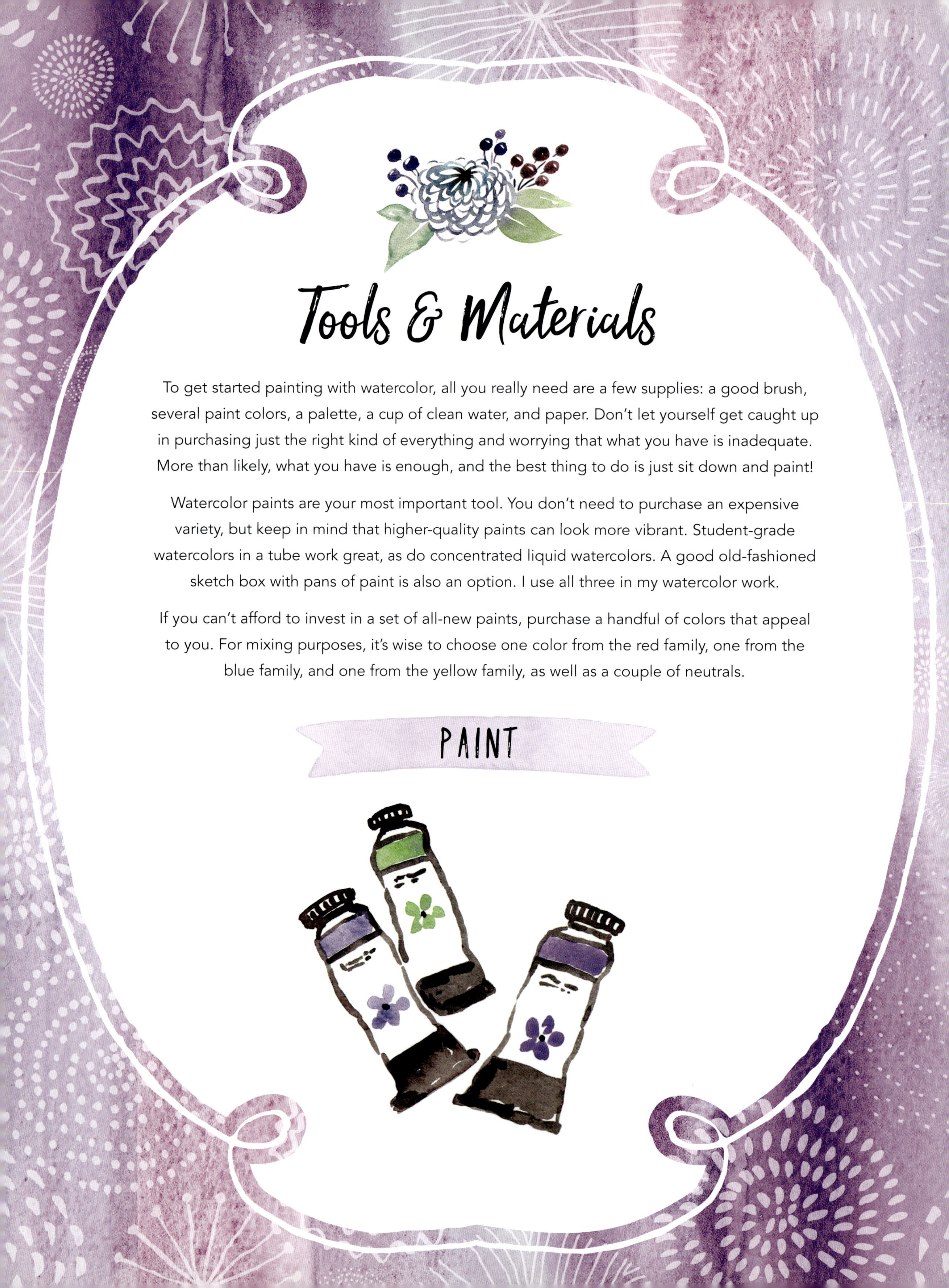

Tools & Materials

To get started painting with watercolor, all you really need are a few supplies: a good brush, several paint colors, a palette, a cup of clean water, and paper. Don't let yourself get caught up in purchasing just the right kind of everything and worrying that what you have is inadequate. More than likely, what you have is enough, and the best thing to do is just sit down and paint!

Watercolor paints are your most important tool. You don't need to purchase an expensive variety, but keep in mind that higher-quality paints can look more vibrant. Student-grade watercolors in a tube work great, as do concentrated liquid watercolors. A good old-fashioned sketch box with pans of paint is also an option. I use all three in my watercolor work.

If you can't afford to invest in a set of all-new paints, purchase a handful of colors that appeal to you. For mixing purposes, it's wise to choose one color from the red family, one from the blue family, and one from the yellow family, as well as a couple of neutrals.

PAINT

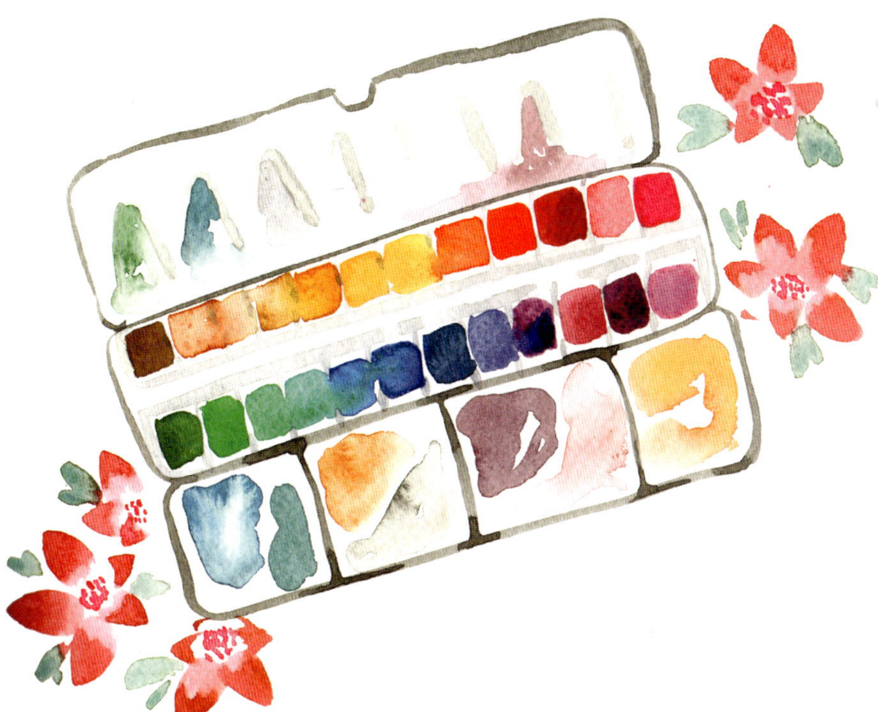

PALETTE

Unless you purchase a paint box with a built-in palette, you will need a separate palette to put your paints on, as well as for mixing. There are many palettes to choose from, but a simple option often works just as well as the fancier ones.

Keep similar colors next to each other on your palette for easier use.

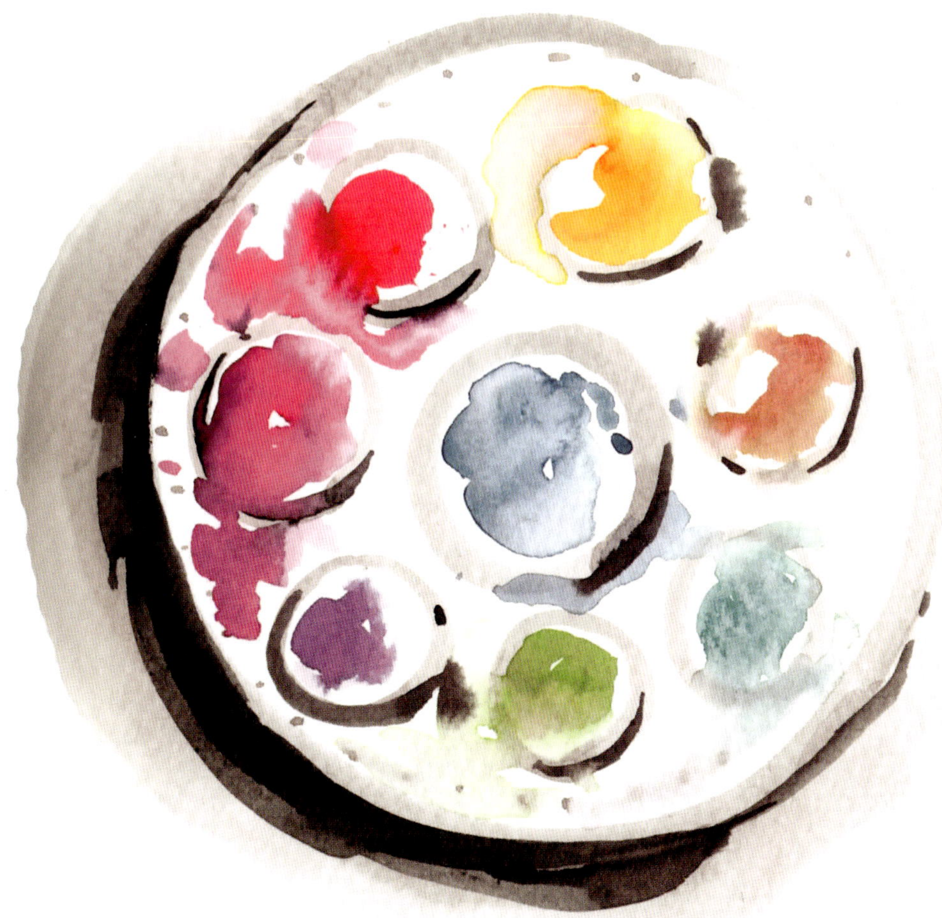

BRUSHES

When I first started painting with watercolor, brushes were one of the most mysterious supplies to me. What kinds did I need, and what sizes should they be? What type of fiber did I want, and in what shape? The only way to figure out the style and type of brush you most enjoy working with is through experimentation. Over time, I discovered that I prefer a small, round, size-6 to -8 brush for detail work; a large, round, size-16 brush for loose floral work; and a water brush for lettering. These are my three workhorse brushes, and I've been using a couple of them for more than 20 years.

Buy the best quality you can afford, and keep in mind that synthetic fibers can make great brushes!

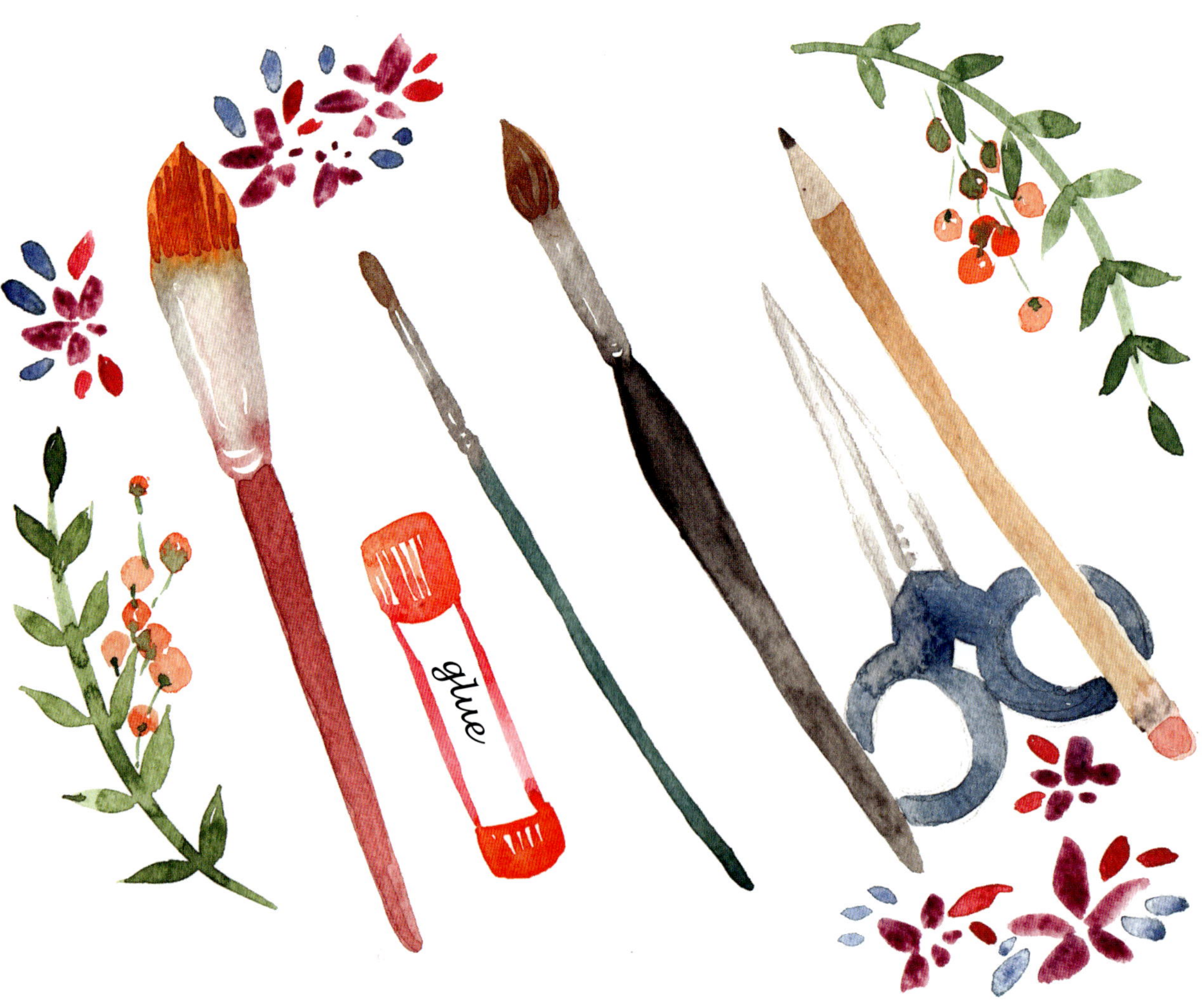

PAPER

For the greatest success when working with watercolor paints, purchase watercolor paper. Watercolor paper comes in hot-pressed and cold-pressed varieties and in three standard weights: 90-lb., 140-lb., and 300-lb. A good all-purpose paper is 140-lb. cold-pressed paper, which is widely available in many sizes. Rough watercolor paper has plenty of "tooth," or raised areas, which add texture to your art. I also like using a 9" x 12" pad. There's no need to spend a lot to get good paper. Local art-supply and craft stores carry high-quality pads at reasonable prices.

You may also find it useful to keep a sketchbook to paint in. Keeping all your pages in one place is a fun way to see how your art progresses over time.

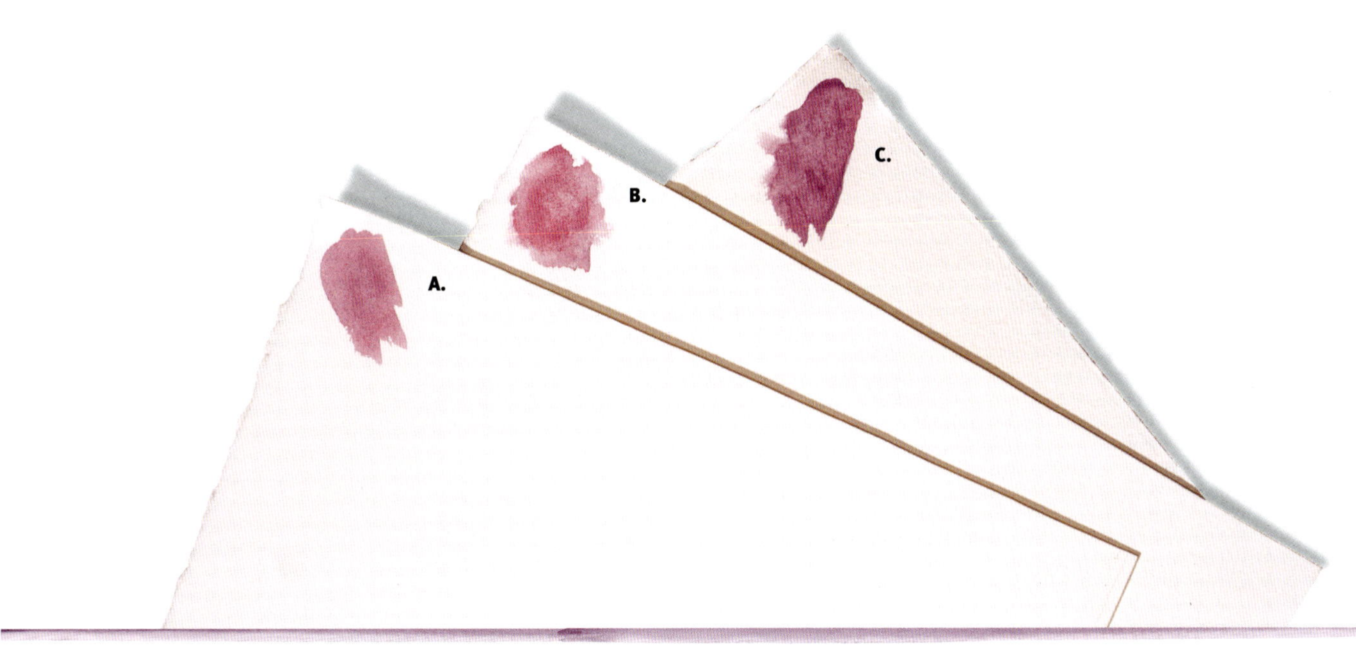

Other Materials

In addition to paint, brushes, and paper, you may want the following items:

Water cup: I use an old jam jar with a folded paper towel placed underneath on which to dab my brush.

Pencil: Keep it handy for drawing guidelines.

Large tray: This is great for holding your supplies, especially if there's room for your pad of paper too. Then, when you are finished working, you can simply pick up the tray and put it away.

Watercolor Techniques

Learning a few simple watercolor techniques will make painting much more accessible and enjoyable for you! Here are some techniques you may want to use while painting colorful flowers using watercolor.

WASH

This technique is used to cover a large area with flat color. To create a wash, load your brush with a wet consistency of your chosen color, and then drag the side of the brush across the paper.

Add visual interest to a flat wash by dropping in another paint color while the first layer remains wet.

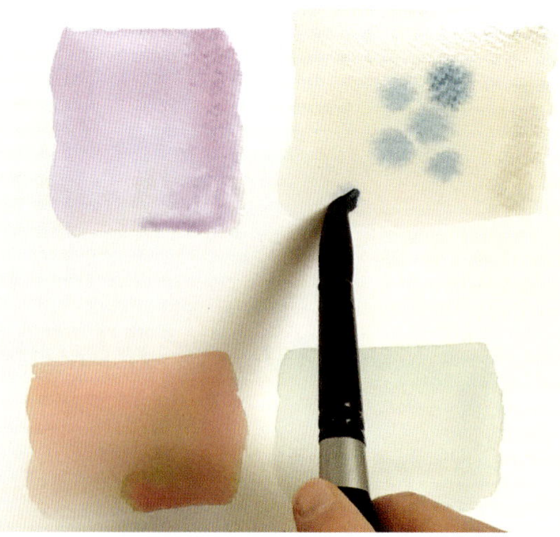

WET-INTO-WET

This technique can be used for all kinds of subjects and lends a spontaneous feel to a painting.

First, create a wet silhouette of the object you wish to paint.

Then load your brush with color, and touch the brush to the outline of the wet area.

For this flower, I also defined its center with a separate touch of color.

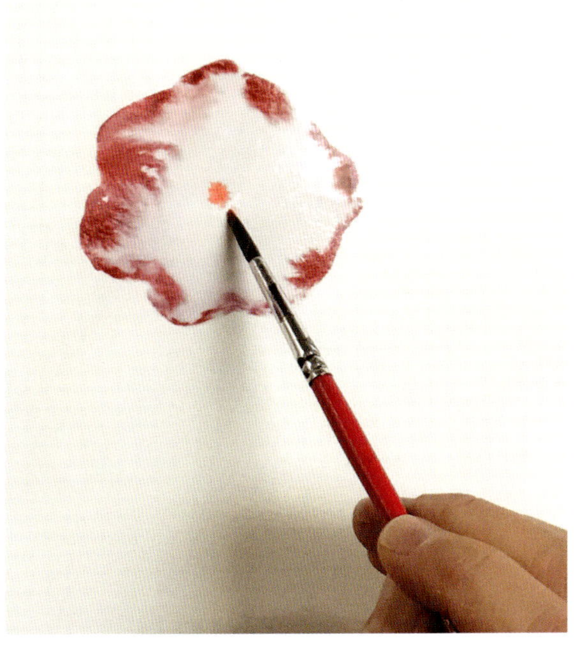

DRYBRUSHING

Useful for creating foliage and other accents, the drybrush technique offers you more control over your paint. Simply load your brush with color, and paint directly onto dry paper.

Varying the speed at which you make your brushstrokes can give them a feathery look.

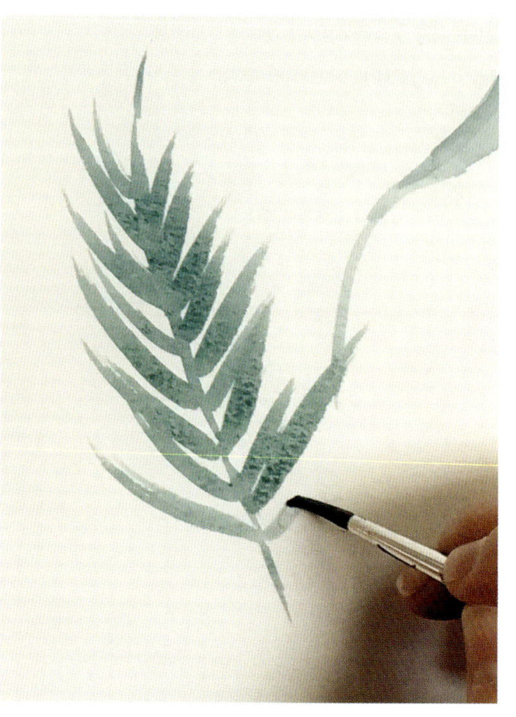

STAMPING

For this method, use your brush or another absorbent material to soak up the paint, and then stamp the shape onto your paper.

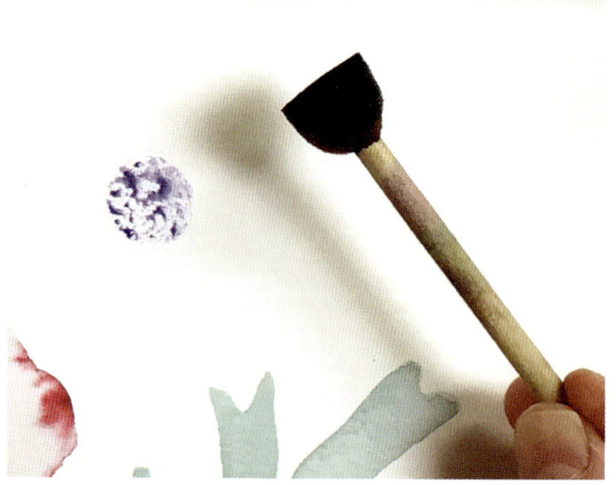

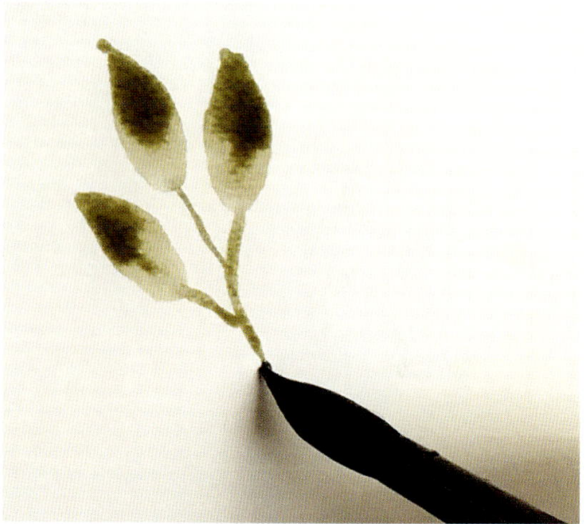

Add stems to connect your stamped shapes and create beautiful botanical foliage.

LAYERING

This technique can be used to create depth in a painting and simply means painting a second or third layer of color over a base color. Be sure to let the base color dry fully or the colors will bleed into each other.

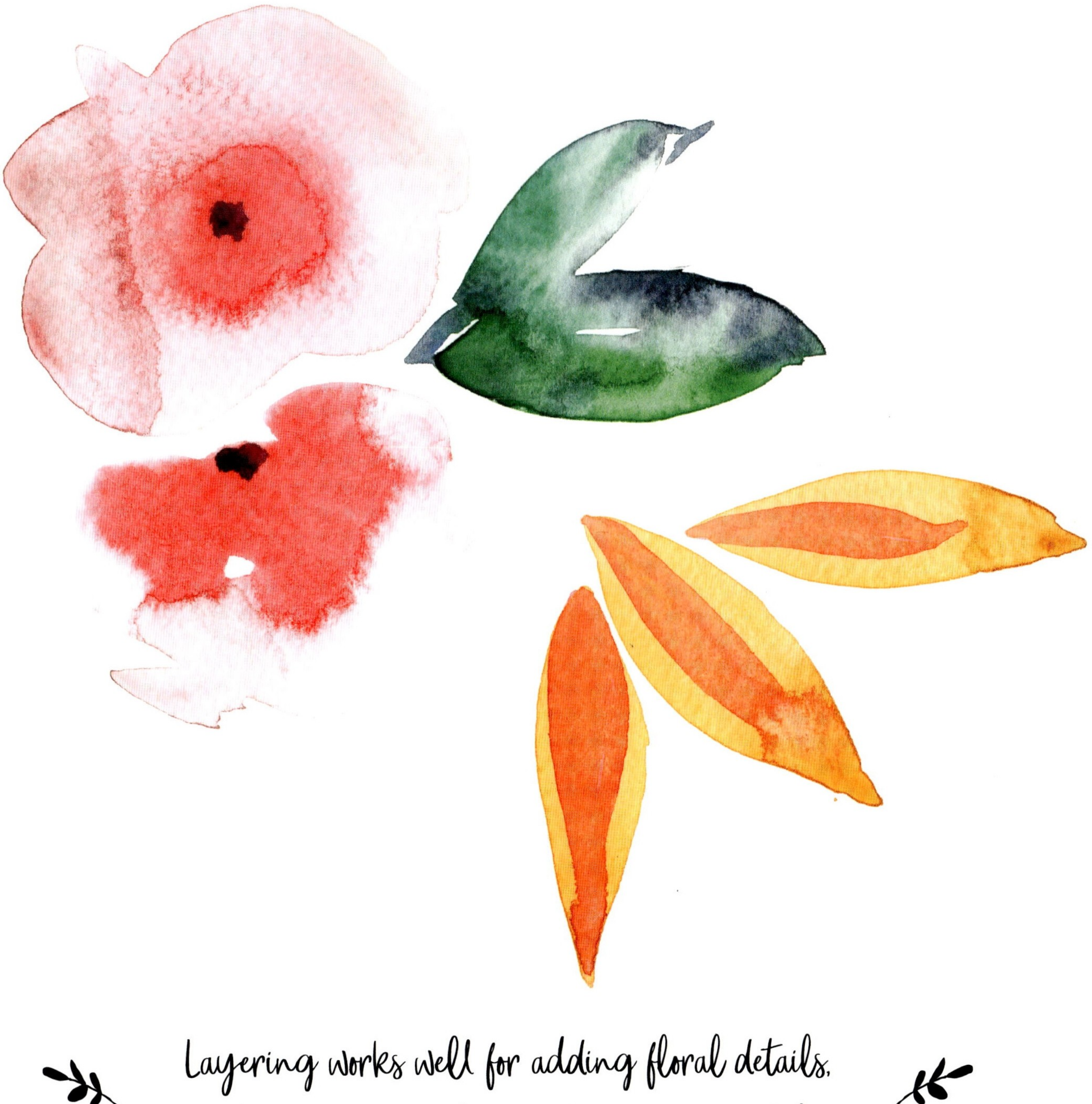

Layering works well for adding floral details, such as veins in a leaf or shadows on a petal.

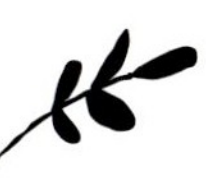

PATTERNS

Another fun way to use your brush: combining its basic marks to create all-over patterns. For these examples, I used the natural shape of my brush to make marks in a sequence and form a patterned effect. Patterns make a lovely element to add into the background of a floral piece.

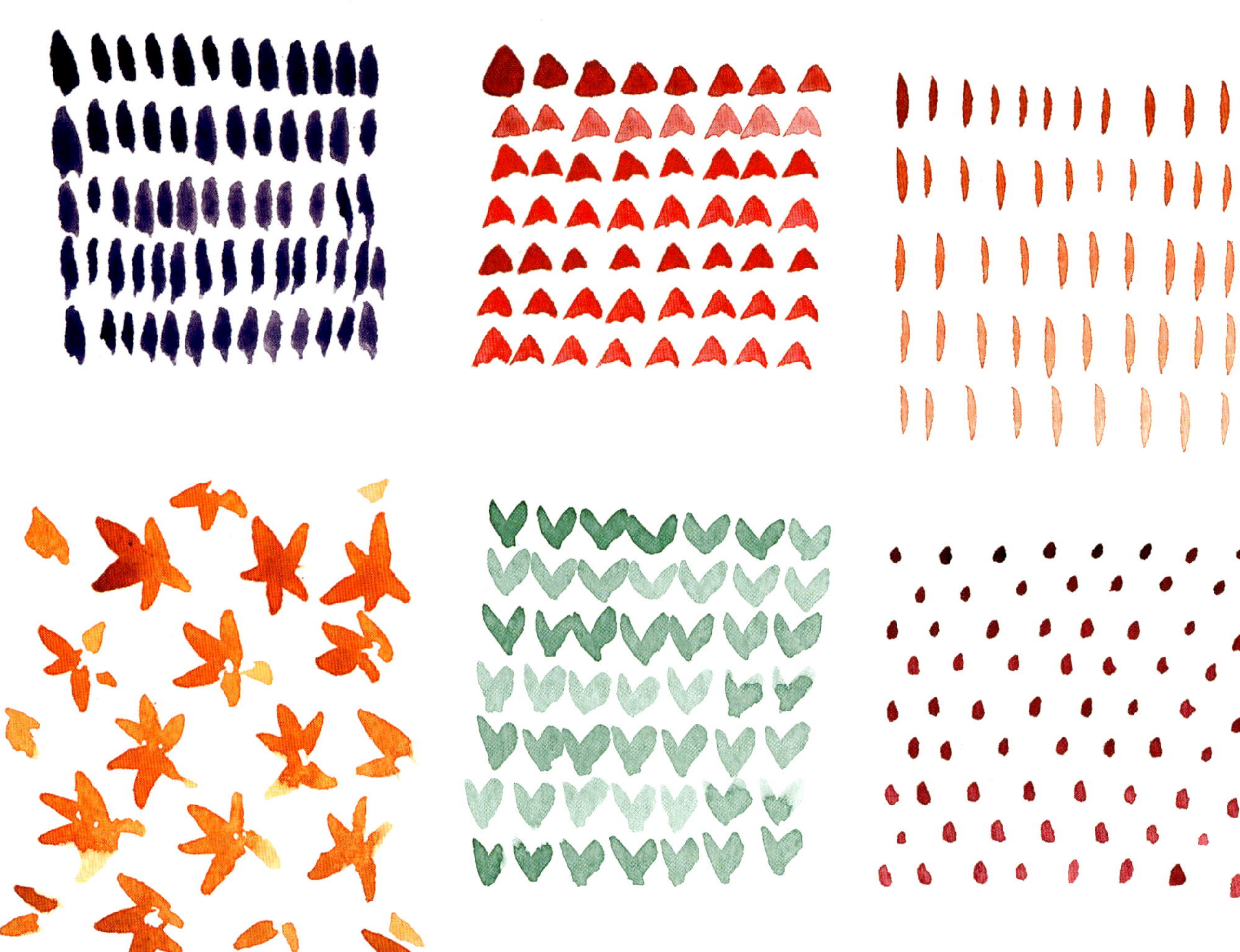

Techniques are useful and important for learning how to paint, but nothing can replace the simple act of painting itself. Playing with your paints and brushes is the one thing that will help you improve your skills the most. Try to paint a little bit each day, and soon you will notice an improvement. The projects in this book are designed to give you a guided way to practice your painting while simultaneously creating beautiful artwork.

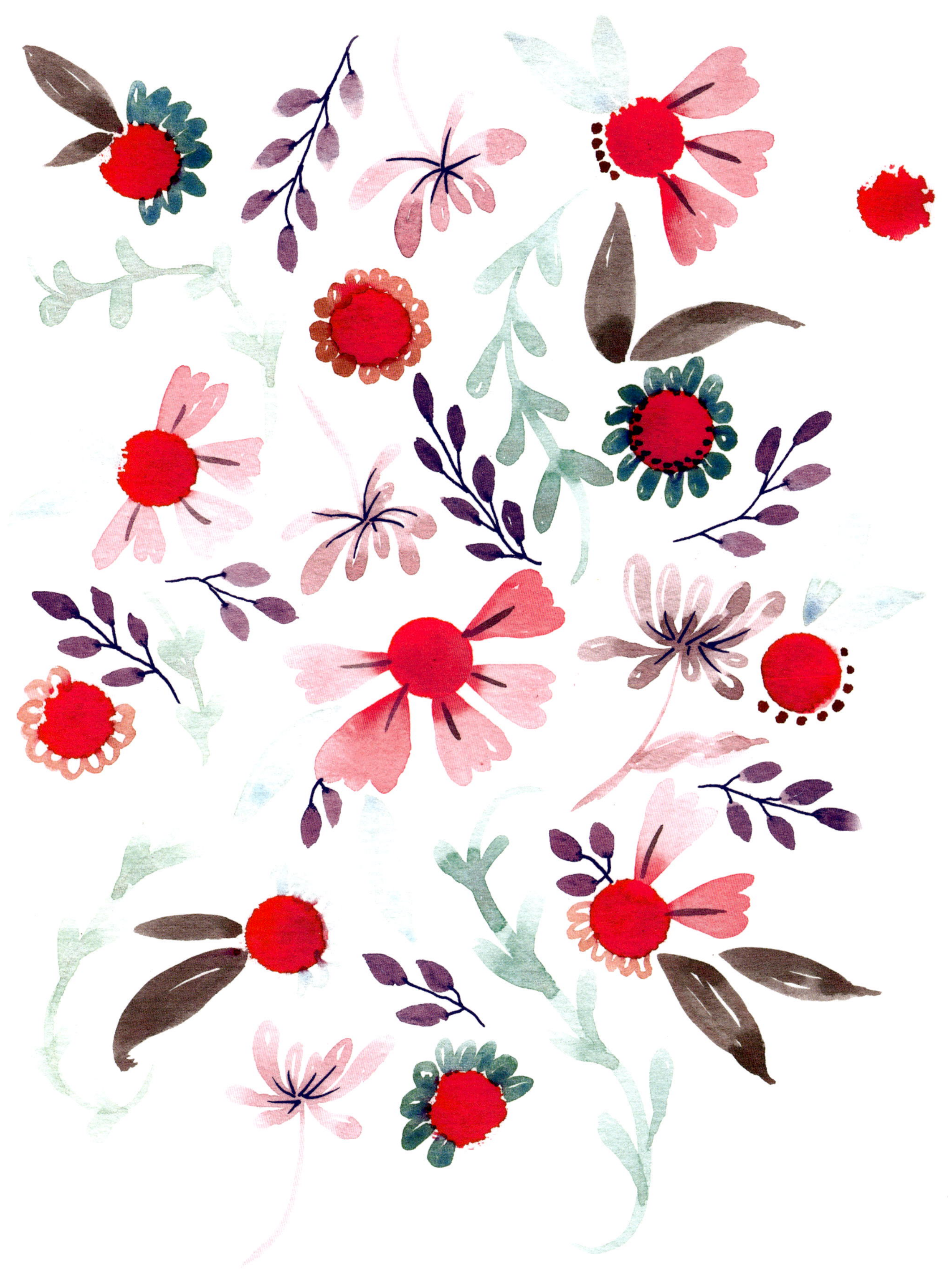

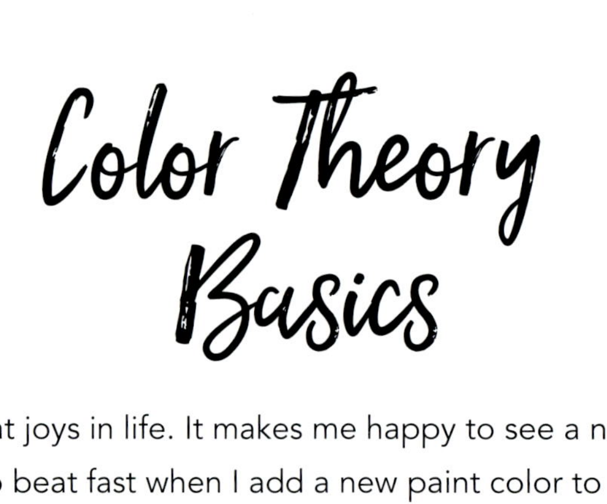

Color Theory Basics

Color is one of my great joys in life. It makes me happy to see a new color scheme, and my heart really starts to beat fast when I add a new paint color to my palette. If you can approach color with a playful, curious, and observant spirit, you will have the most success.

I often choose a color palette based on a combination I've seen, but my favorite combinations come through experimentation. There is just no substitute for practice! And what type of practice is more fun than playing with color?

One way that I play with color is by keeping a color sketchbook. I collect inspiring color combinations from magazines and catalogs, cutting and pasting as I find hues I love, and develop new color palettes this way. Ultimately, color is about what you like, but it will help if you learn the theories behind color. This will allow you to maximize your creativity!

THE COLOR WHEEL

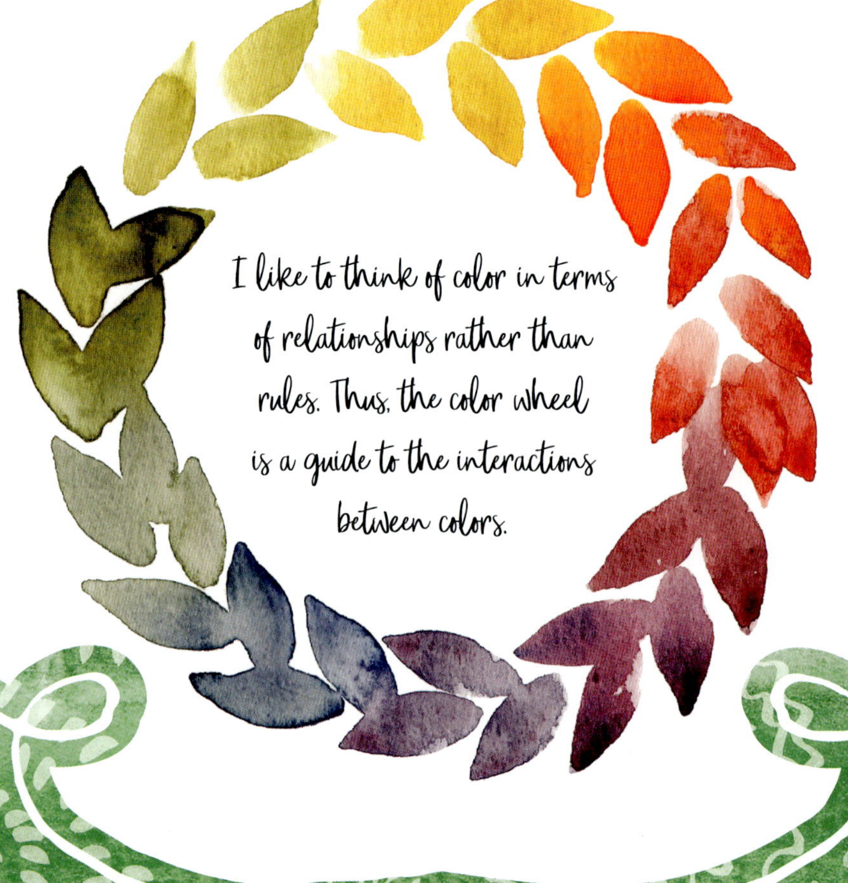

I like to think of color in terms of relationships rather than rules. Thus, the color wheel is a guide to the interactions between colors.

Primary Colors

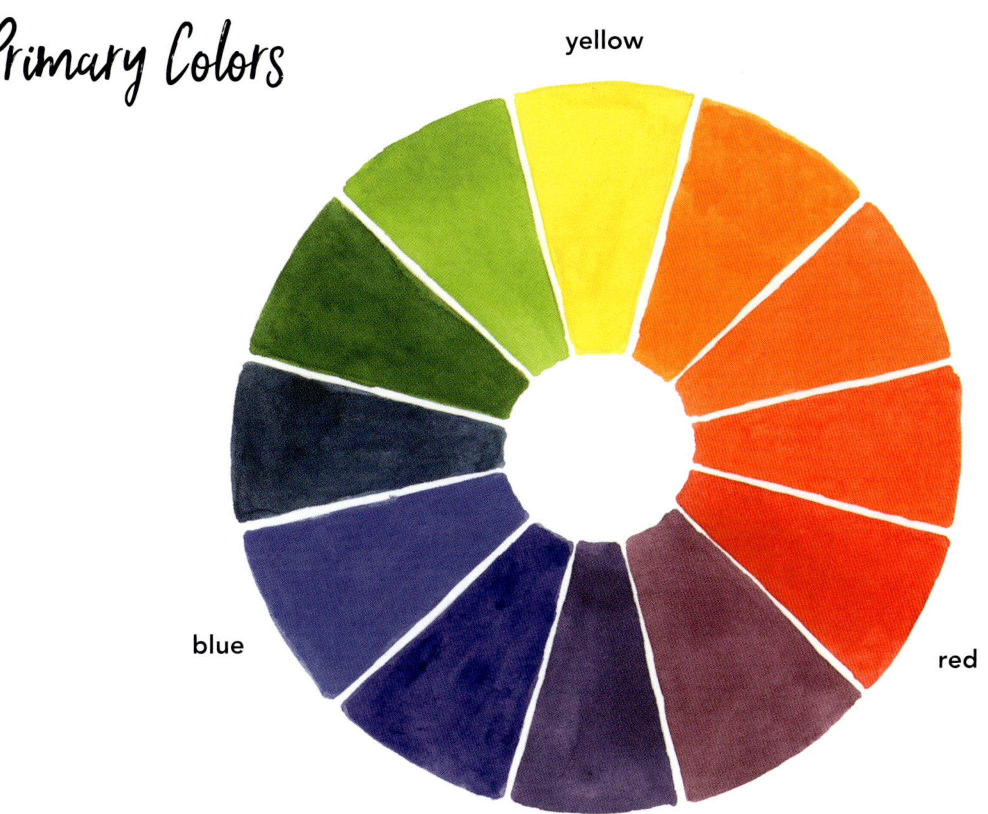

Let's start with the three primary colors: **red**, **yellow**, and **blue**. These colors cannot be mixed from other colors.

Secondary Colors

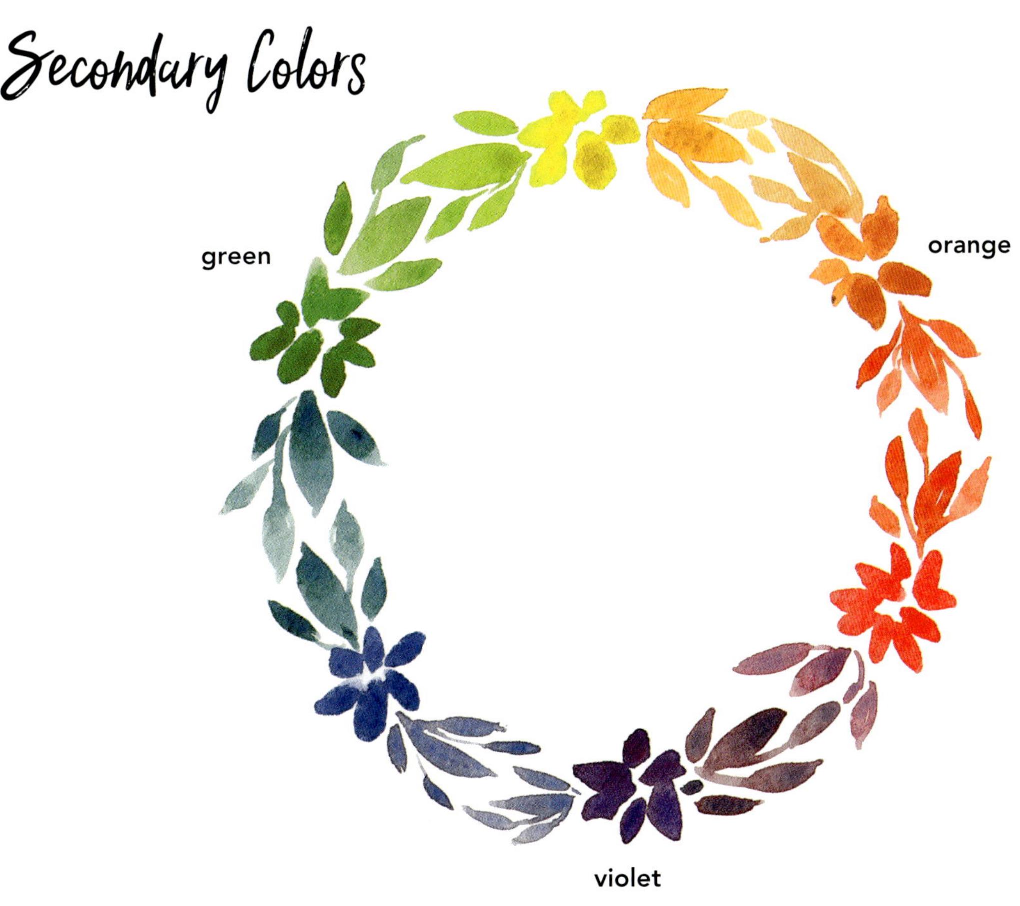

Between the primary colors sit the secondary colors: **orange**, **green**, and **violet**.

More Color Categories

Then there are the tertiary colors, which land between the primary and secondary colors. There are six tertiary colors: red-orange, yellow-orange, yellow-green, blue-green, blue-violet, and red-violet.

Colors directly across from each other on the color wheel are called "complementary colors," and they bring out the best in one another, making for a vibrant combination. Some examples of complementary color combinations are red and green, blue and orange, and yellow and violet. Analogous colors sit next to each other on the color wheel, and they create a more sedate combination.

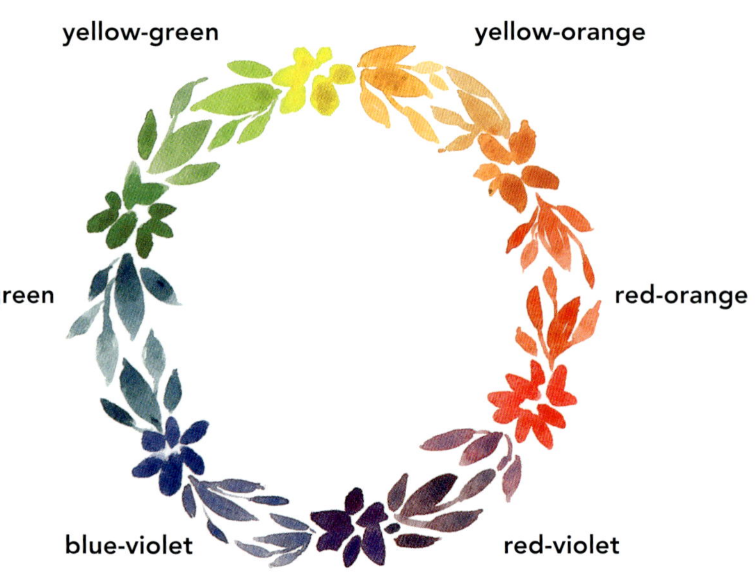

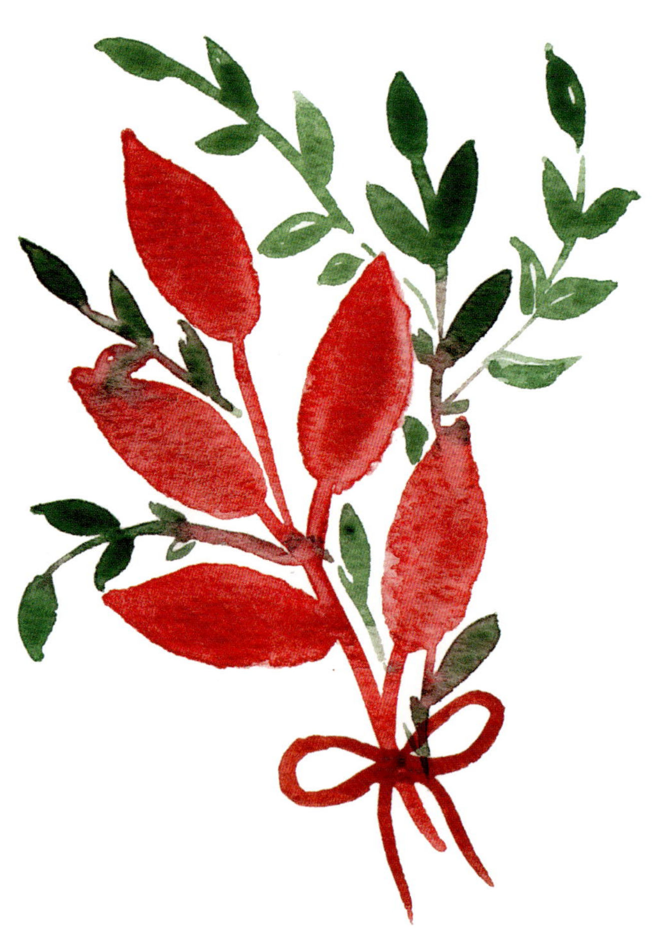

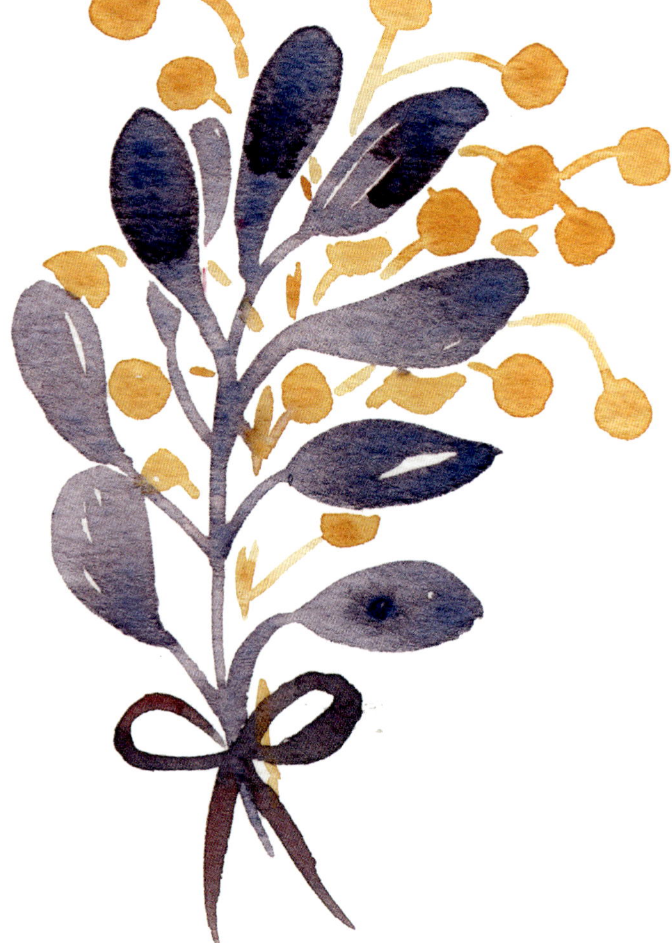

Complementary Colors

COLOR TEMPERATURE

Think about how color evokes a mood or recalls to memory a certain location or feeling. It's no coincidence that the tropics are often represented with reds, oranges, pinks, and other bright, vibrant colors. We describe a color as warm or cool depending on its proximity to yellow (warm) or blue (cool) on the color wheel. Warm colors (right) include reds, oranges, pinks, and yellows. Cool colors (below) are greens, blues, and violets.

When choosing a color palette, it is sometimes helpful to keep these relationships in mind, especially if your painting needs a little pop of something to make it interesting. For example, if you are working with warm, analogous pinks, oranges, and yellows, a subtle touch of a cool blue or violet might give your painting that necessary final touch.

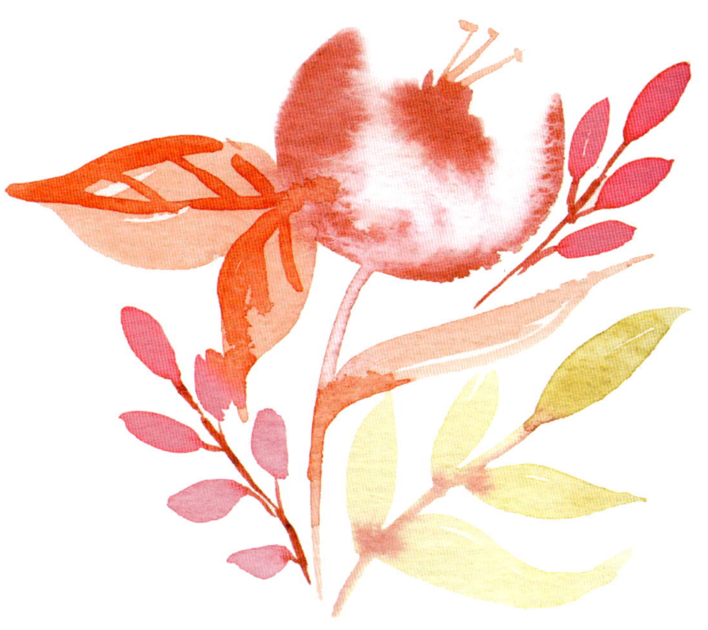

Warm Colors

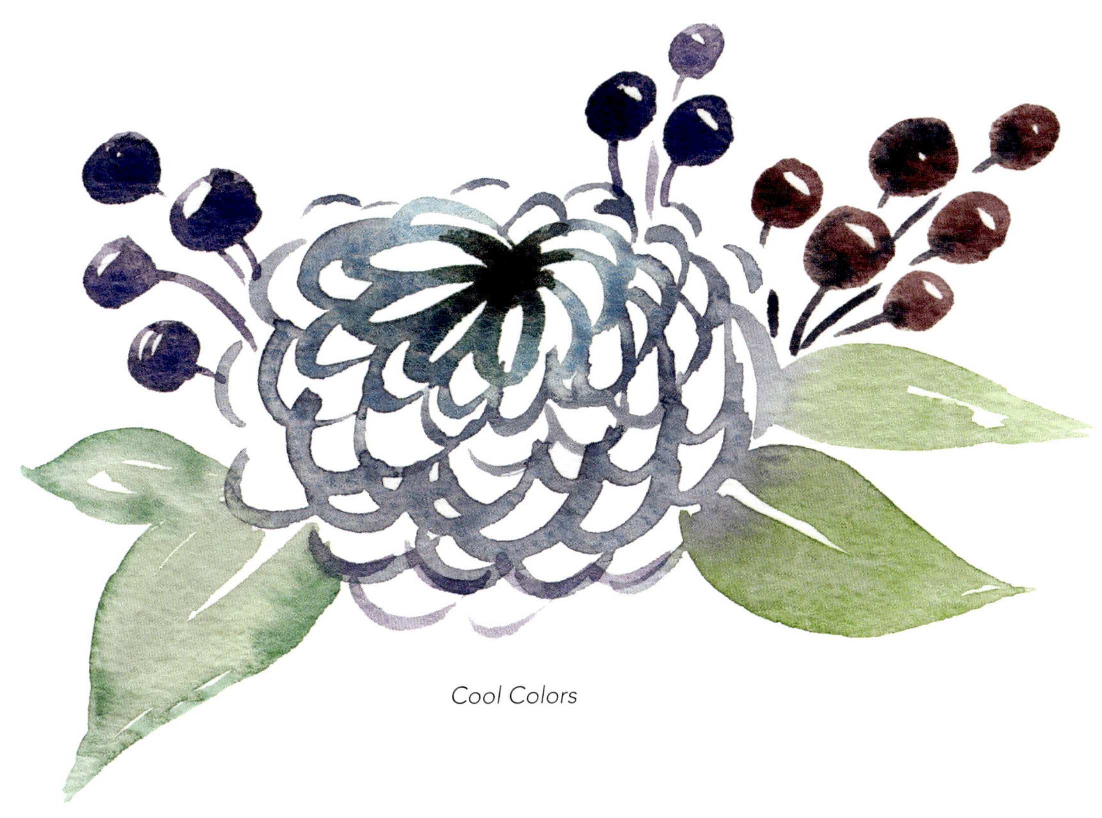

Cool Colors

DRAB COLORS

No painting is complete without a few drab colors—"ugly" colors, as I like to call them. These are the colors that your elementary-school art teacher described as "muddy" and discouraged you from mixing. But now you can mix your muddy colors with abandon and put them to good use at the same time!

Ugly colors can elevate a painting by creating depth and interest. Grays, browns, and muddy greens and blues all fall into this category. These colors are a great way to clean off your palette too. Just mix all the colors on your palette into one color, water it down, and you've achieved your very own ugly color.

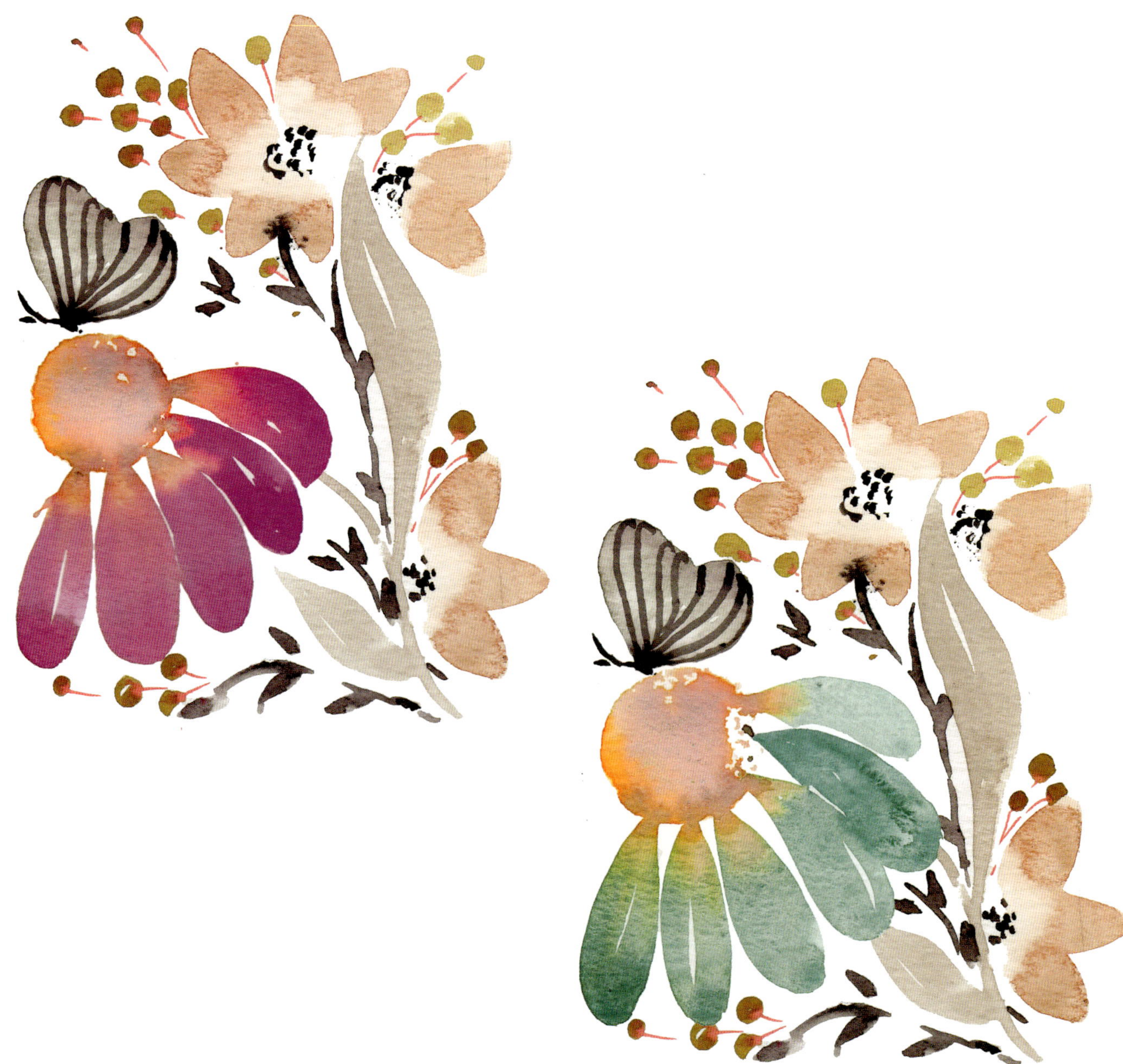

Challenge Yourself

You will always be more naturally drawn to certain colors than others. In my case, I love brights, especially pinks!

Sometimes, in order to increase the number of colors I'm comfortable using, I will intentionally pick a color that I don't really like and play with it. By experimenting with adding colors from the rest of my palette, I can often come up with a new scheme that I *bm*really like.

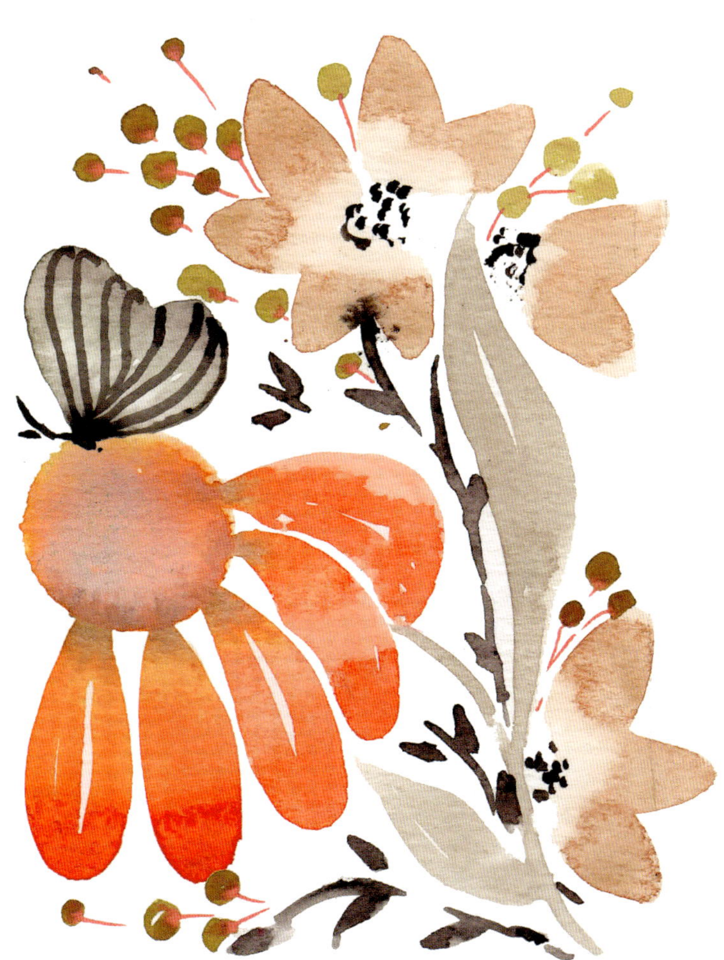

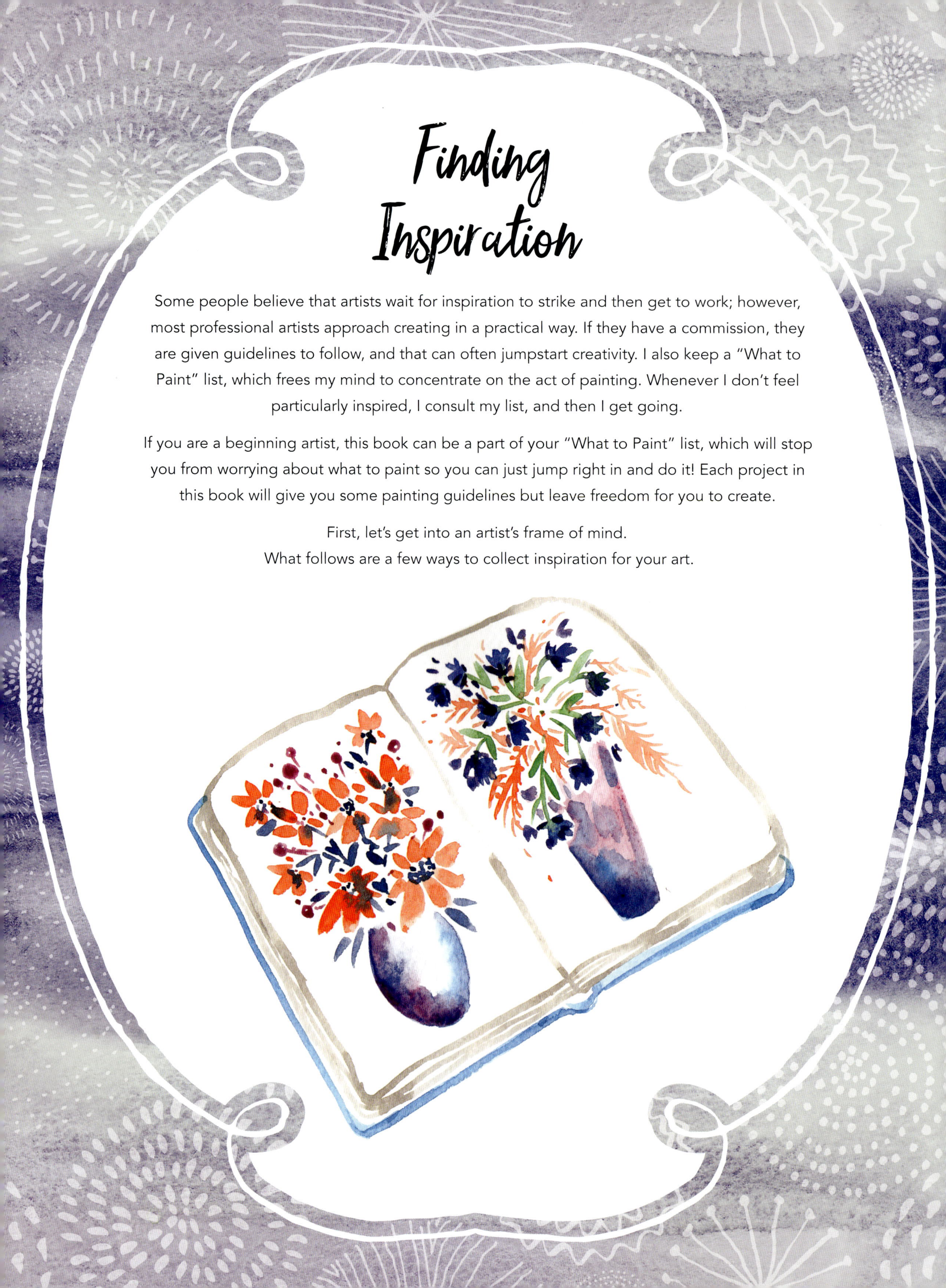

Finding Inspiration

Some people believe that artists wait for inspiration to strike and then get to work; however, most professional artists approach creating in a practical way. If they have a commission, they are given guidelines to follow, and that can often jumpstart creativity. I also keep a "What to Paint" list, which frees my mind to concentrate on the act of painting. Whenever I don't feel particularly inspired, I consult my list, and then I get going.

If you are a beginning artist, this book can be a part of your "What to Paint" list, which will stop you from worrying about what to paint so you can just jump right in and do it! Each project in this book will give you some painting guidelines but leave freedom for you to create.

First, let's get into an artist's frame of mind.
What follows are a few ways to collect inspiration for your art.

BECOME A VISUAL COLLECTOR

Here's a simple way to begin thinking like an artist: Collect visual inspiration when you're out and about. Let's say you're out shopping for your kids' clothes, and you see a beautiful color palette in an outfit. Snap a photo to use in your next painting. Or maybe you observe a beautiful tile floor in a restaurant. Take a picture; these all-over patterns can make fabulous backgrounds in floral paintings.

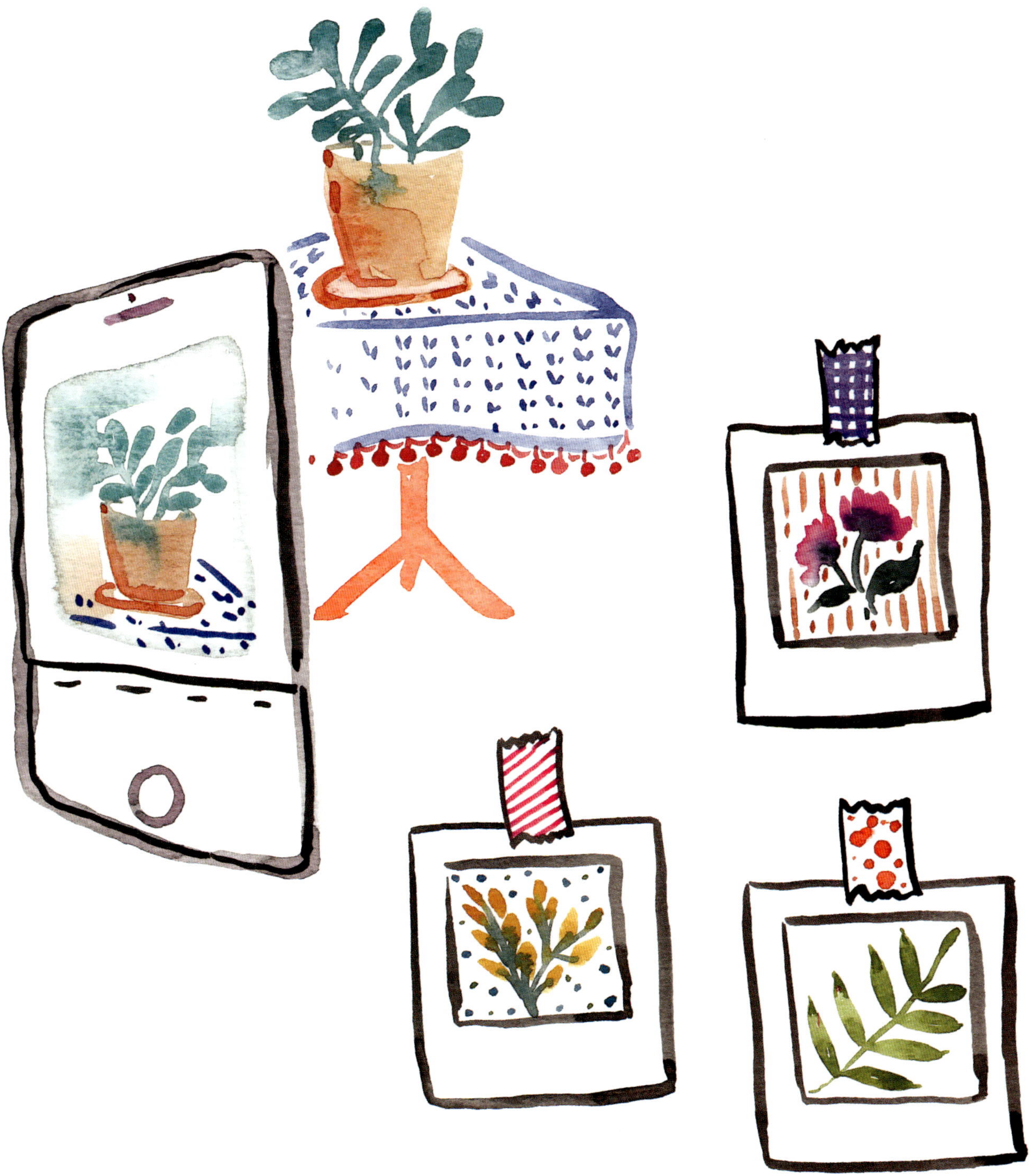

REFERENCE BOOKS

Some of my favorite sources of inspiration are old books. Visit a thrift store or used bookstore, and check out the gardening section. Begin to amass a collection of books that are inspirational to you and can be used as references for new floral and leaf shapes. Also, vintage children's books often have unique color palettes and may provide ready-made inspiration that you can utilize in your painting.

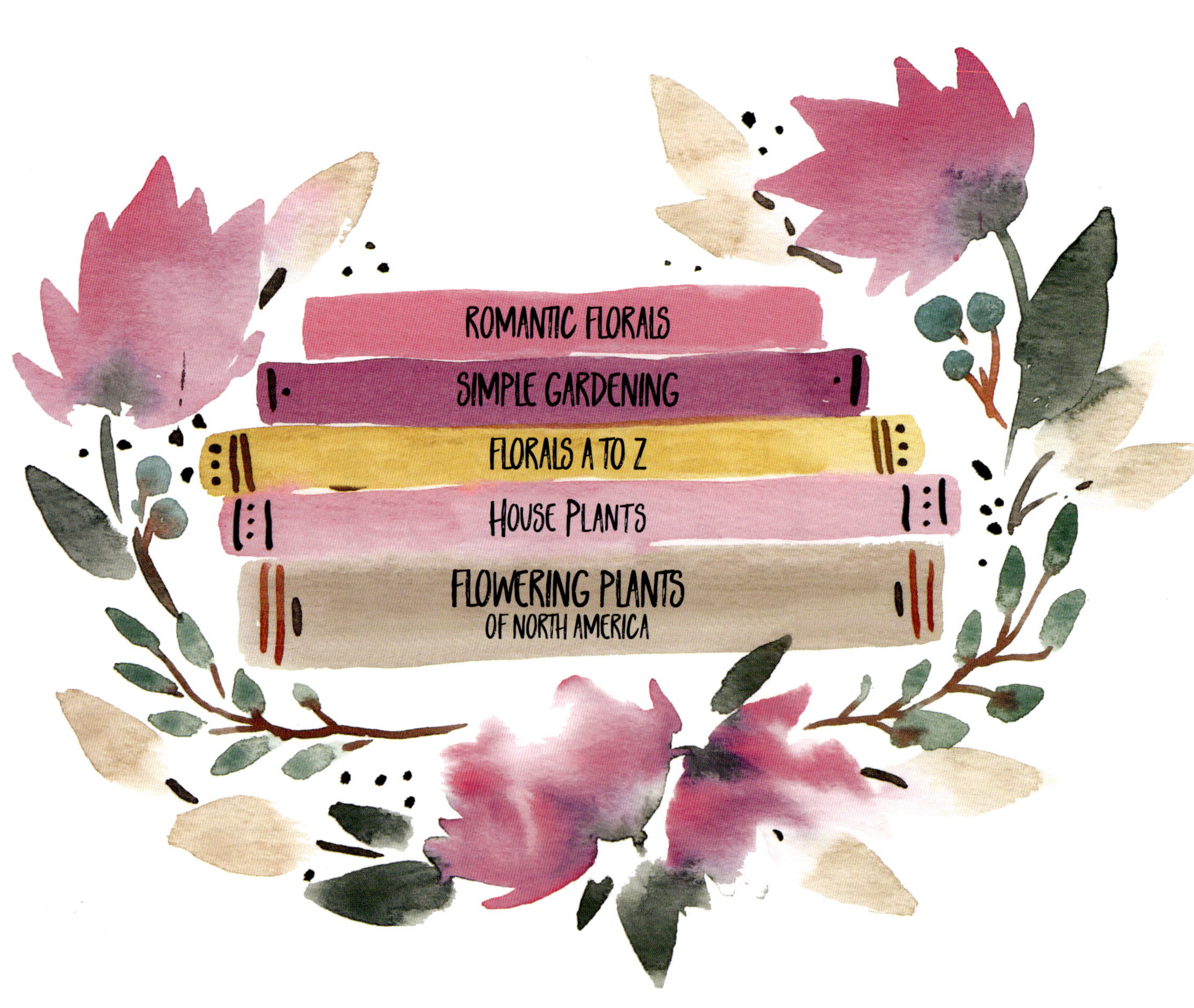

KEEP A COLOR NOTEBOOK

Keeping a sketchbook of inspiring color palettes can be helpful and fun too. This is very simple: Grab a small blank notebook or some loose sheets of paper. Using magazine clippings or paint chips, experiment with putting together different colors until you find some pleasing combinations. Try starting with a color that you wouldn't normally gravitate toward and see if you can create a color palette that you love. Paste the finished colors together on a page to record your unique color palettes. This is a fun exercise to do while traveling or whenever you don't feel like painting.

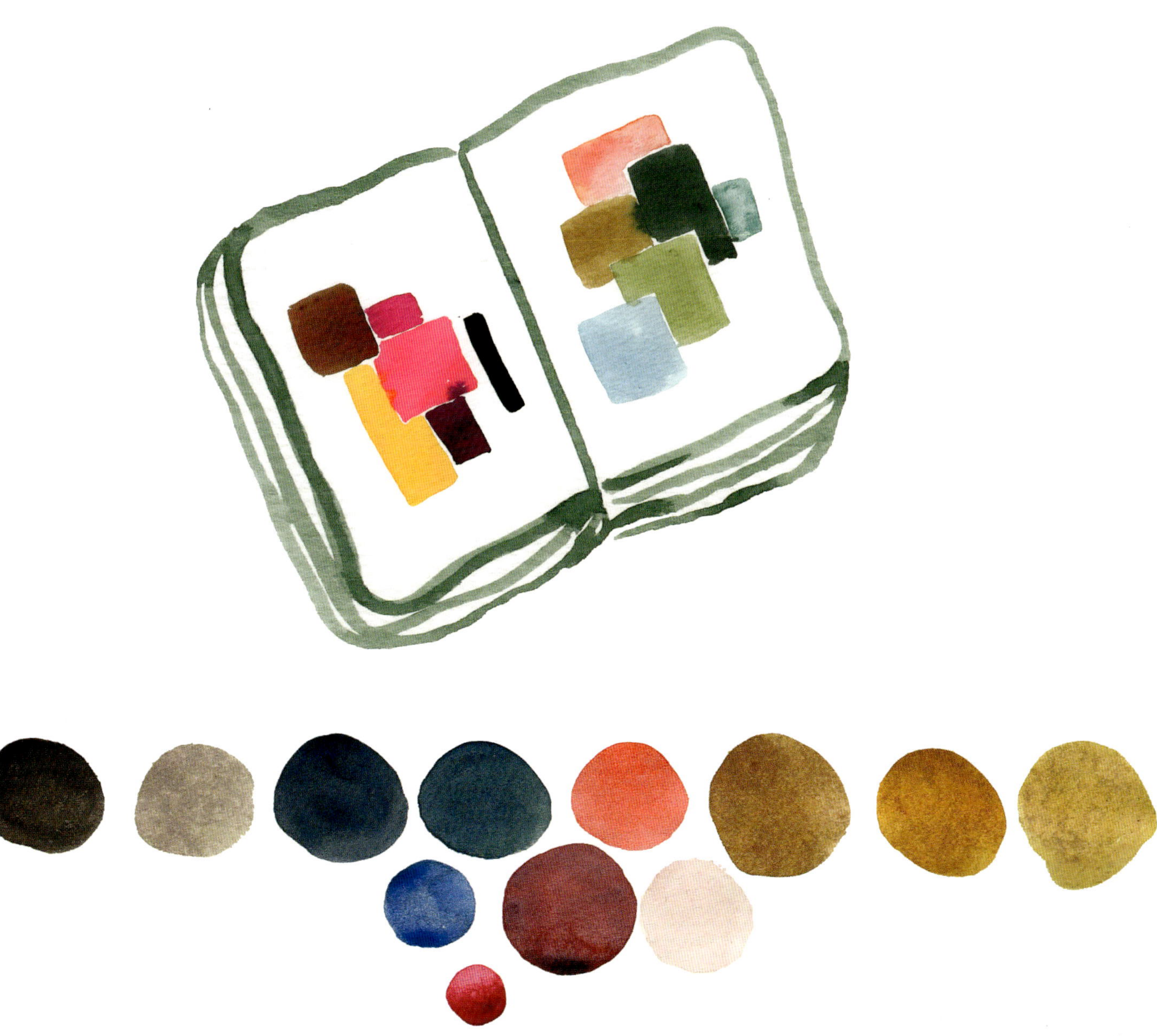

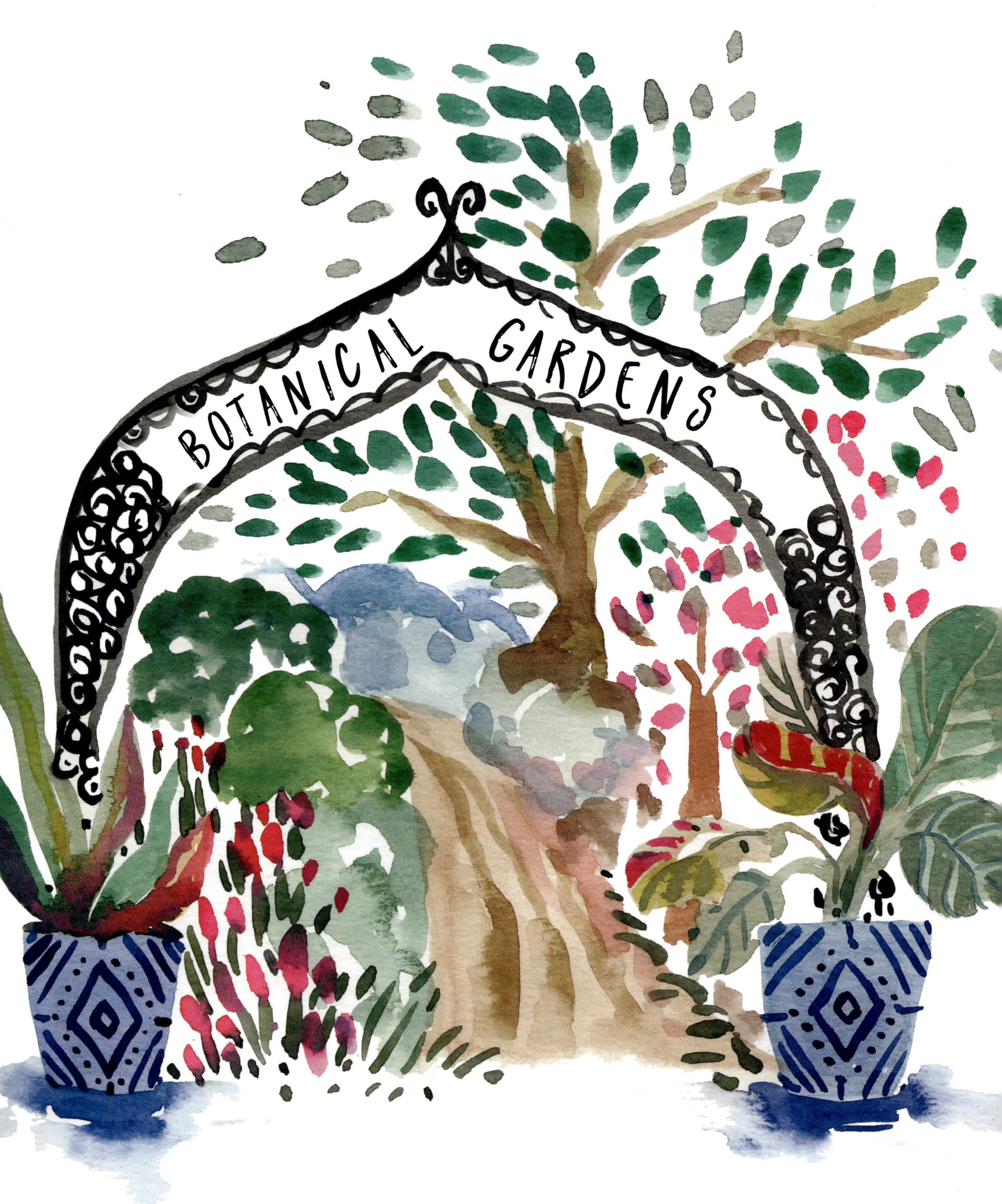
BOTANICAL GARDENS

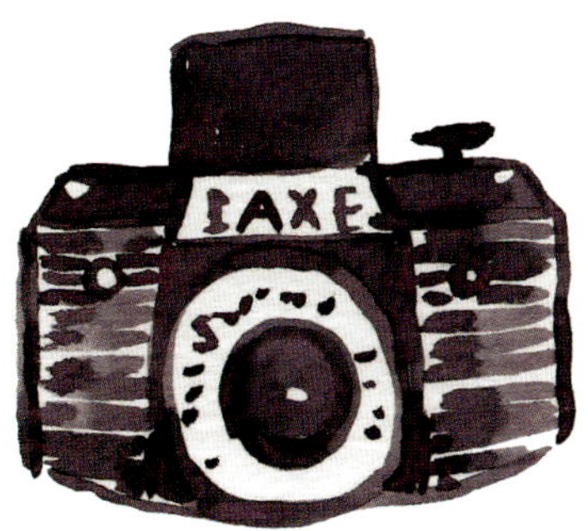

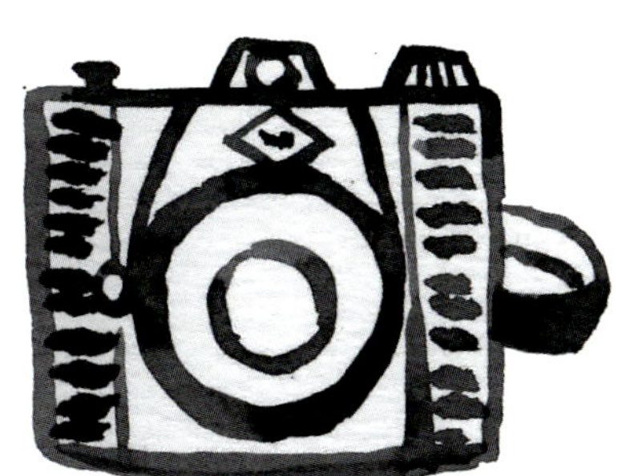

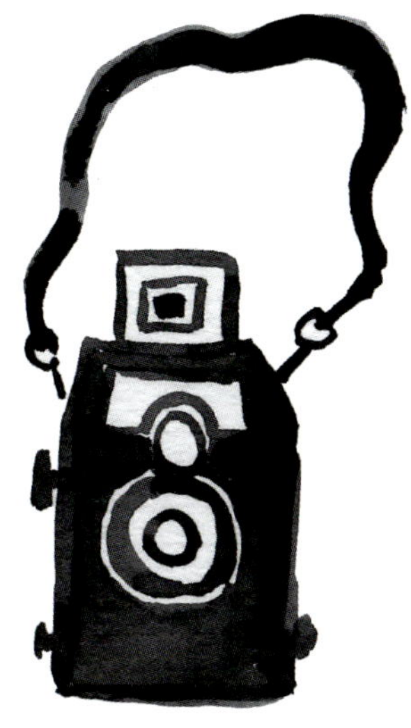

TAKE A FIELD TRIP

Botanical gardens and nature preserves don't just make for fun day trips; they can provide a wealth of natural inspiration as well. Remember to bring your camera so you can snap pictures of unique floral shapes.

The great thing about being a visual collector is that you don't have to spend a dime. Simply observe the details around you, and record them in a photo to help jog your memory later.

You can work on your art even when you're not painting!

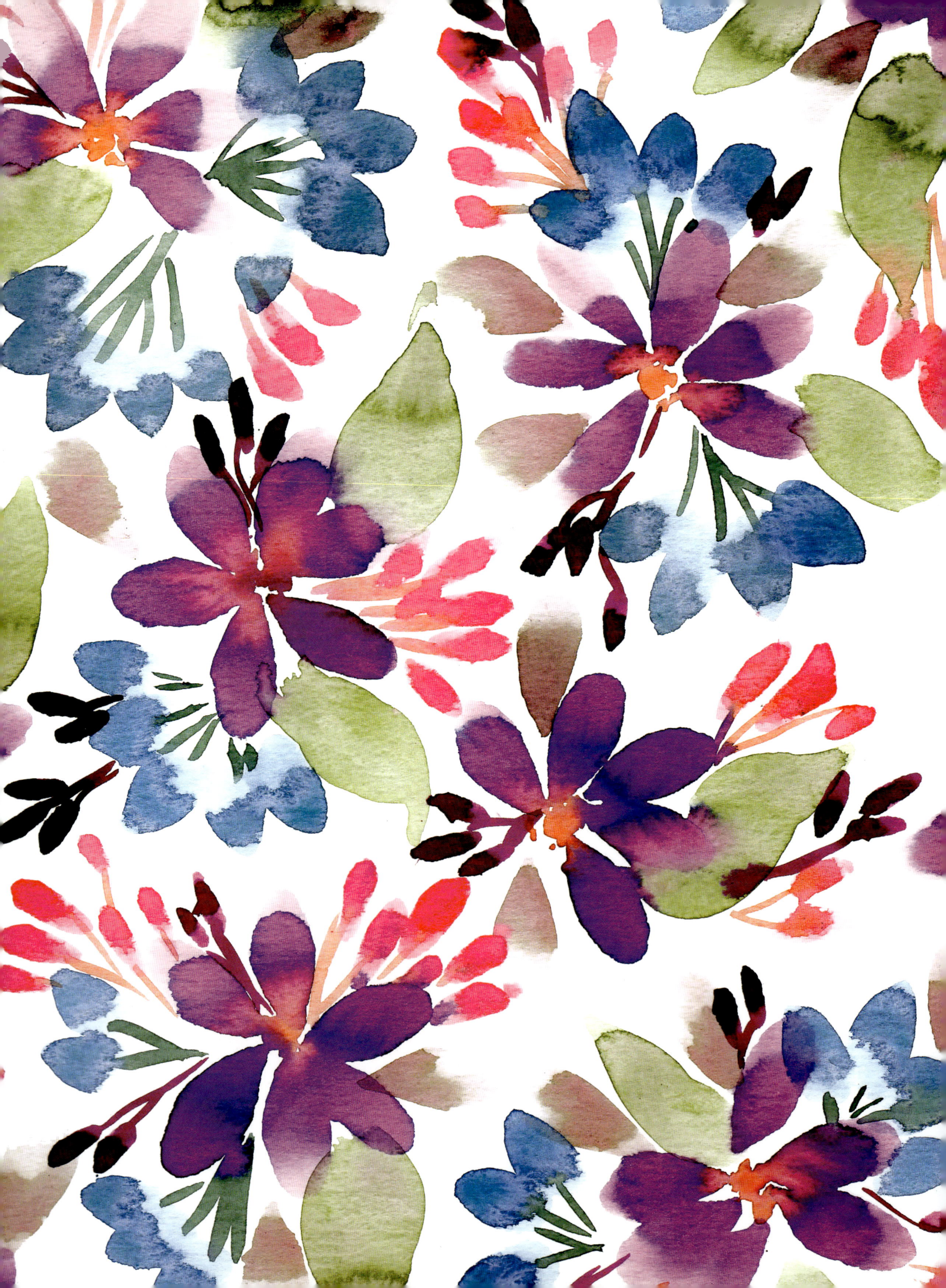

STEP-BY-STEP PROJECTS

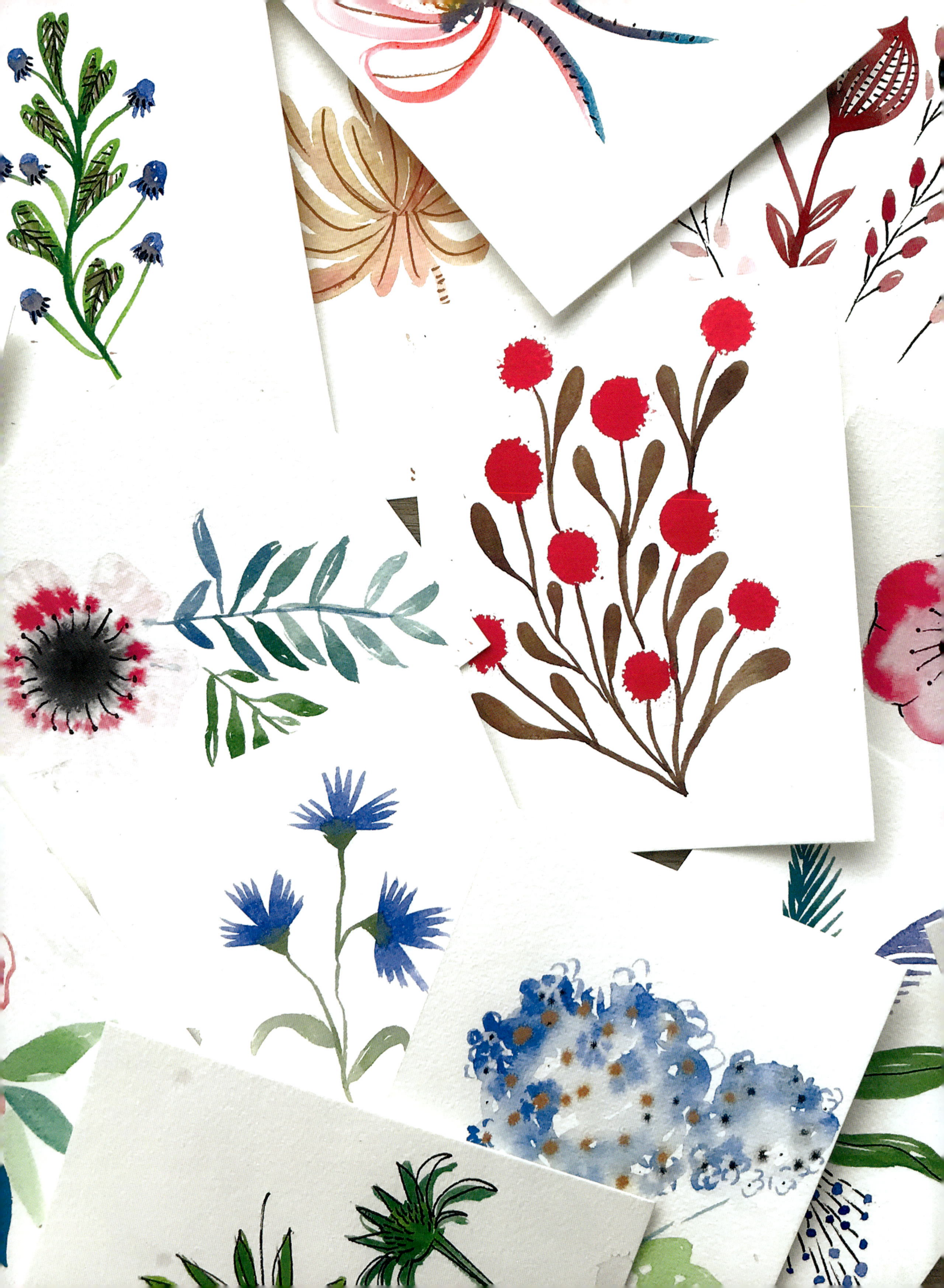

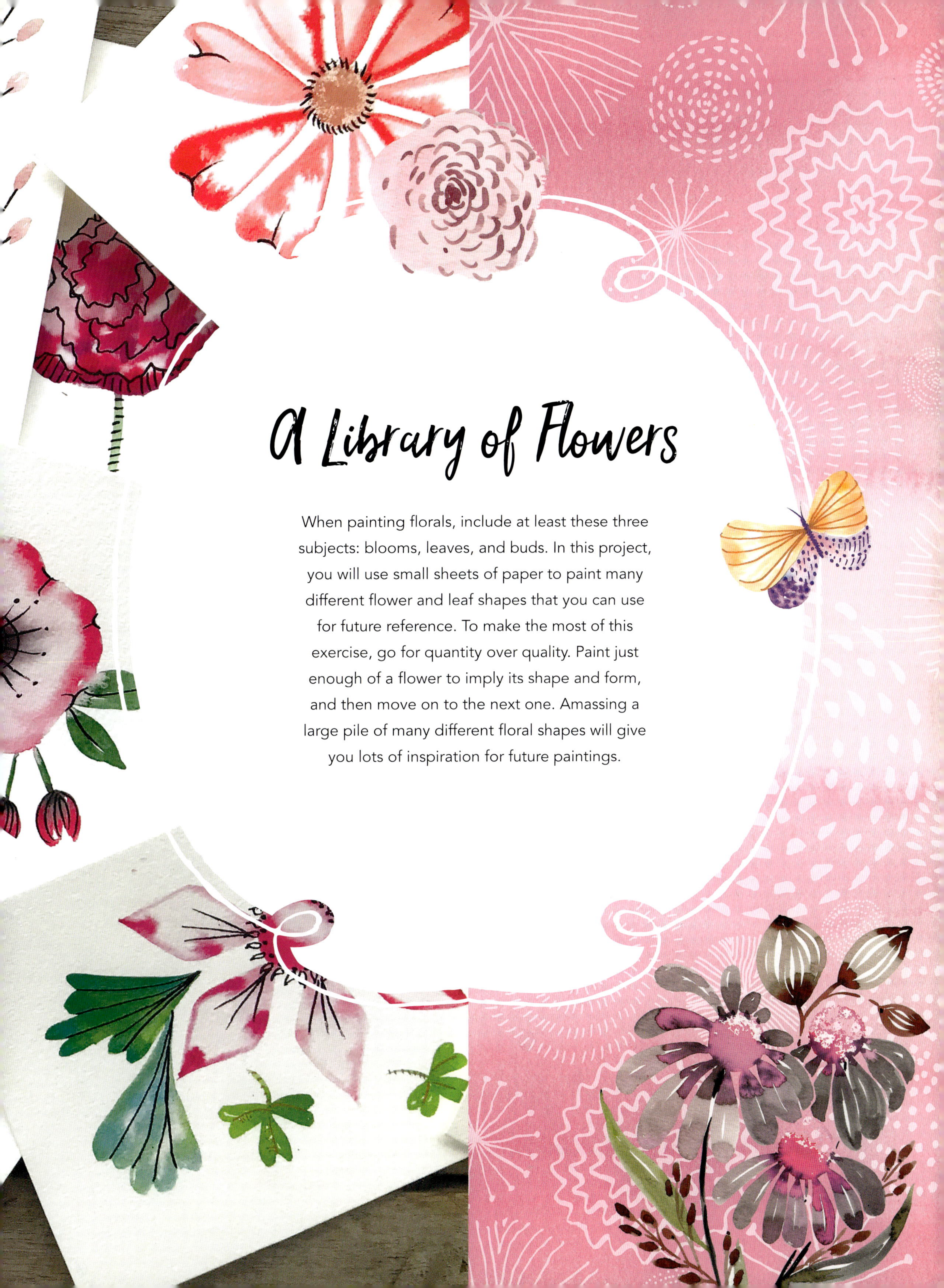

A Library of Flowers

When painting florals, include at least these three subjects: blooms, leaves, and buds. In this project, you will use small sheets of paper to paint many different flower and leaf shapes that you can use for future reference. To make the most of this exercise, go for quantity over quality. Paint just enough of a flower to imply its shape and form, and then move on to the next one. Amassing a large pile of many different floral shapes will give you lots of inspiration for future paintings.

BLOOMS

Blooms are the focal flowers in a bouquet. To help you visualize the various shapes that blooms come in, borrow some gardening or flower books from your local library, and use the shapes you observe to inspire your blooms. Now, let's paint your first bloom!

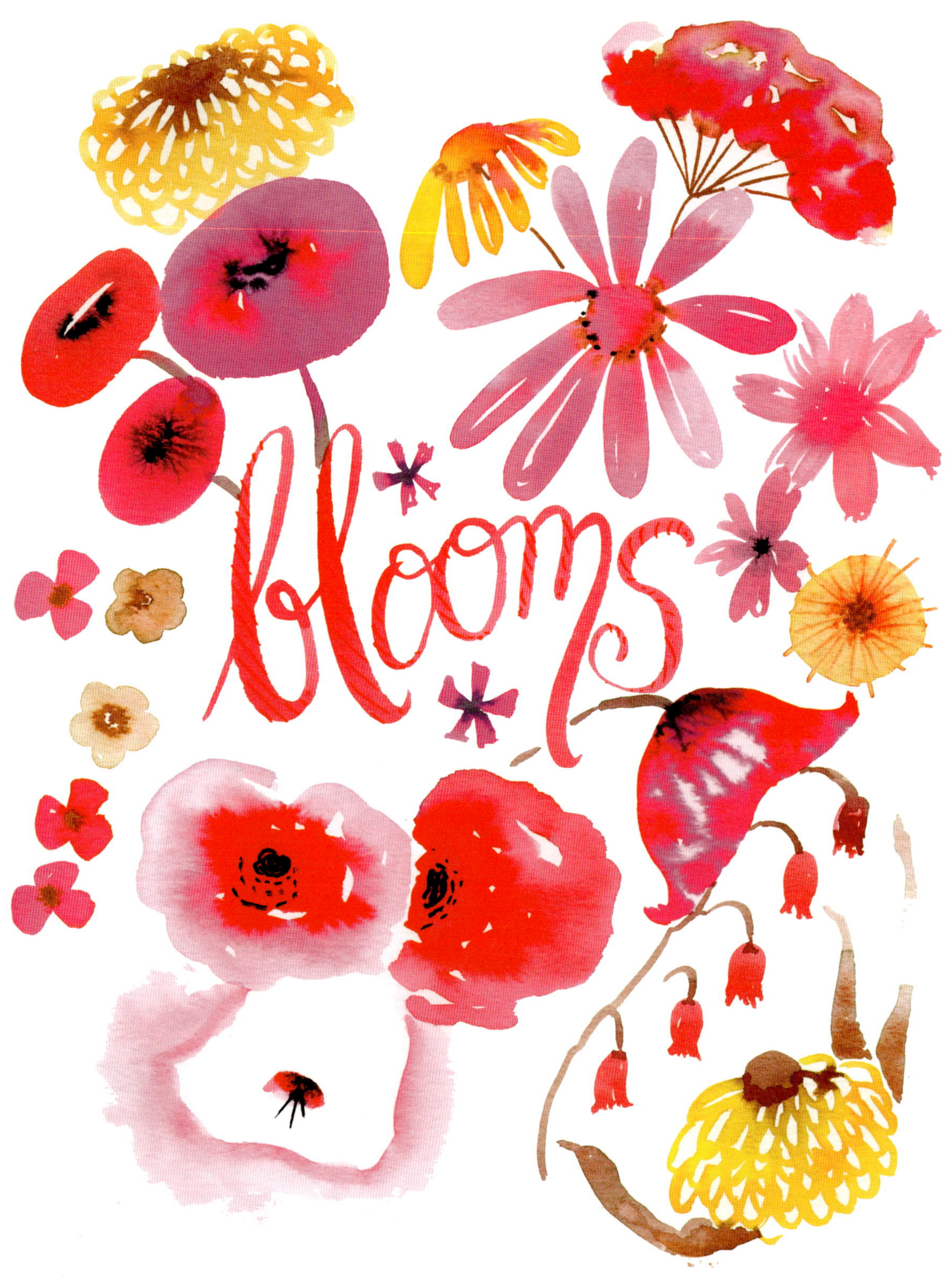

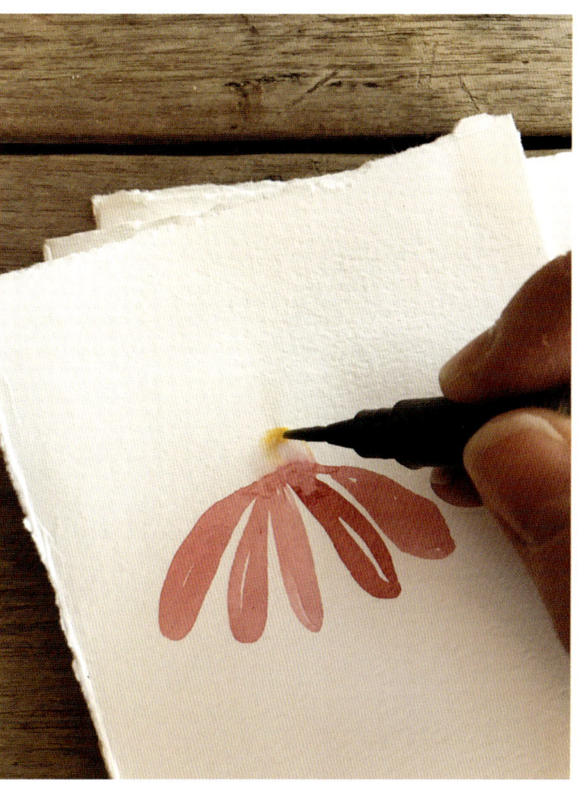

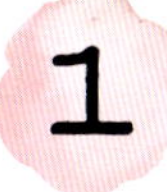

Blooms usually extend from a middle point. This flower will be shown from the side, so the center will be at the top with the petals extending downward.

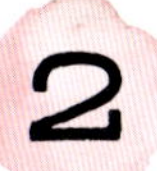

Add a drop of water to create the center of the flower, and then add some yellow or orange paint.

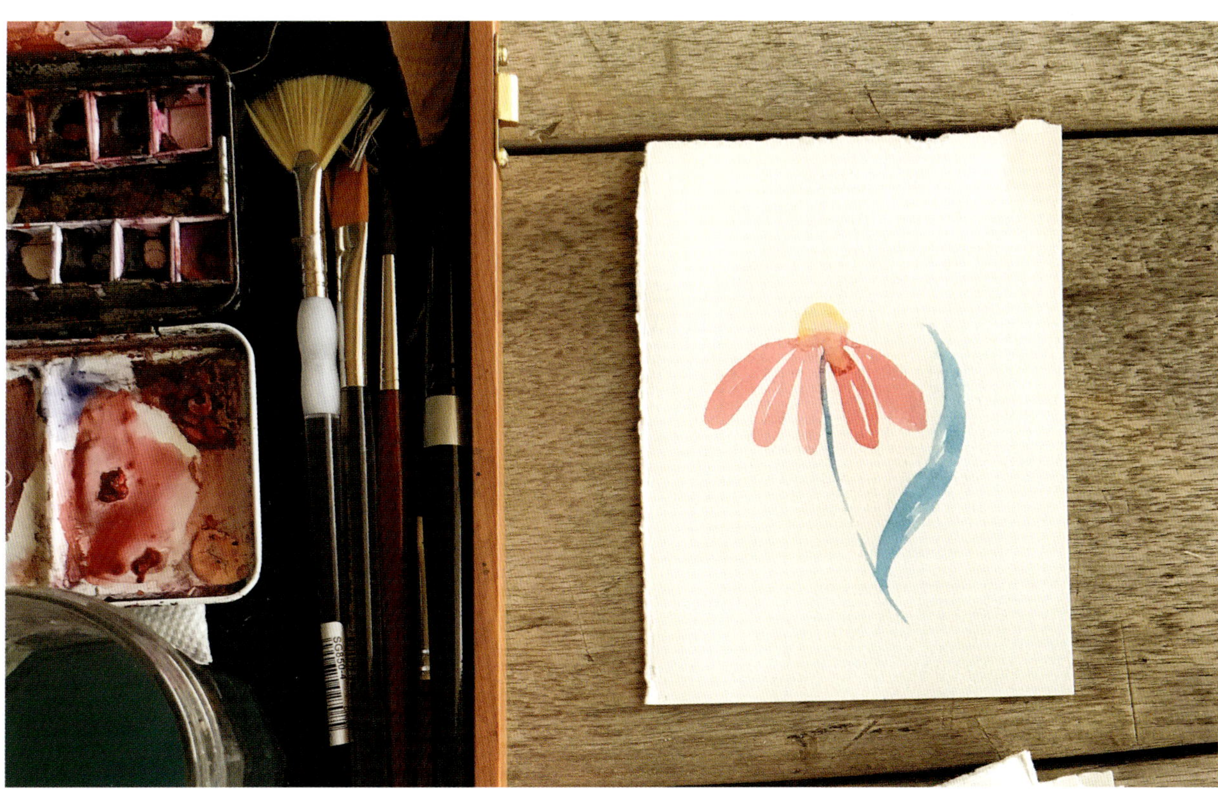

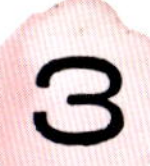

Add a stem and a simple leaf.

Rose

It's time to paint specific kinds of blooms, starting with a rose.

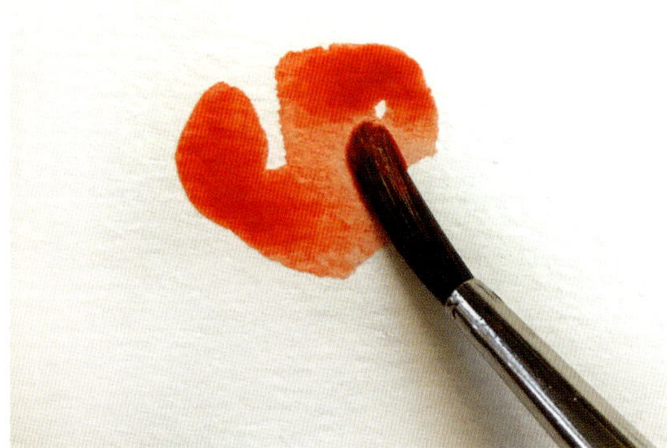

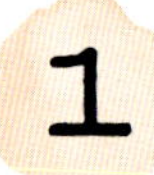

Begin with the color in its center.

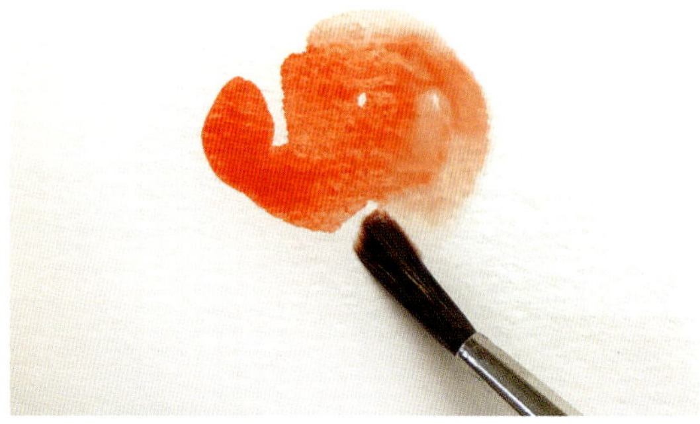

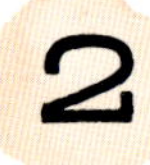

Rinse your brush, fill it with clean water, and then pull the color from the center of the flower with your brush.

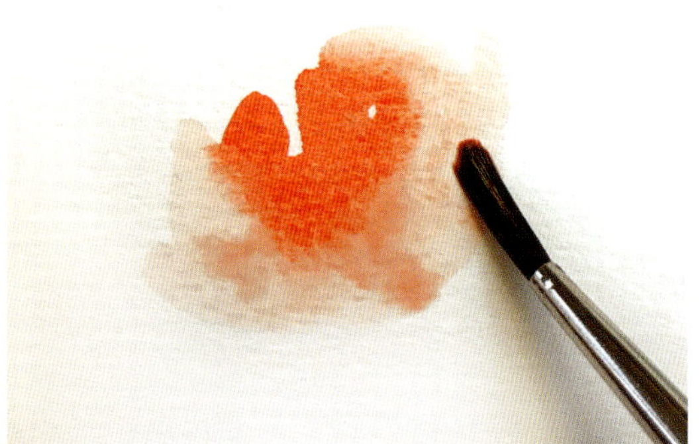

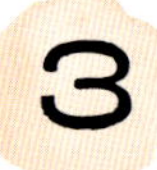

Continue cleaning your brush and pulling out the color in a fluffy shape to imitate the softness of a rose.

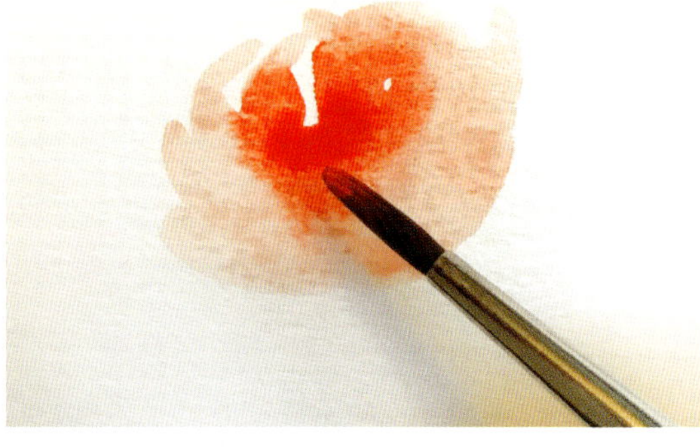

4 Now fill your brush with concentrated color, and dab a little into the center of your rose.

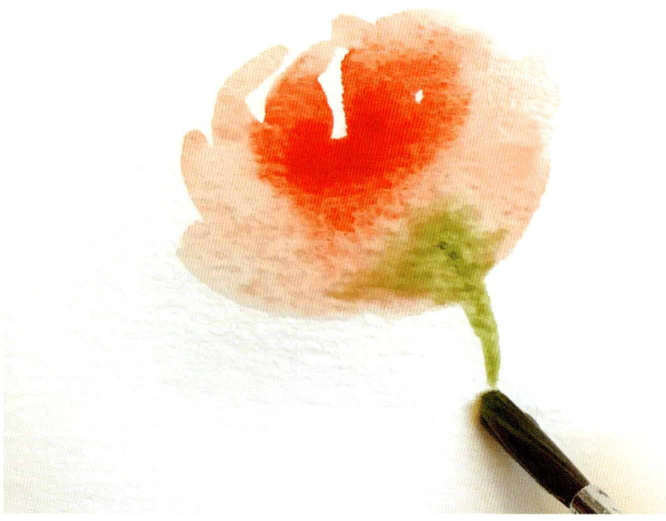

Add a green stem to the bottom, and voilà! You have a rose.

Zinnia

Now let's paint my favorite flower: the zinnia! I like to paint zinnias from the side, showing just a bit of the top-center.

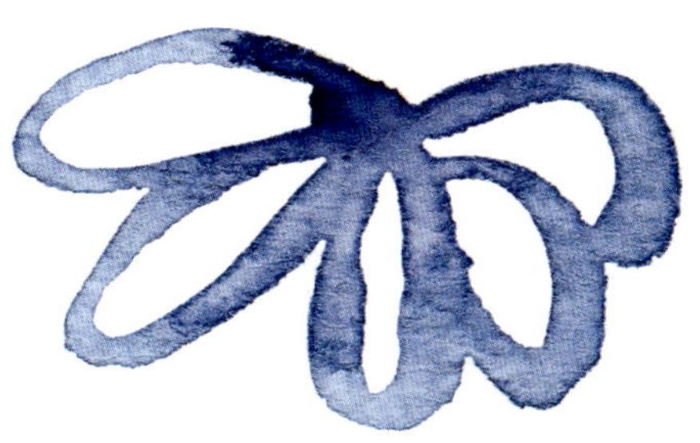

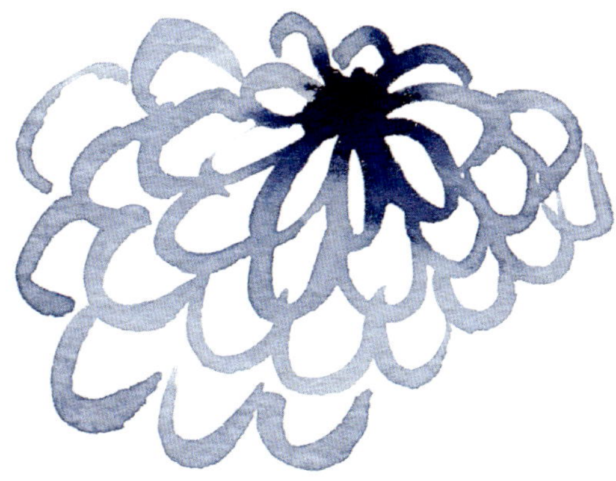

1 Starting at the center, loosely paint rounded petals coming down and around.

2 Continue adding petals, and drop a darker color into the center of the flower.

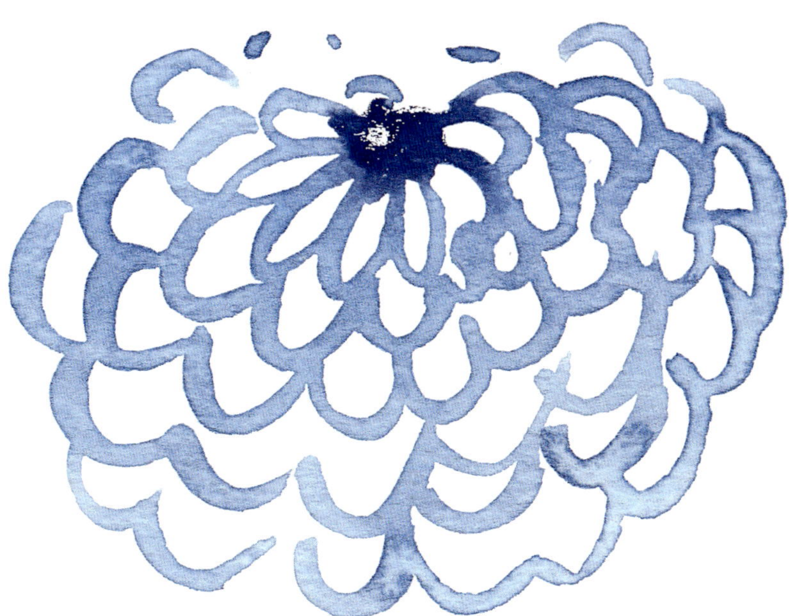

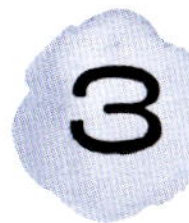

3 Add petals until you are happy with the shape of the flower.

LEAVES

Leaves are fun to paint because, like blooms, they feature a wide variety of shapes and colors. As you paint your library of leaves, try to create a new shape on each sheet of paper, and also use a different shade of green. Look at my leaf cheat sheet below, and you'll see that almost every leaf shape is a slightly different green color than the one next to it.

Here is where your color theory training (pages 16–21) will come in handy. Try adding a bit of blue to one green or a little yellow to another. What about pairing yellow-brown leaves with green ones? Muted, dirty greens make lovely colors for leaves!

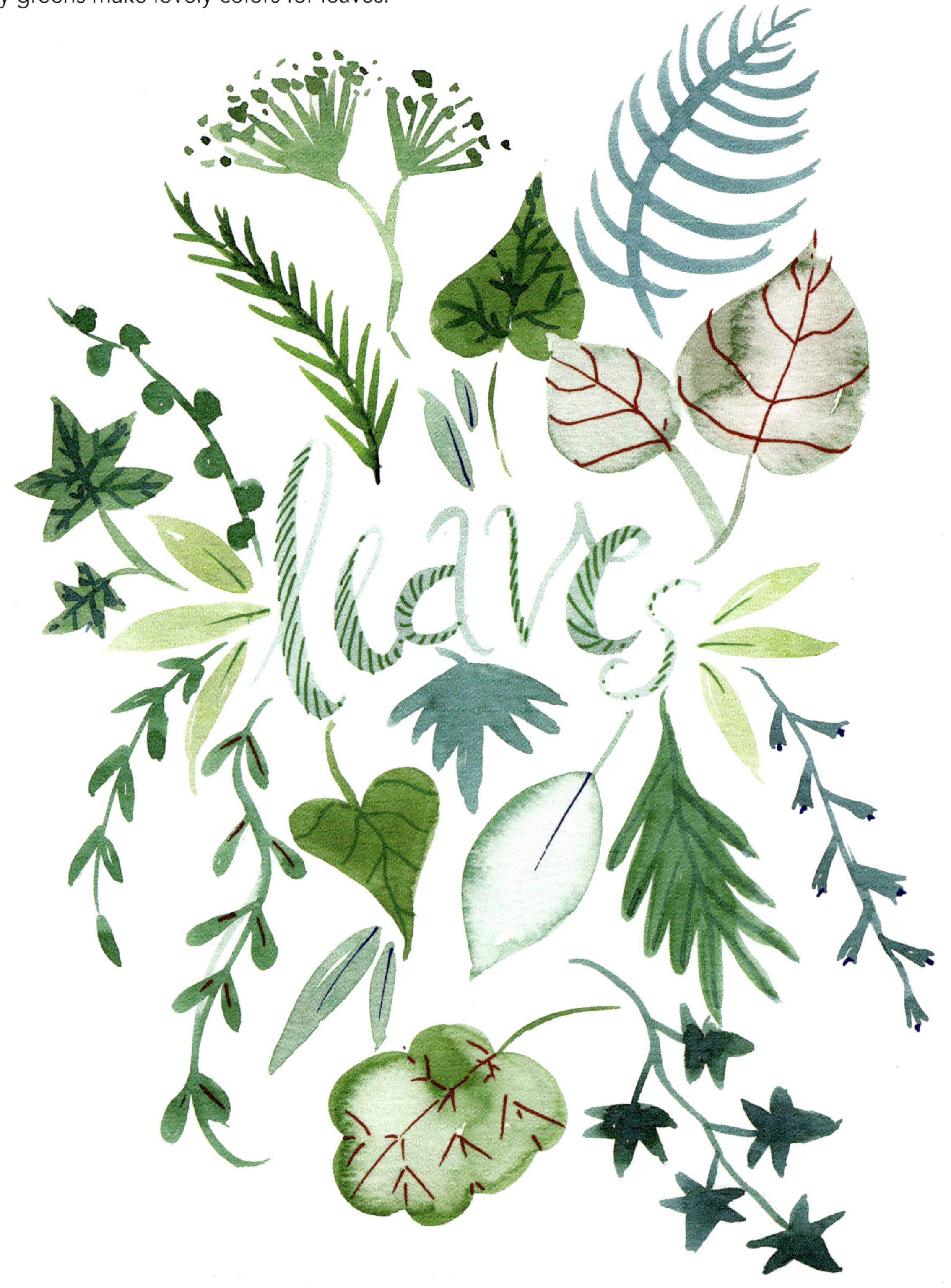

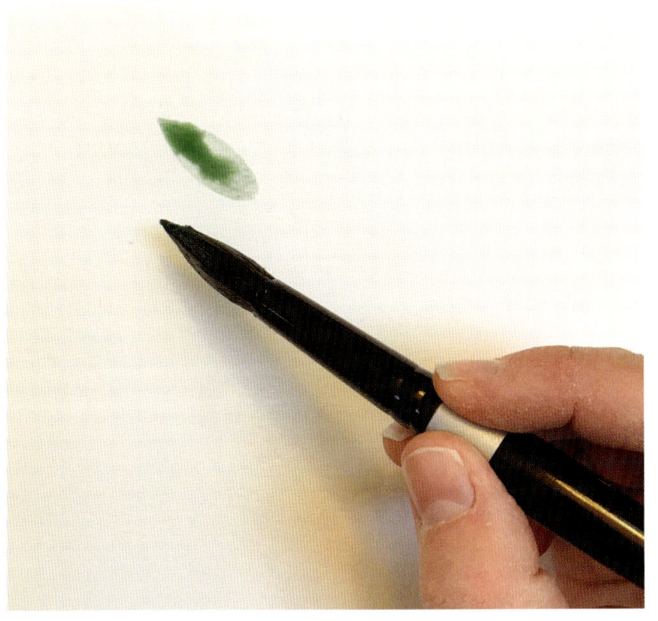

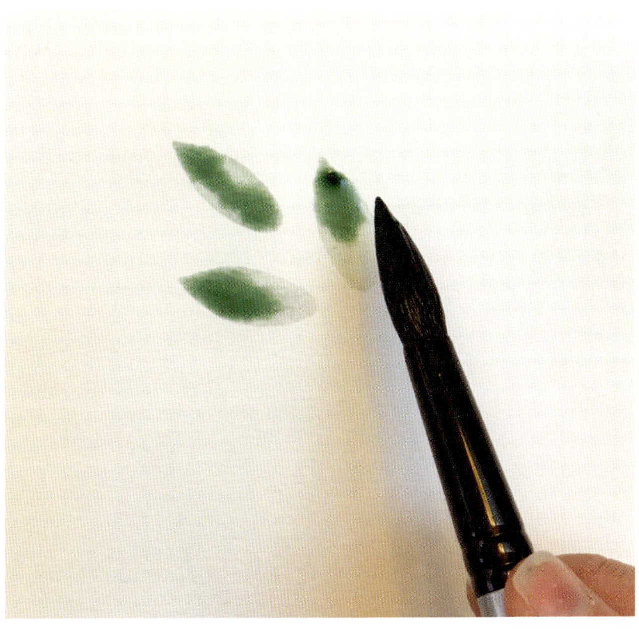

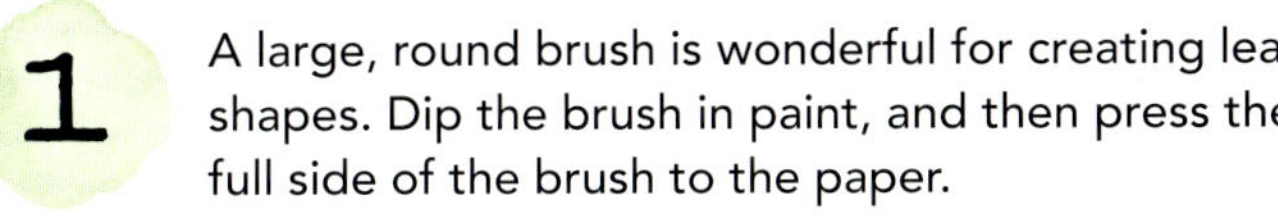

1 A large, round brush is wonderful for creating leaf shapes. Dip the brush in paint, and then press the full side of the brush to the paper.

2 Make a series of shapes to create a larger leaf form.

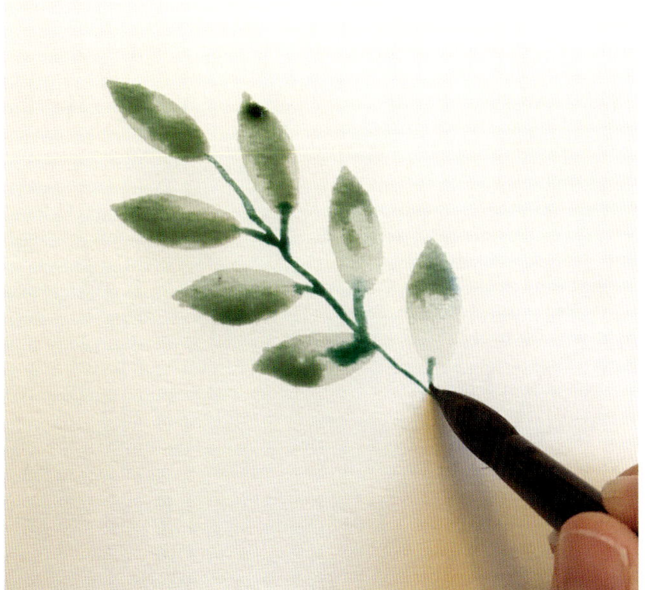

3 Connect the leaves to a stem. Use just the tip of your brush to create the stem.

An easy way to create leaves is to use the natural shape of your brush to suggest their form.

BUDS

In a painting, buds can act as filler flowers that enhance the main blooms. Painting a variety of buds is a great way to fill in the awkward white spaces in your painting, and they can also serve as an unexpected pop of color when necessary. They provide the finishing touch in a painting.

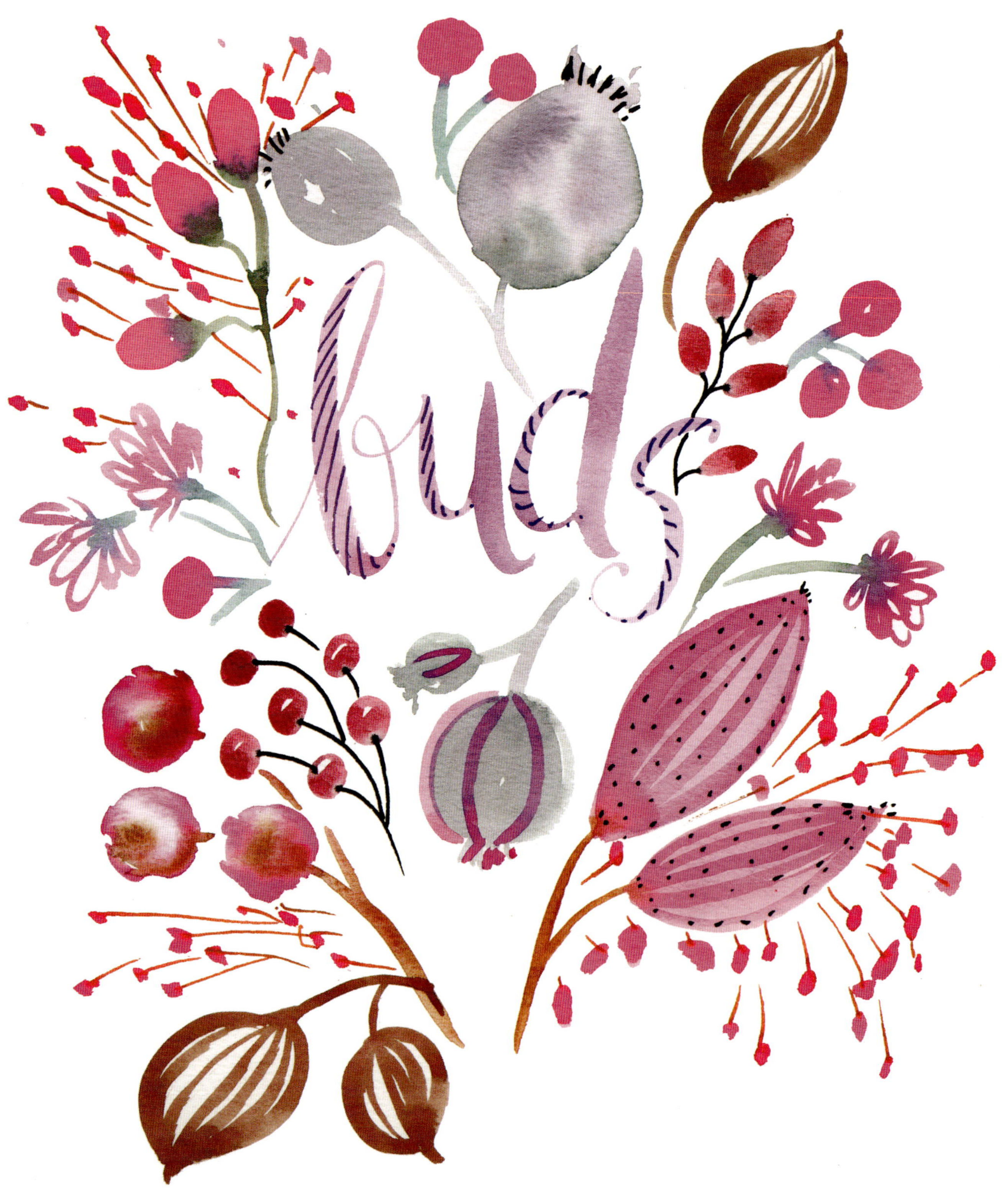

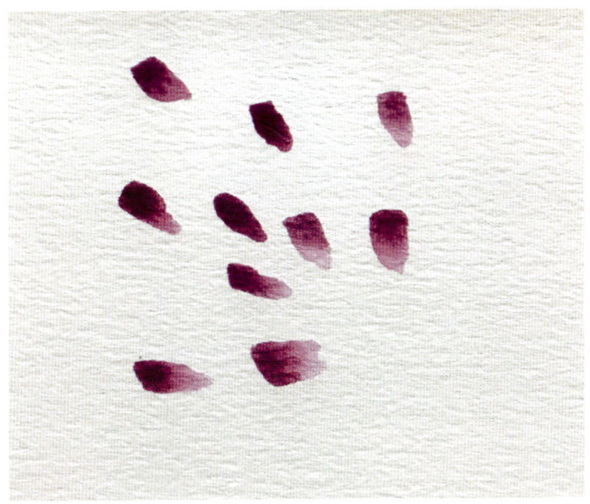

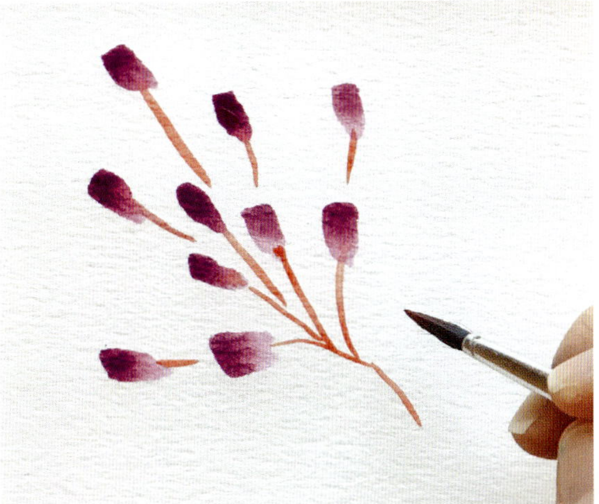

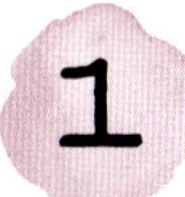

Using the side of a small, round brush, dab marks in a spraylike shape.

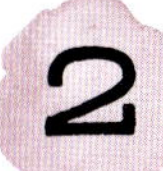

Add stems to the buds, angling the lines toward a central stem at the bottom of the spray.

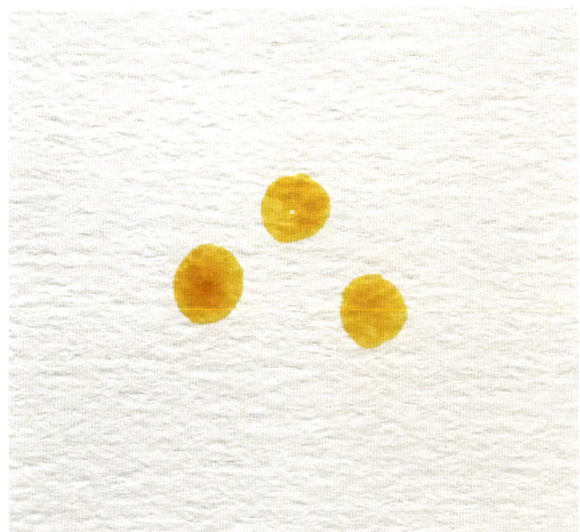

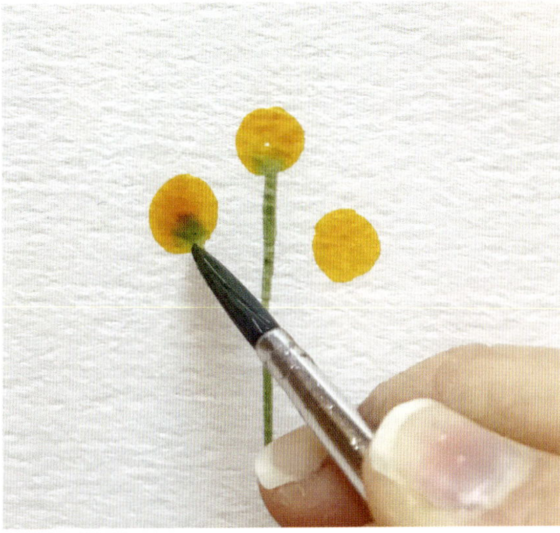

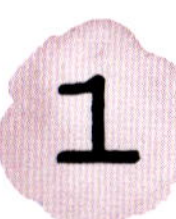

Here is another easy bud that you can use to fill out your florals.

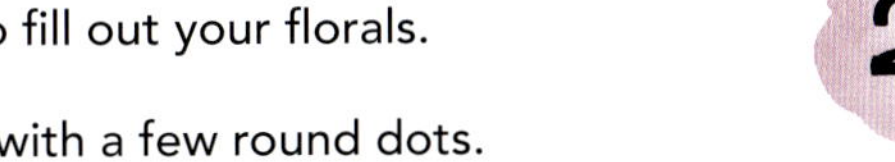

Start with a few round dots.

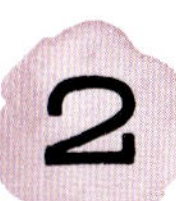

Choose a color for the stem, and touch your brush to the still-wet bud. Then extend the stem downward.

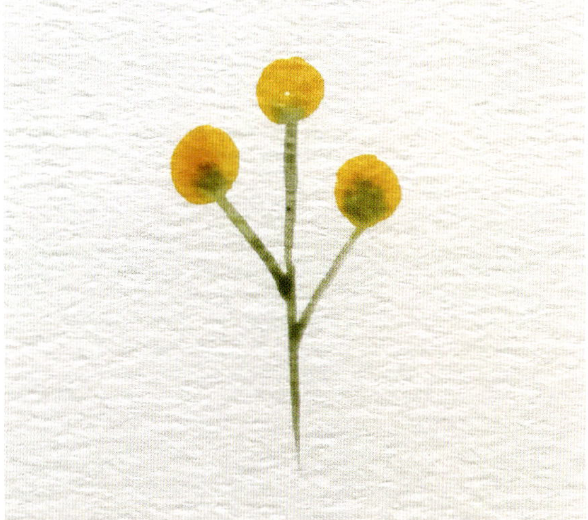

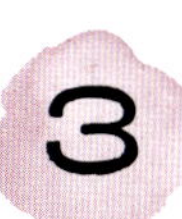

Angle the stems toward each other and connect them.

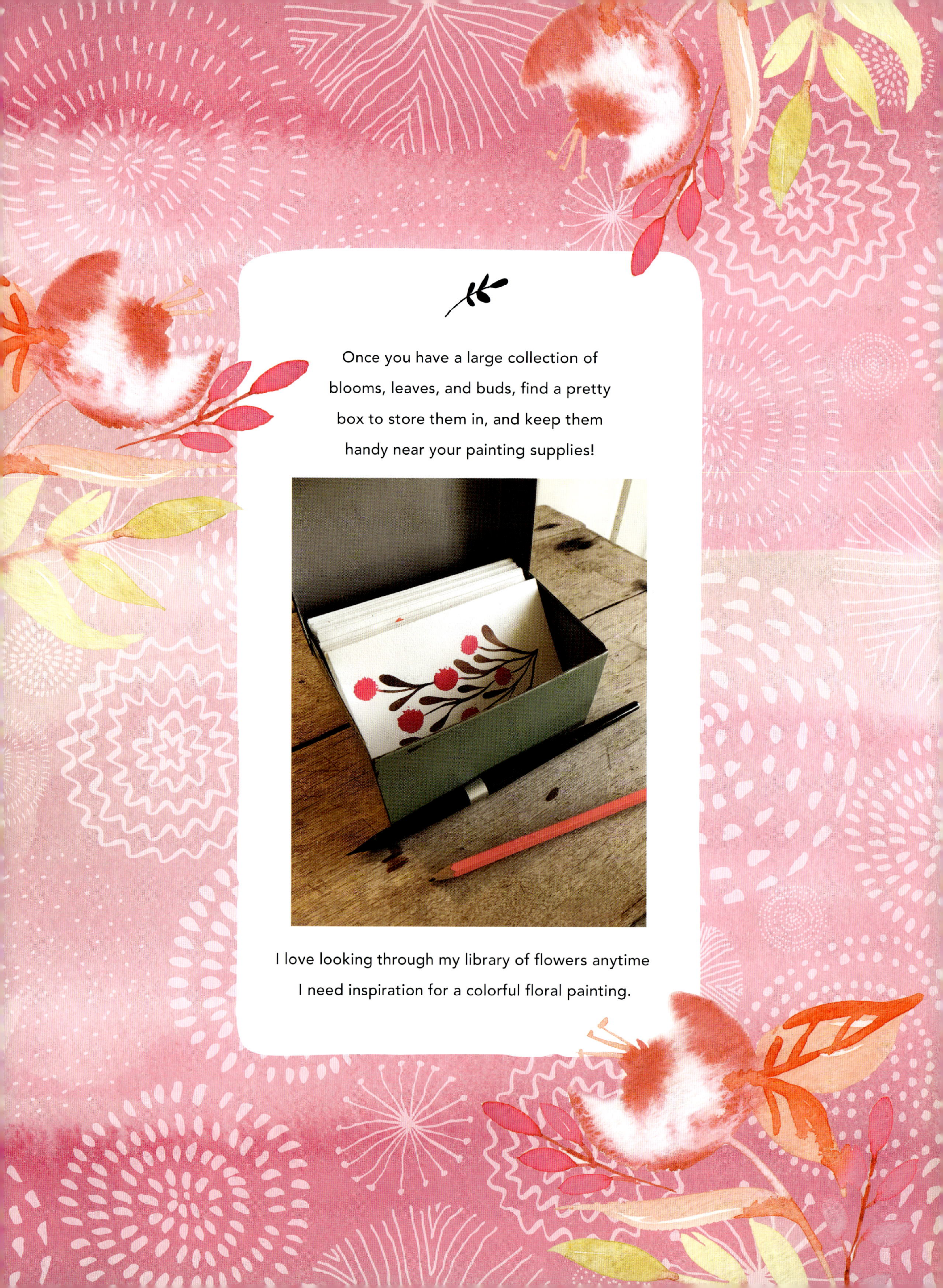

Once you have a large collection of blooms, leaves, and buds, find a pretty box to store them in, and keep them handy near your painting supplies!

I love looking through my library of flowers anytime I need inspiration for a colorful floral painting.

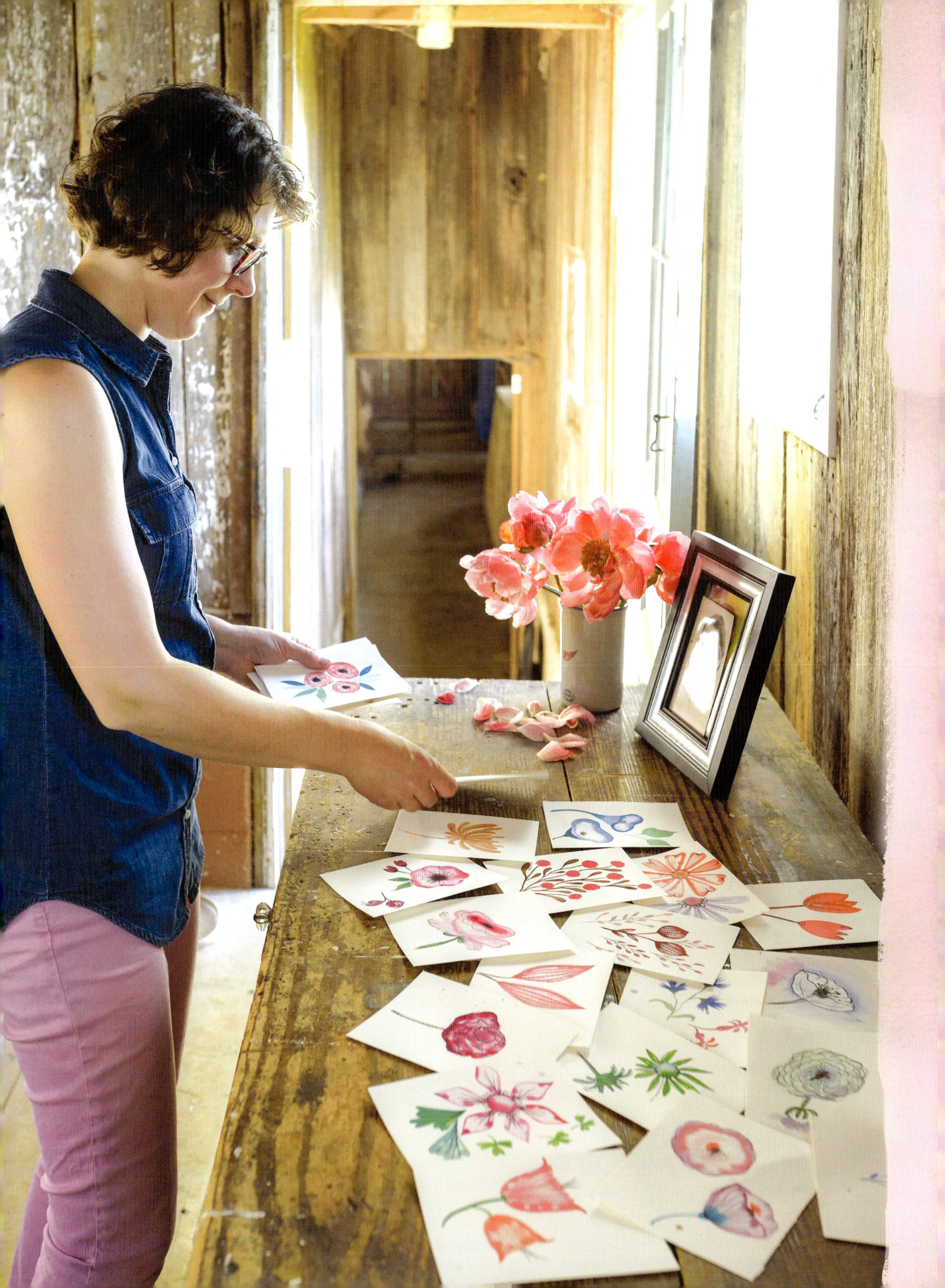

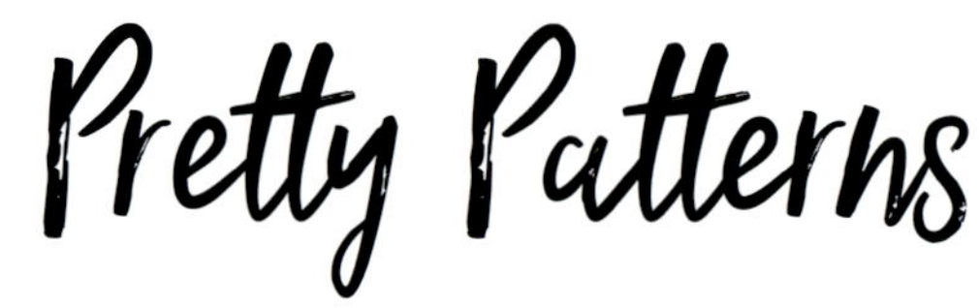

Pretty Patterns

Creating patterns out of watercolor florals is easy to do, and the results are always so pretty! The key to forming a pattern is repetition, and this is also what makes patterns fun to paint. Look around your home to observe the many different uses of patterns in your world: rugs, cushion covers, dishes, linens, maybe even the outfit you're wearing right now—many feature patterns.

Use the artwork you created for the "A Library of Flowers" project on pages 30-41, and choose one focal bloom, one secondary bloom, a couple of different leaves, and a couple of bud shapes. Then consider your color palette. You can use the colors I've chosen, or you can go rogue and make up your own. Don't overthink it—just get started!

Perhaps a color palette in your home will inspire the pattern you will create for this project!

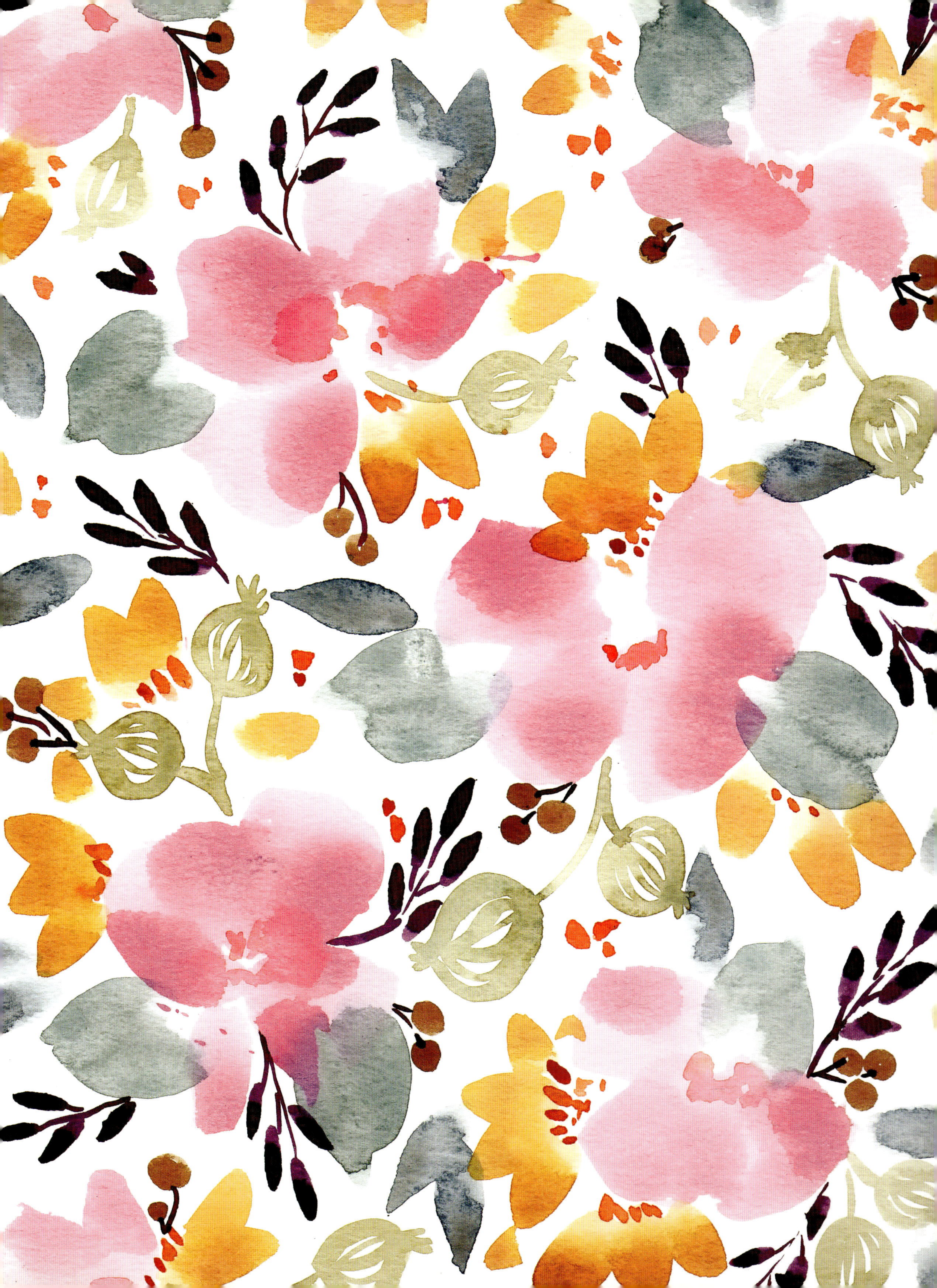

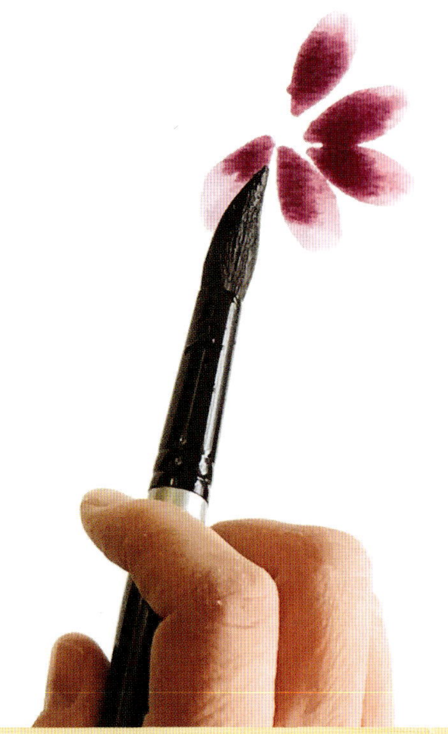

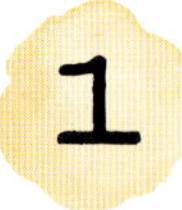

Start by painting your focal bloom. I used my largest round brush on its side and mimicked the shape of petals, which I then formed into a bloom.

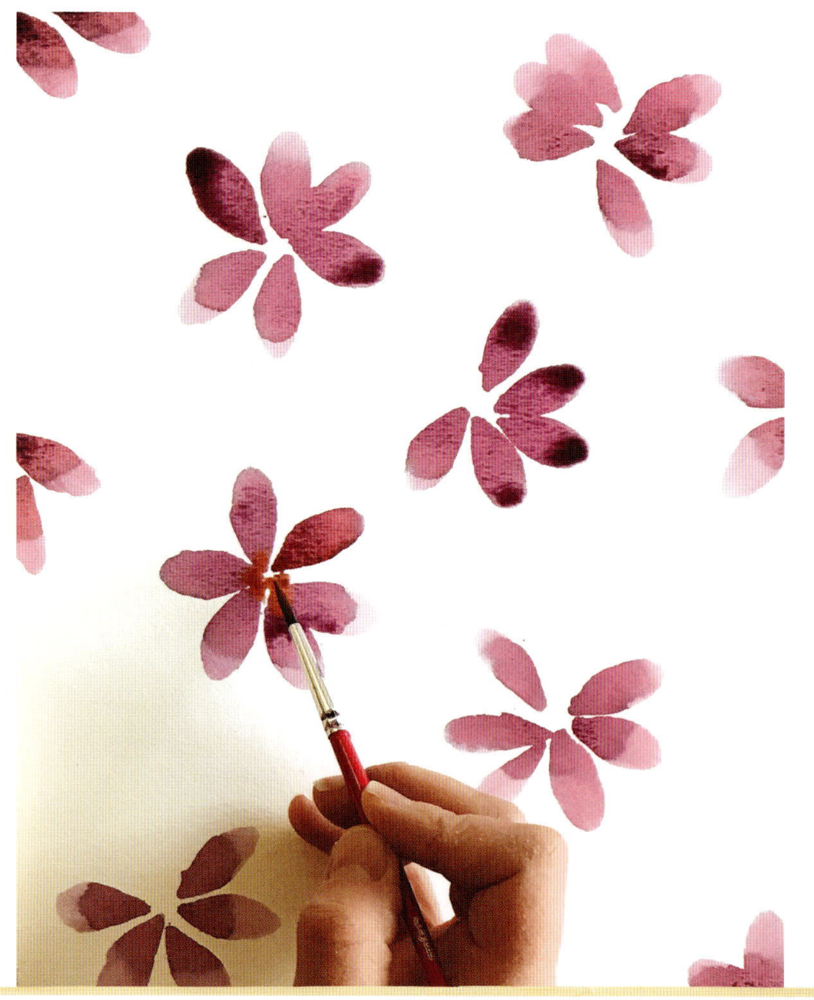

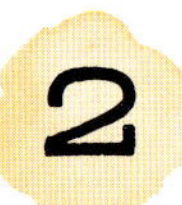

Repeat the flower throughout the page, and remember to include some partial blooms near the edges of the paper to indicate that the pattern continues indefinitely.

With a smaller brush and a different paint color, tap some color into the centers of the blooms you just painted.

3

Paint some secondary blooms extending from the focal blooms. Paint a couple of smaller secondary blooms next to each other, and add tiny stems to these to visually connect them to the focal blooms.

4

Using a large brush and a new paint color, press the brush into a leaf shape that extends from the focal blooms.

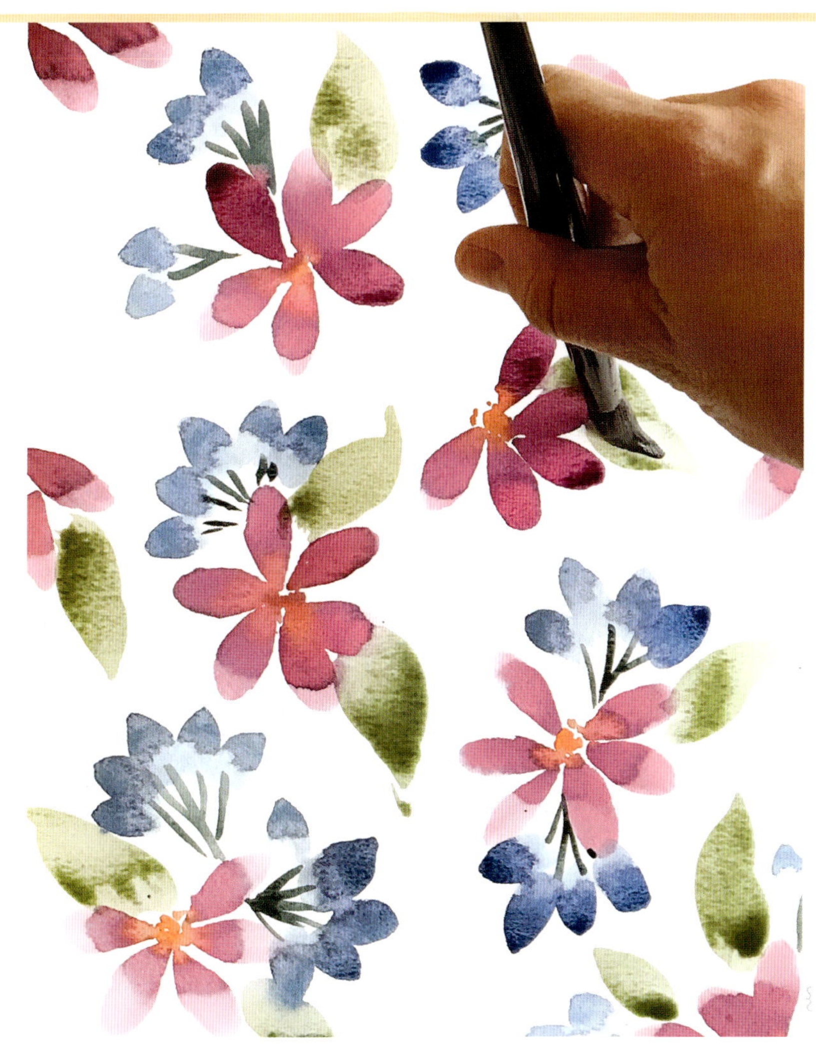

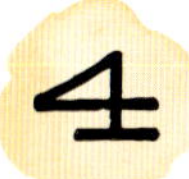

Strive for balance in your painting.

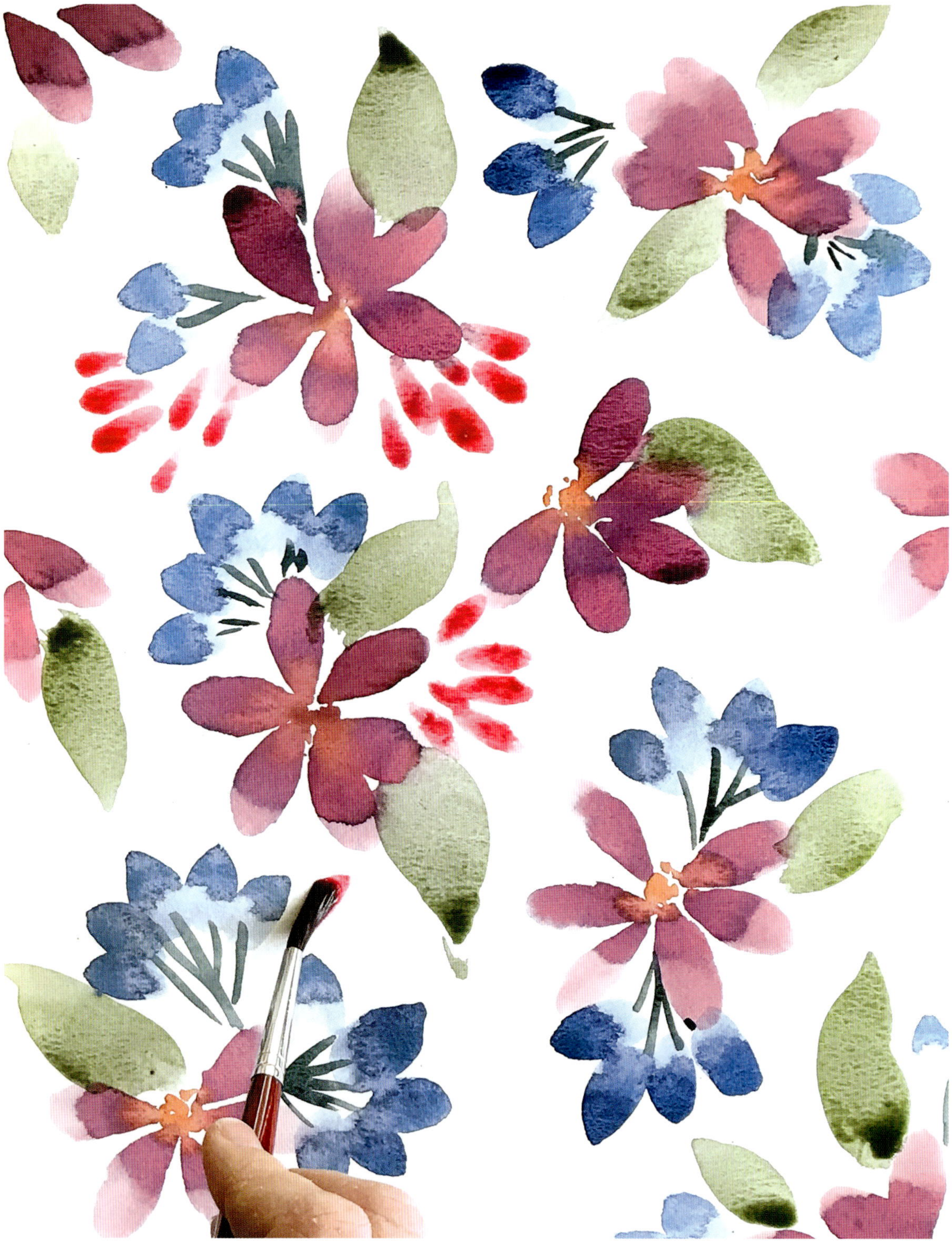

Add some buds. Using a smaller brush, press the color onto the page, and cluster a group of buds around the focal bloom.

6

With an "ugly" color (see page 20), draw stems moving from the buds toward the focal bloom.

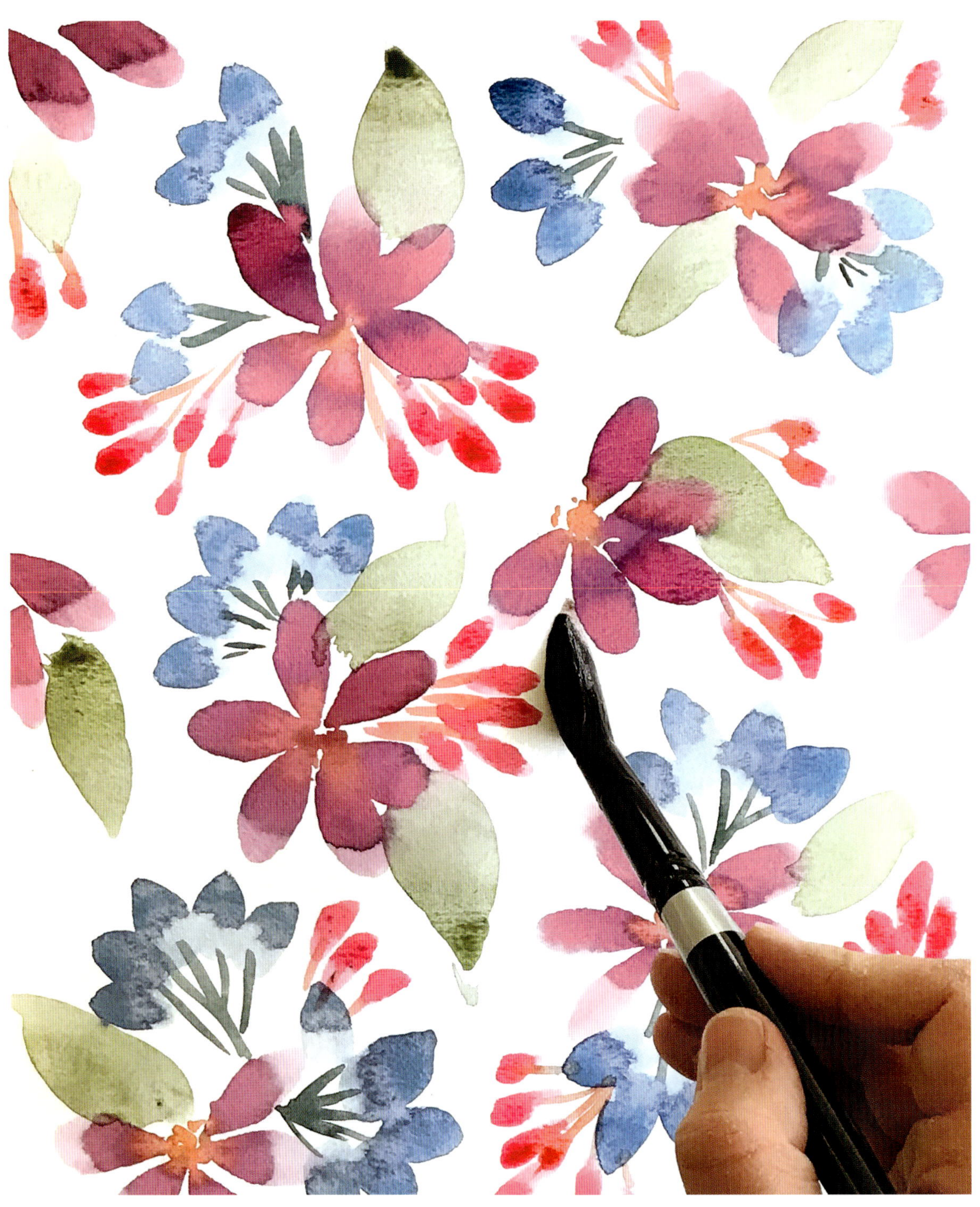

7 There are some white spaces left that can be filled with another neutral "ugly" color. Using the side of your brush, press leaflike shapes evenly around the page.

Your eye will tell you when the painting looks pleasing and balanced.

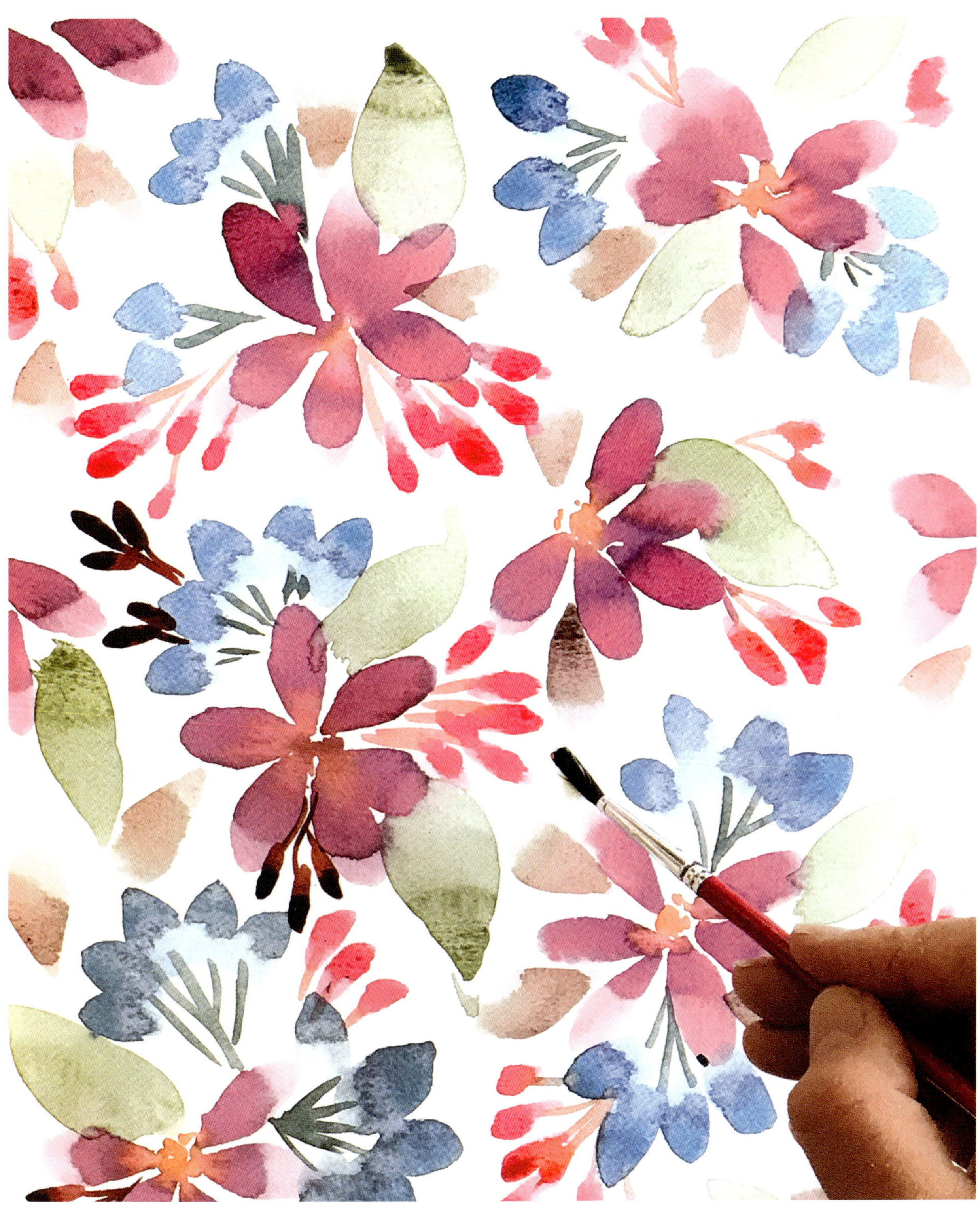

8 With an eye-catching color, create some smaller bud or leaflike forms extending from each cluster of blooms and leaves. Because this is a pattern, once again strive for balance when placing your colors and shapes.

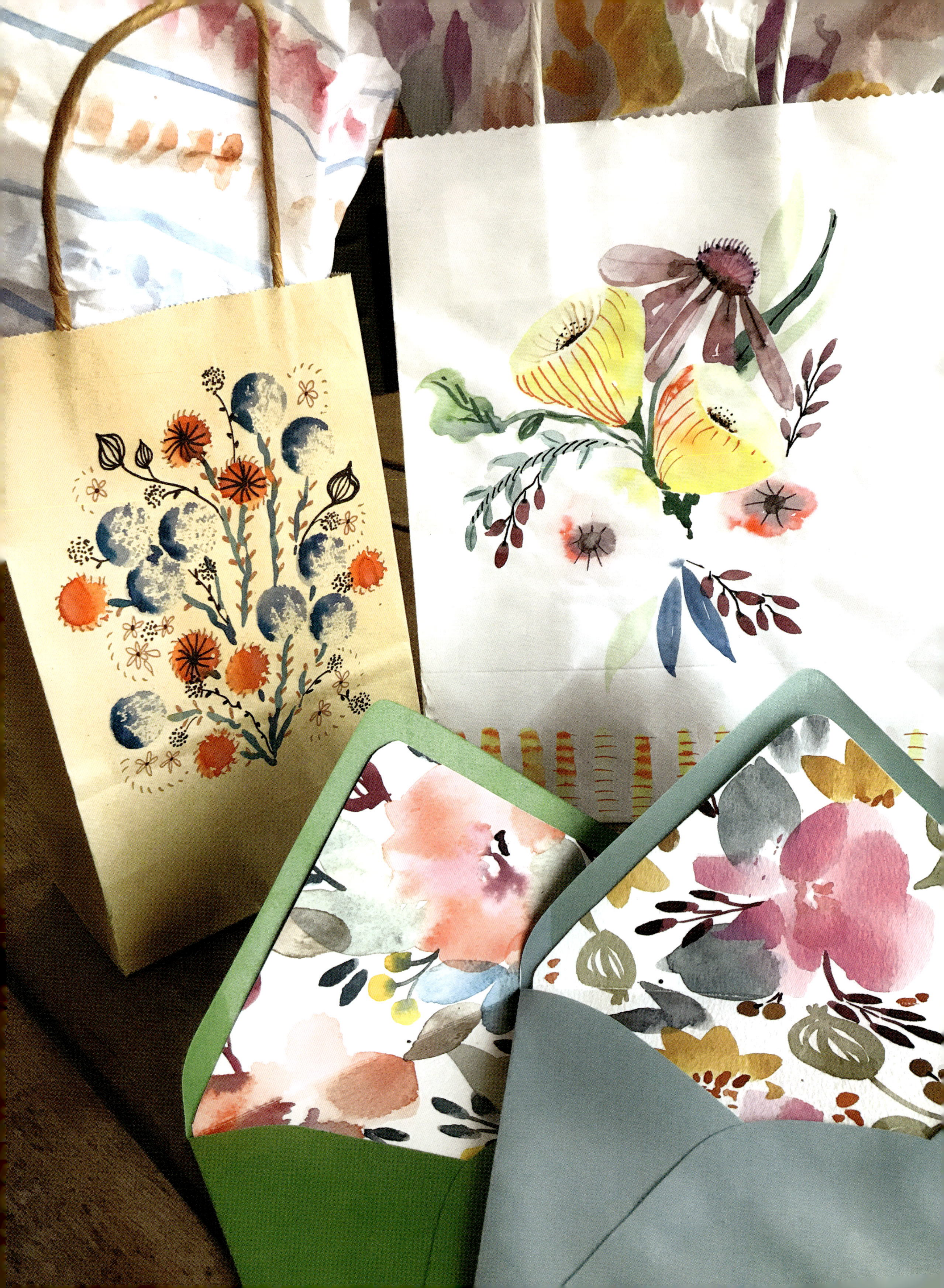

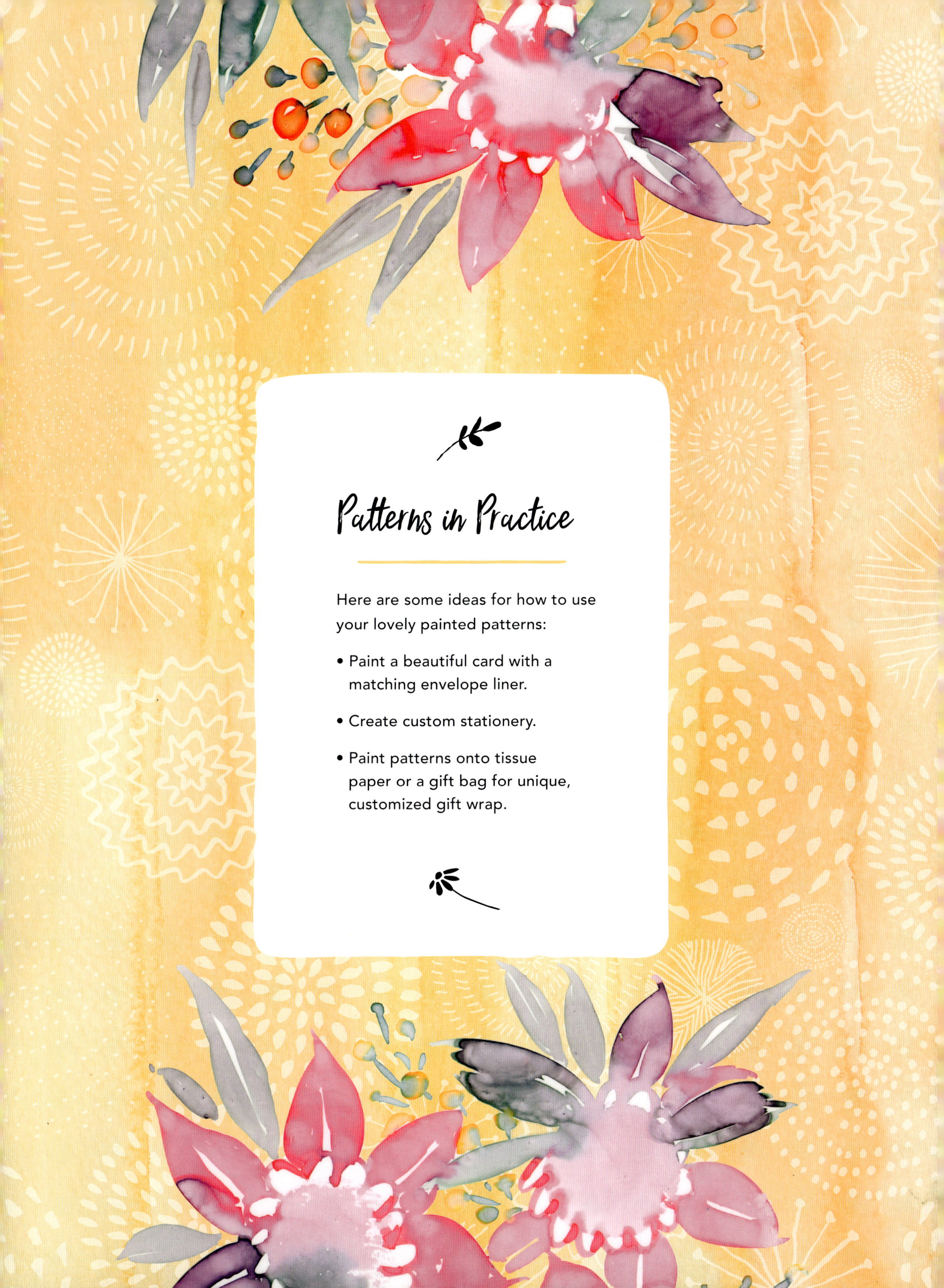

Patterns in Practice

Here are some ideas for how to use your lovely painted patterns:

- Paint a beautiful card with a matching envelope liner.
- Create custom stationery.
- Paint patterns onto tissue paper or a gift bag for unique, customized gift wrap.

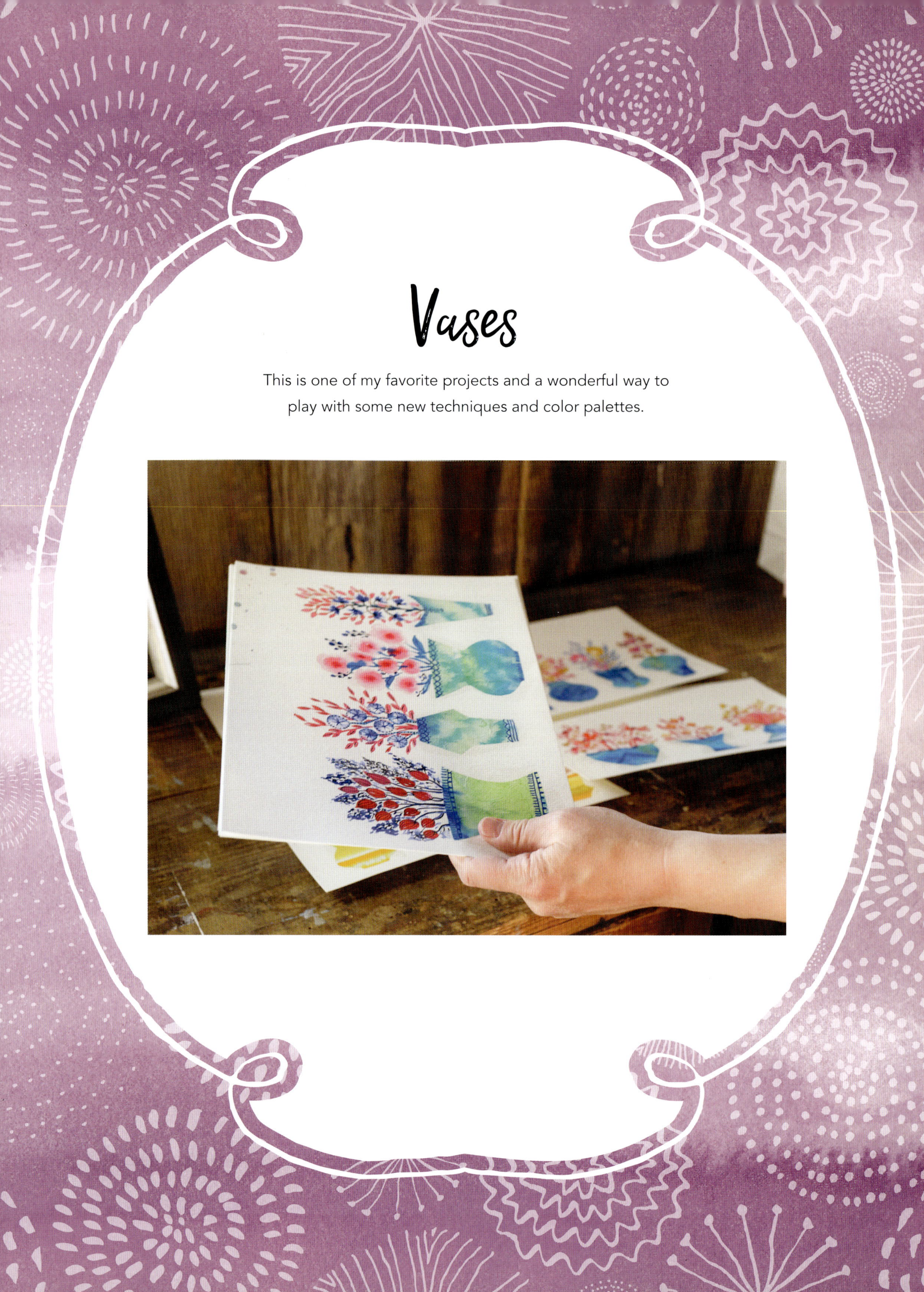

Vases

This is one of my favorite projects and a wonderful way to play with some new techniques and color palettes.

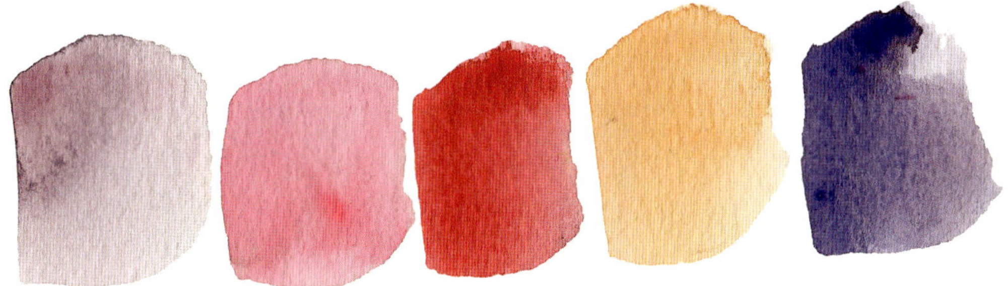

1

Start by choosing a palette of four or five colors.

I chose a warm, mostly analogous color palette of purples, pinks, and oranges with a pop of blue.

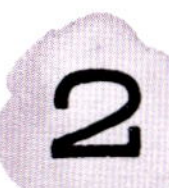

Now let's play with a new technique that will add some texture to your piece: painting on tissue paper.

Grab a piece of white tissue paper (about 5" x 7" in size). With a plastic garbage bag or something similar over your work surface, place the tissue paper matte side up. Now, using the colors you've chosen, paint over the entire sheet of tissue paper. Then lift it off the plastic and let it dry.

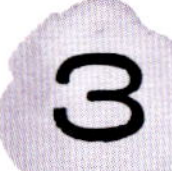

Prepare a sheet of watercolor paper by trimming away its edges and giving it a hand-ripped deckle edge.

First, mark some guidelines for your ruler so that you can rip in a straight line. Then align the ruler to the guidelines, and carefully rip off the remaining flap of paper.

Turn the watercolor paper horizontally; this will form the background for your three vases.

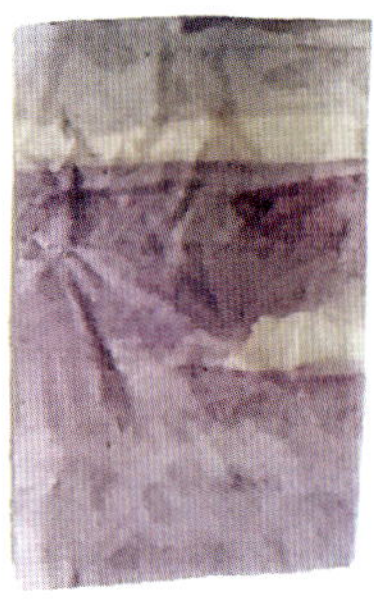

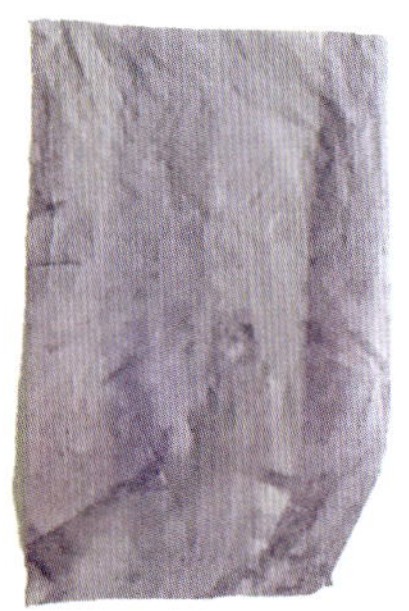

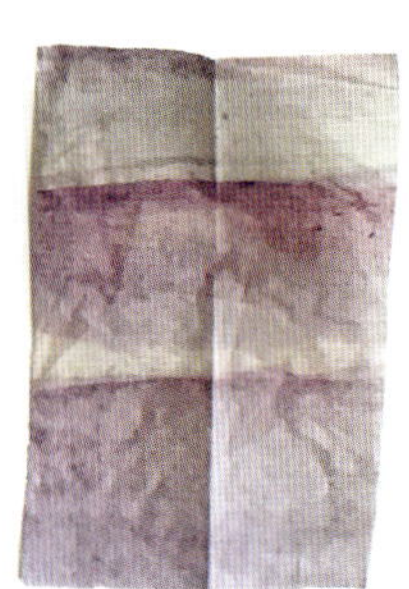

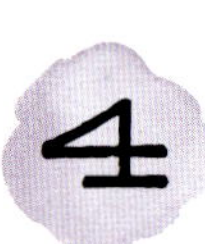

Cut three small pieces from the painted tissue paper.

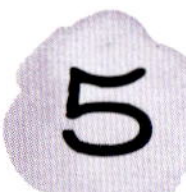

Fold each piece of cut tissue paper in half lengthwise and cut out half of a vase, so that when you open your tissue paper, you will have a symmetrical shape. Cut out three vases of different shapes, and then glue these pieces to the watercolor paper, leaving room above the vases to paint bouquets of flowers.

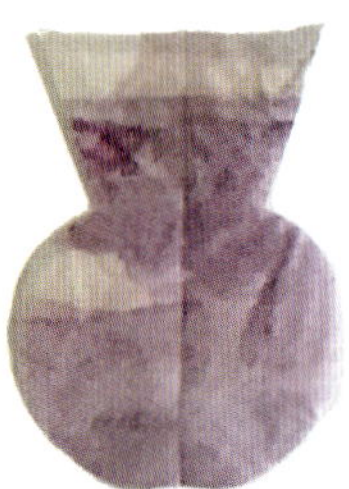

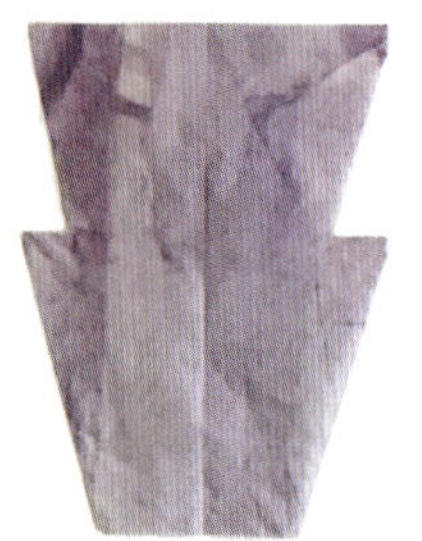

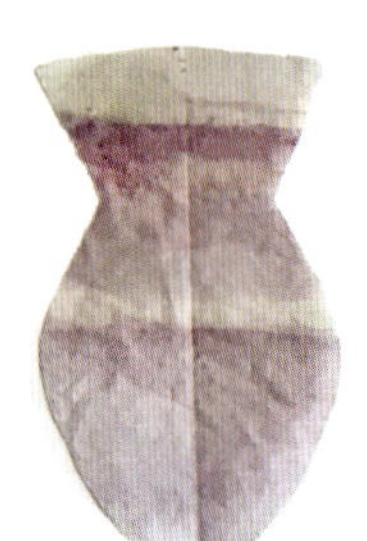

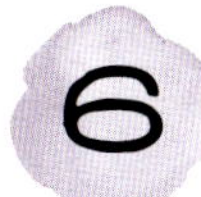

Beginning with the center vase, pick one bloom shape to paint multiple times in a bouquet. These flowers can be somewhat stylized, as they will be small.

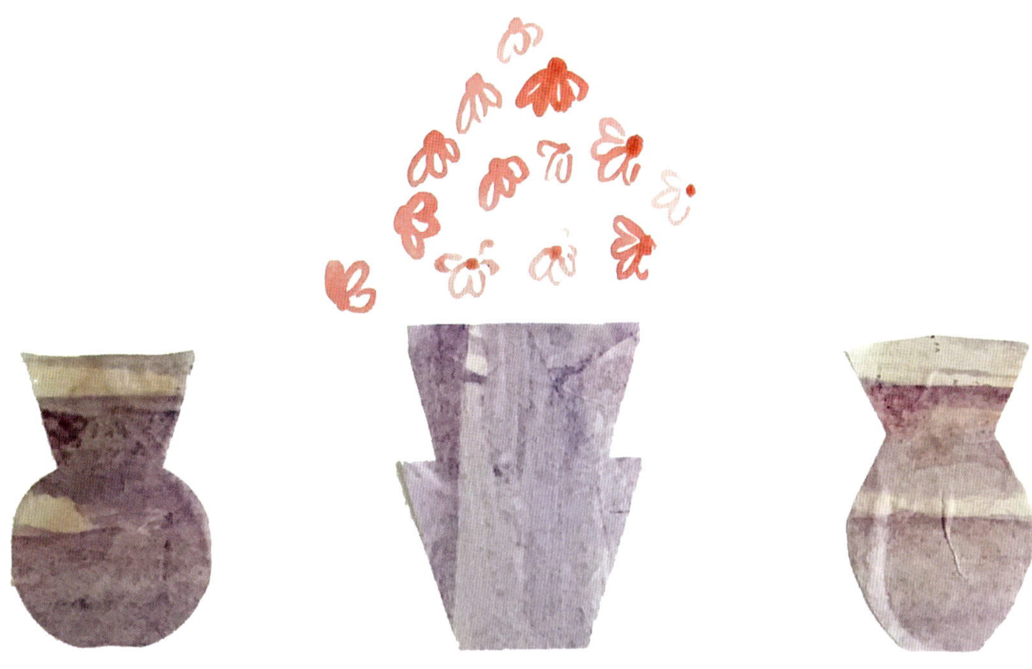

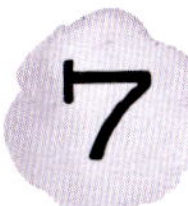

Keeping to your chosen color palette, add details, like stems, leaves, and other elements, to complete your bouquet. Also add a few details to the vase itself.

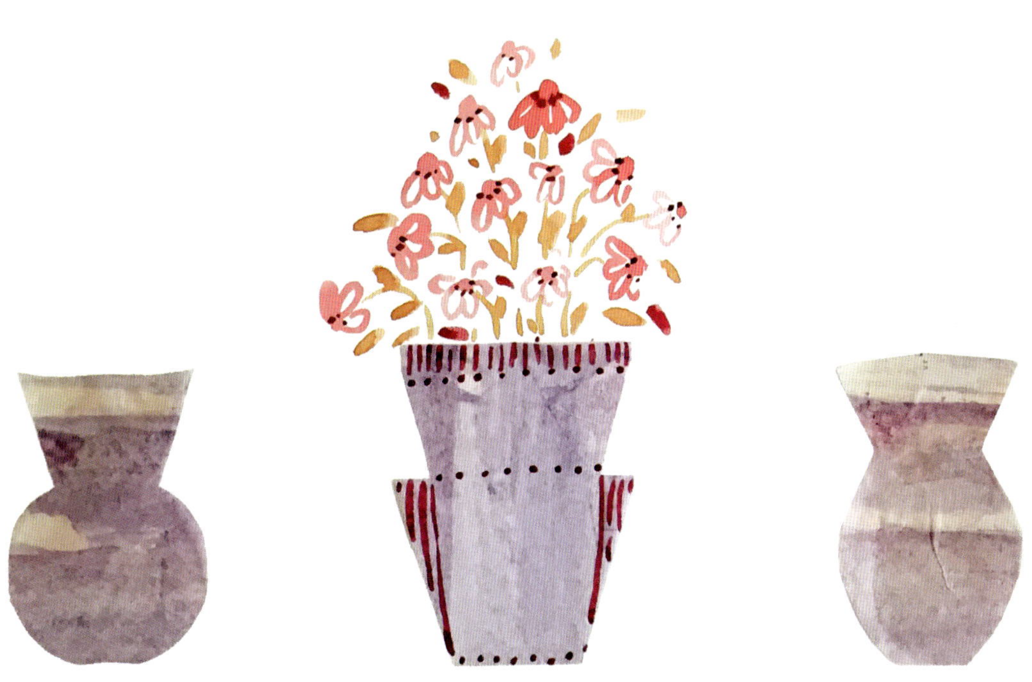

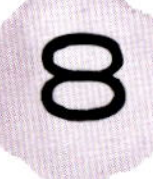

8

Complete the remaining vases using different florals and leaves. Try to use all the colors within your chosen palette while maintaining a balanced look.

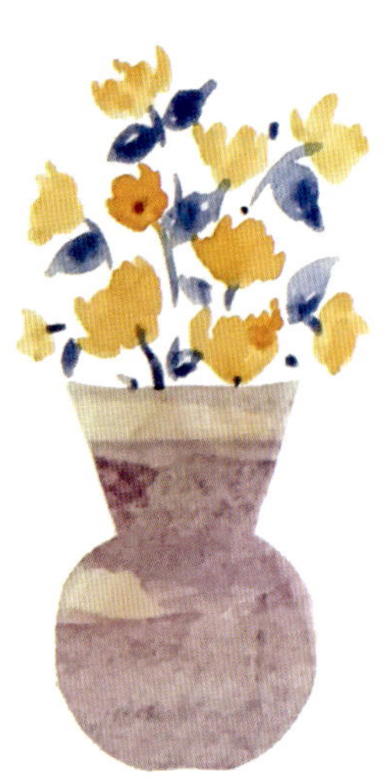

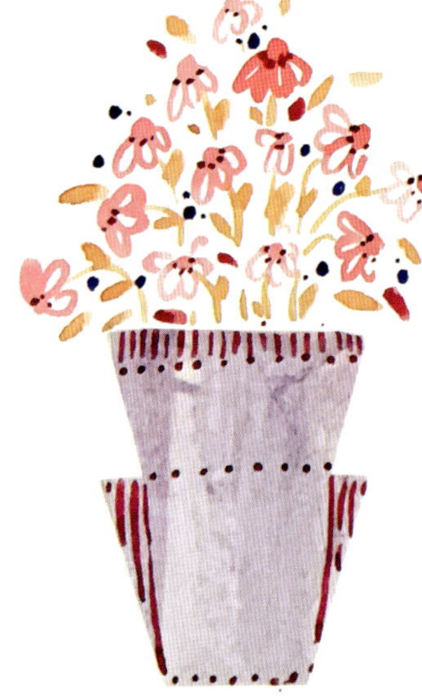

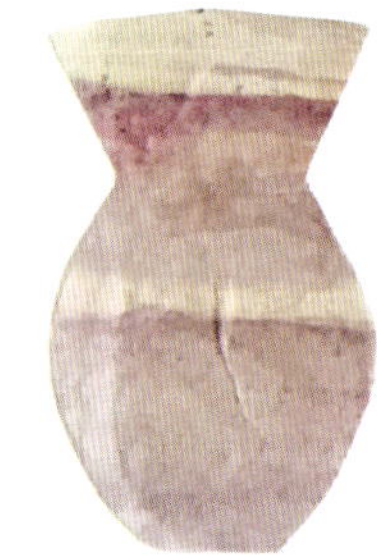

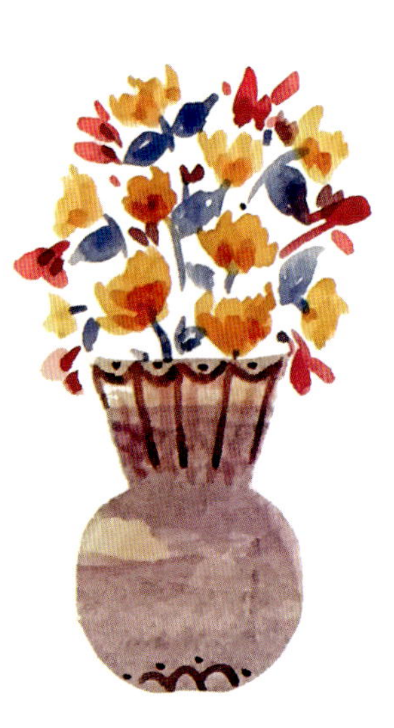

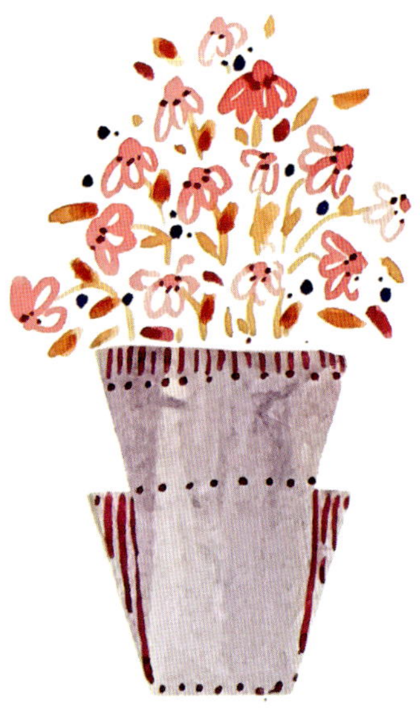

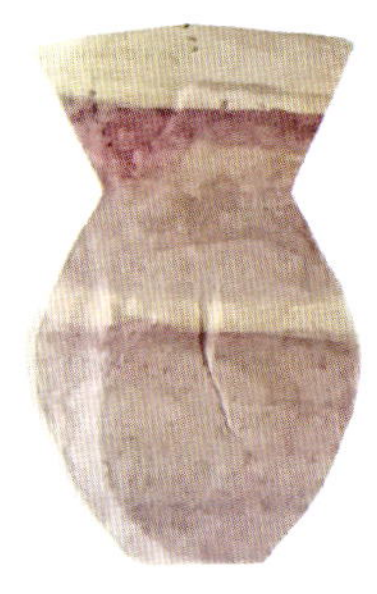

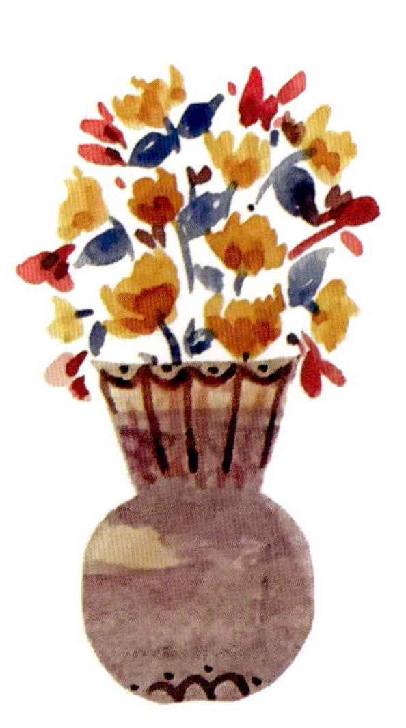

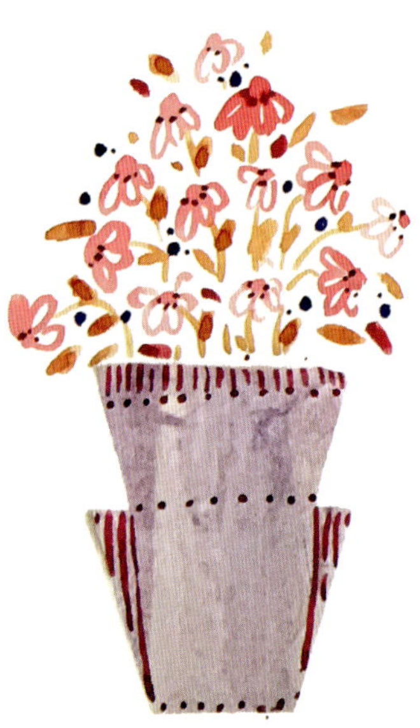

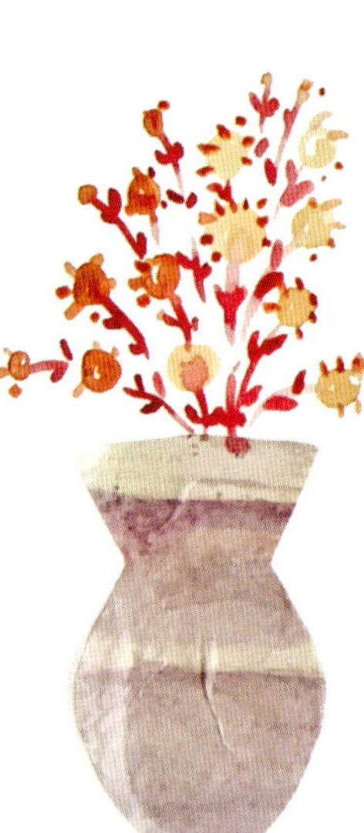

Here is the finished piece.

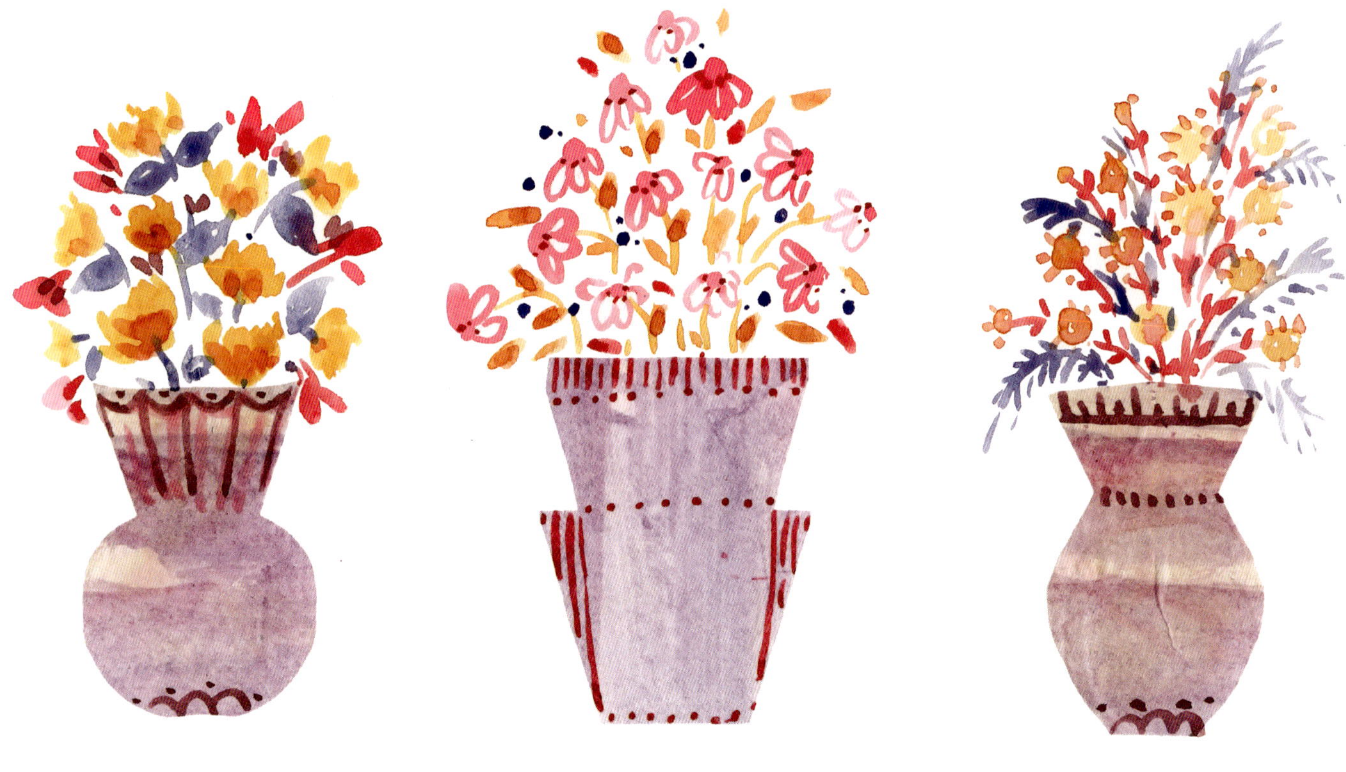

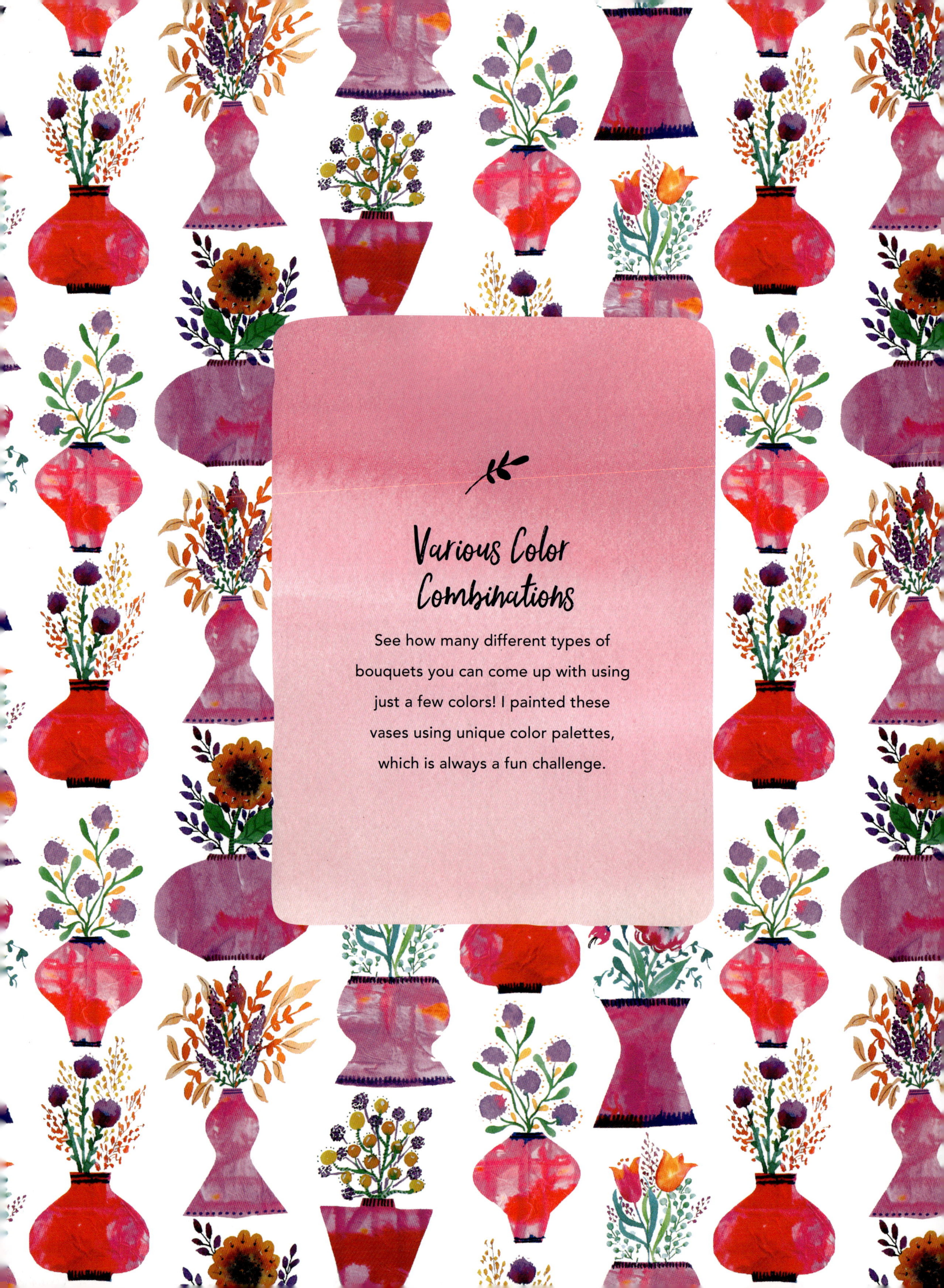

Various Color Combinations

See how many different types of bouquets you can come up with using just a few colors! I painted these vases using unique color palettes, which is always a fun challenge.

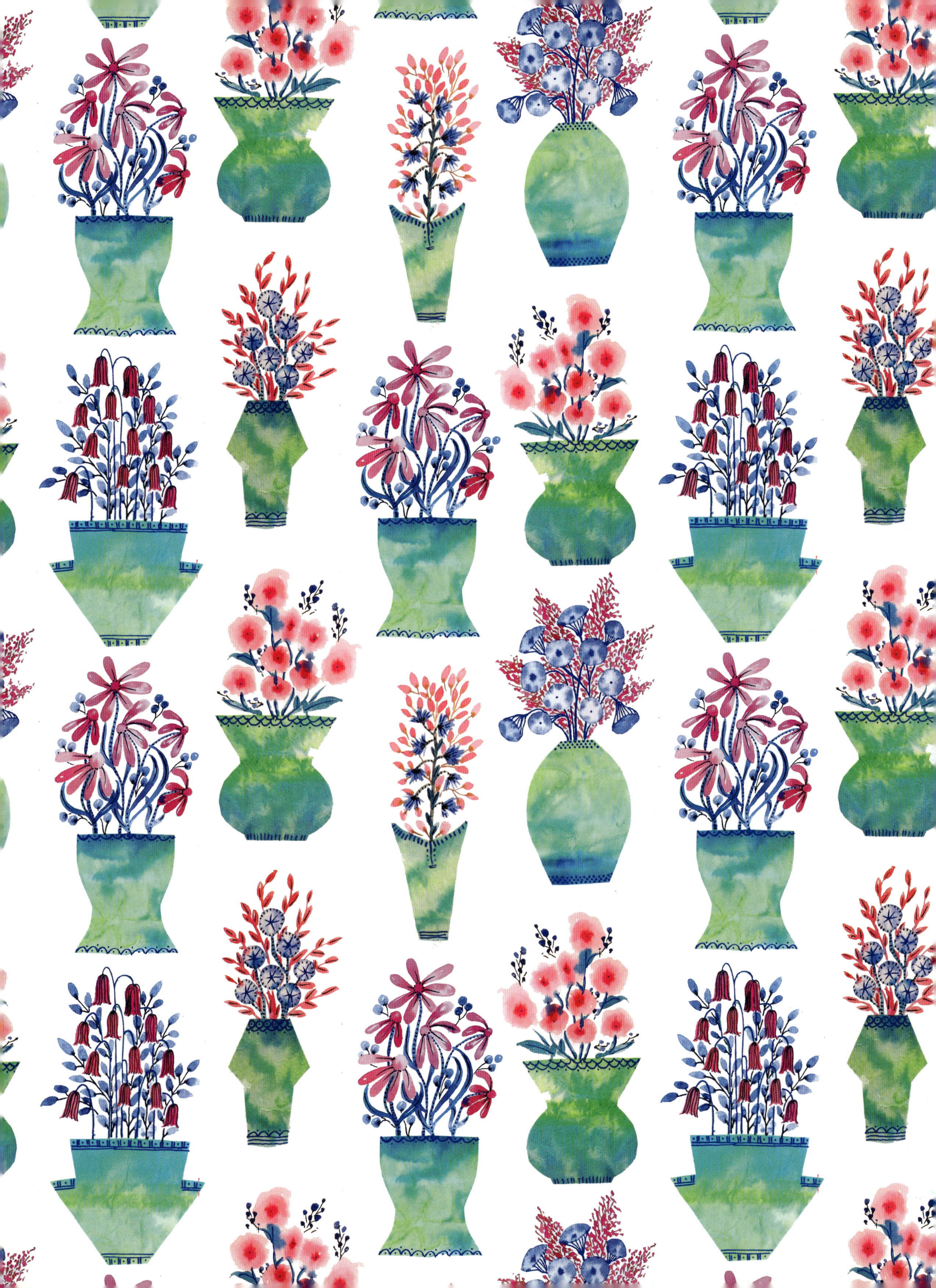

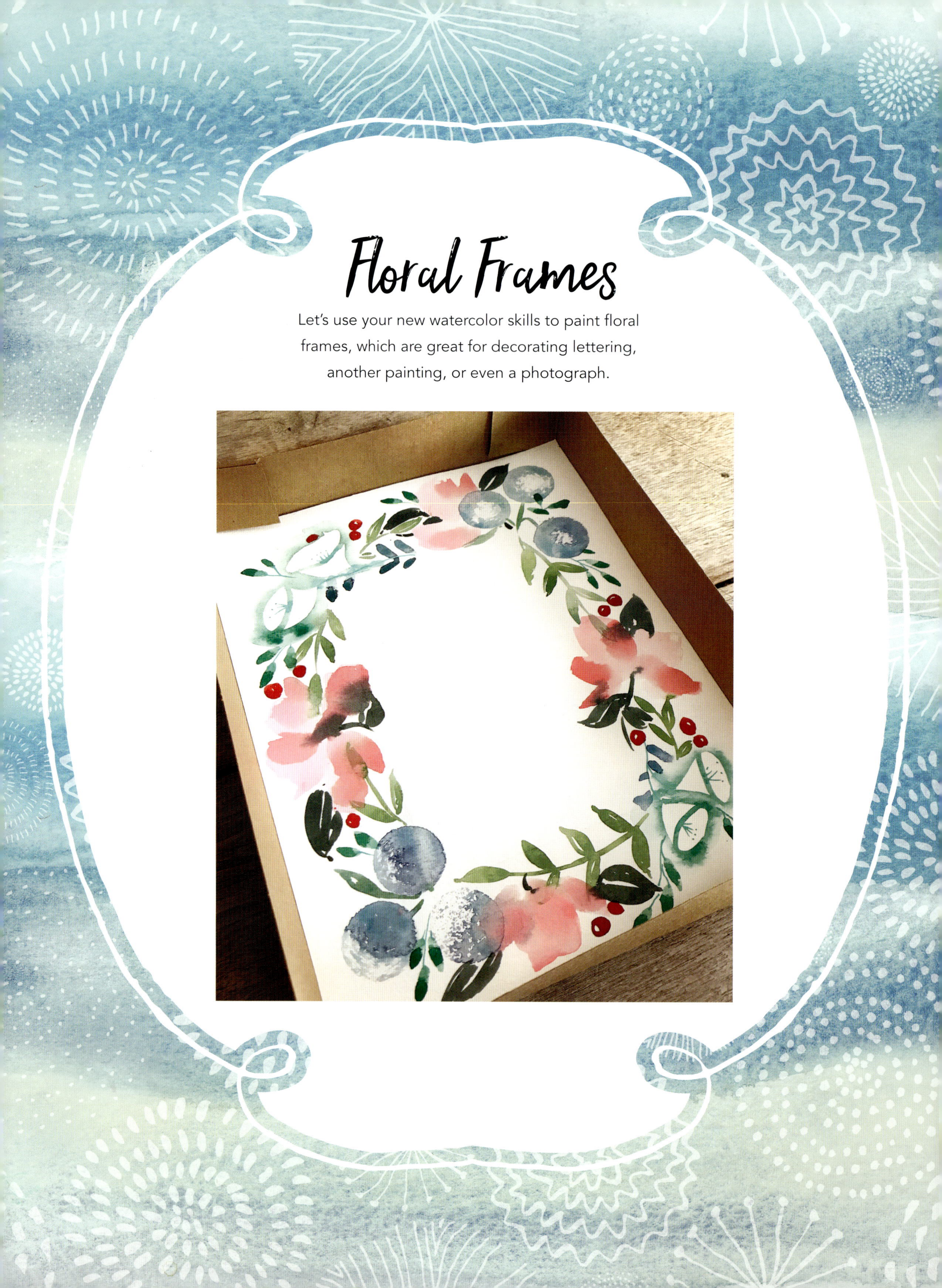

Floral Frames

Let's use your new watercolor skills to paint floral frames, which are great for decorating lettering, another painting, or even a photograph.

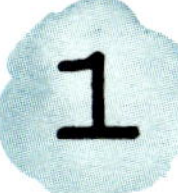

First, find a "template" for your frame. Look around your home for a circular or square object that's smaller than a sheet of watercolor paper. Then center the object on your paper, and lightly trace around it with a pencil.

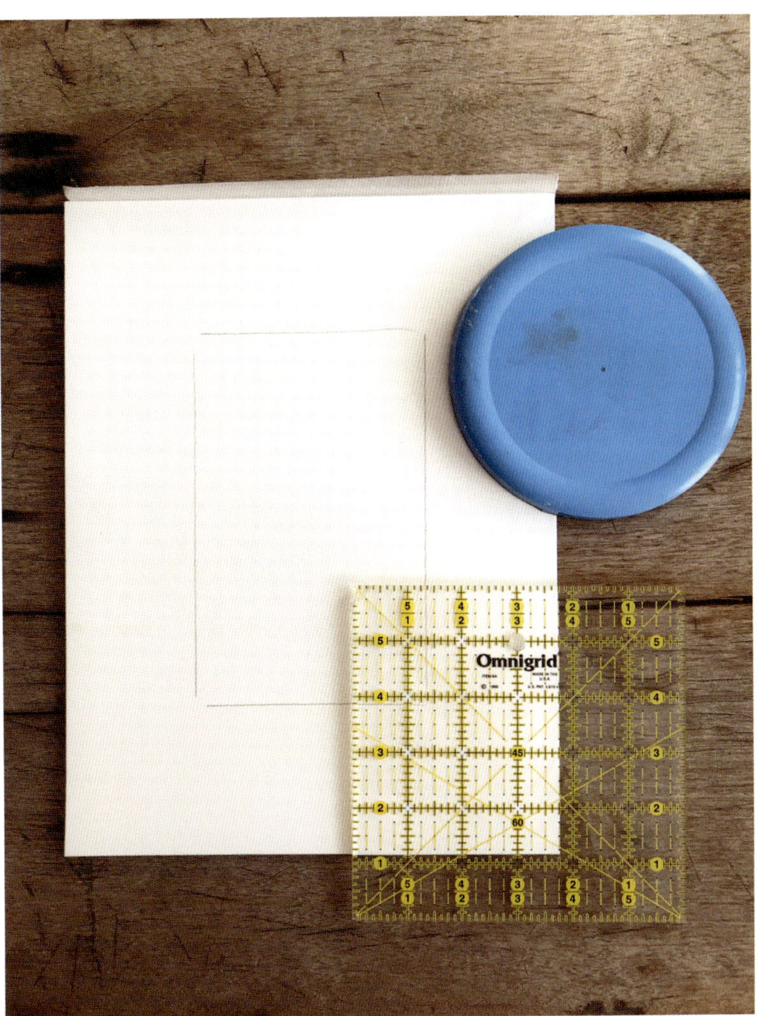

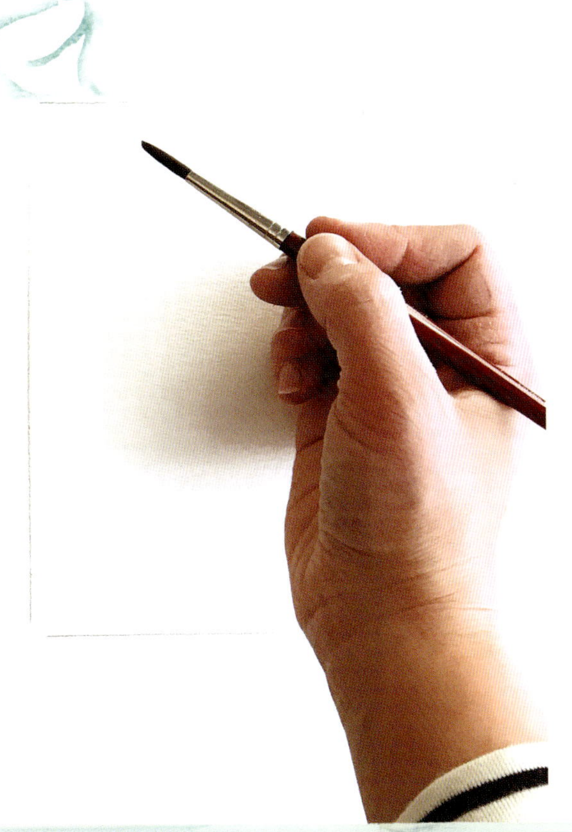

2

Let's paint! For this frame, I've chosen a color scheme of greens and blues with a pop of pink for some contrast. I like to start painting in a corner to immediately define the frame.

Create white flowers by defining the negative space around them.

When painting a frame, the most important thing to keep in mind is balance. If you put flowers in one corner, you should also put them in the opposite corner. This is somewhat intuitive, and as you practice more, it will become second nature.

Add some smaller leaves using another color. I used a darker blue-green.

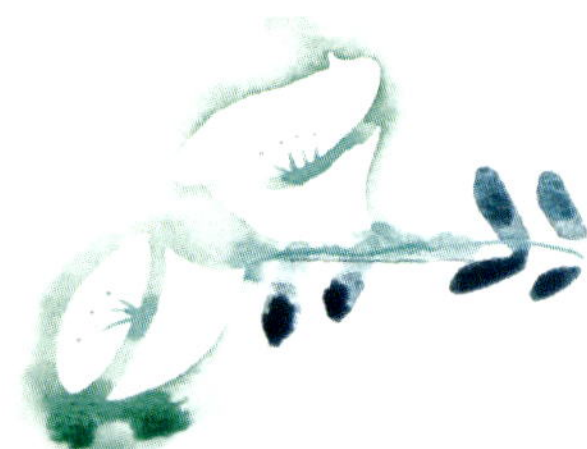

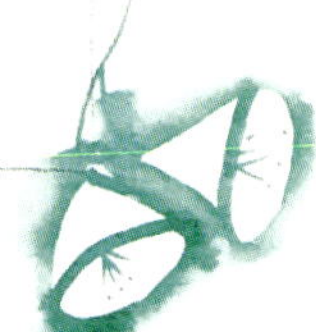

Paint markers work well for adding stems and other details in a controlled way.

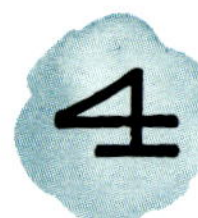

Now, begin to fill in the other two corners. I used a round sponge brush to create a stamped look.

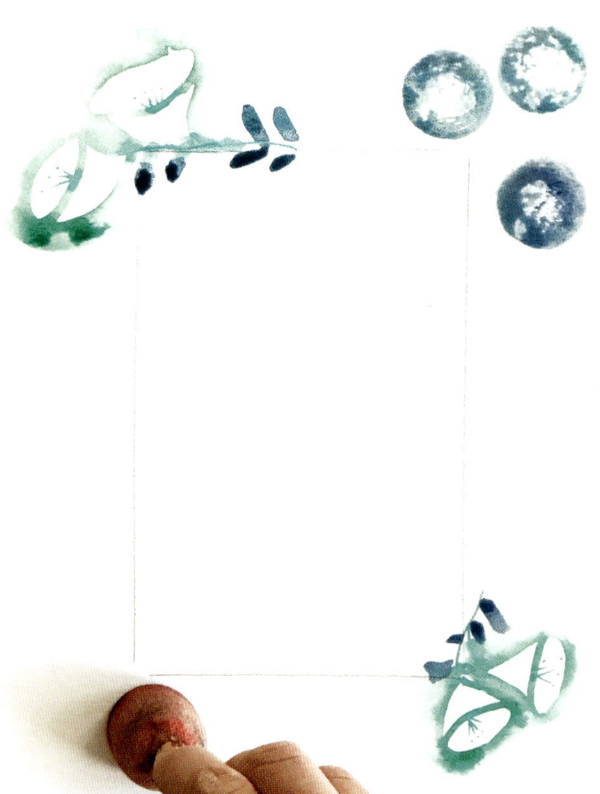

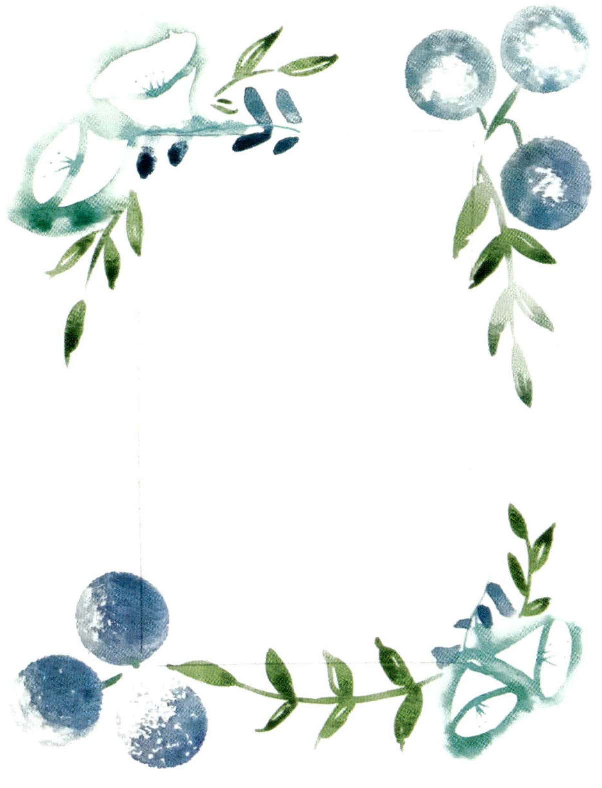

Add leaves branching out from the flowers to help fill space. I used a lighter yellow-green color.

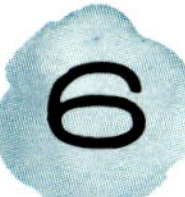

There are still large, open areas on each side of the frame. With a contrasting color, paint some focal blooms. I dragged my large, round brush to create lush, pink petals.

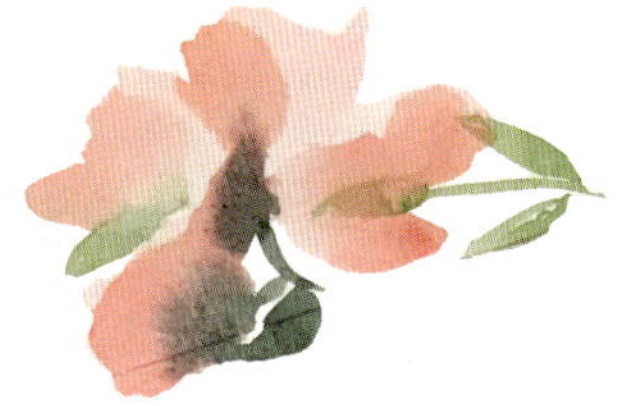
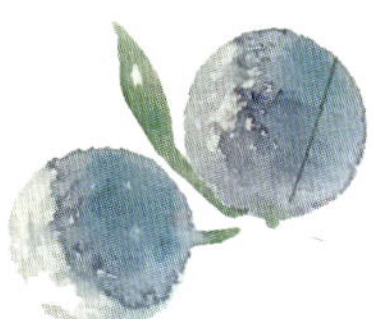
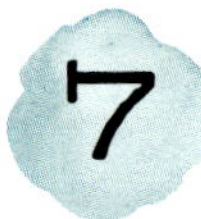

With a darker color, add leaves to your new blooms. I used a dark, earthy green.

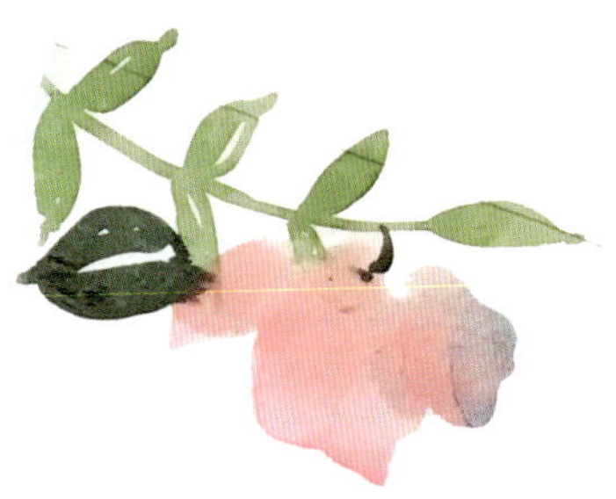
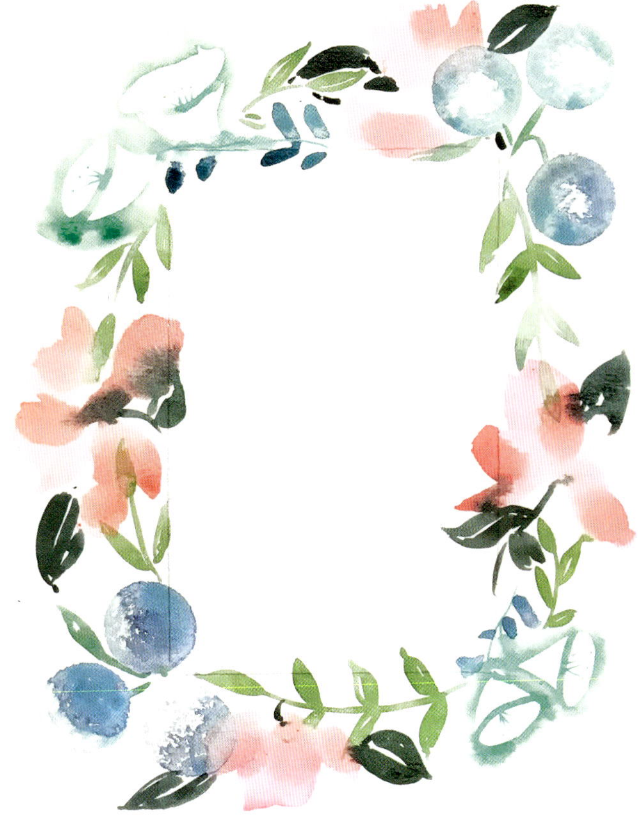
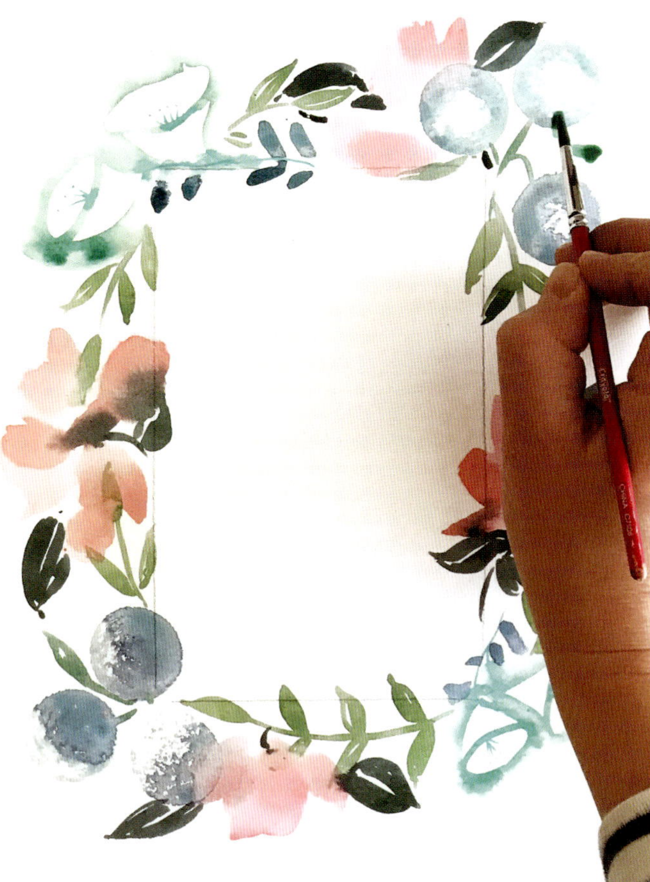
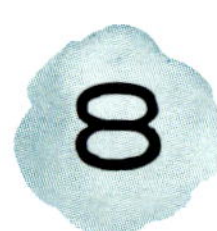

And the finishing touches. I painted some smaller leaves using dark green to help fill in any remaining white areas.

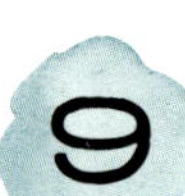

I added dark red berries to my final piece for a fun surprise!

Let your painting dry before erasing the pencil guidelines, and enjoy your finished frame. Wouldn't this make a lovely gift surrounding a precious family photo?

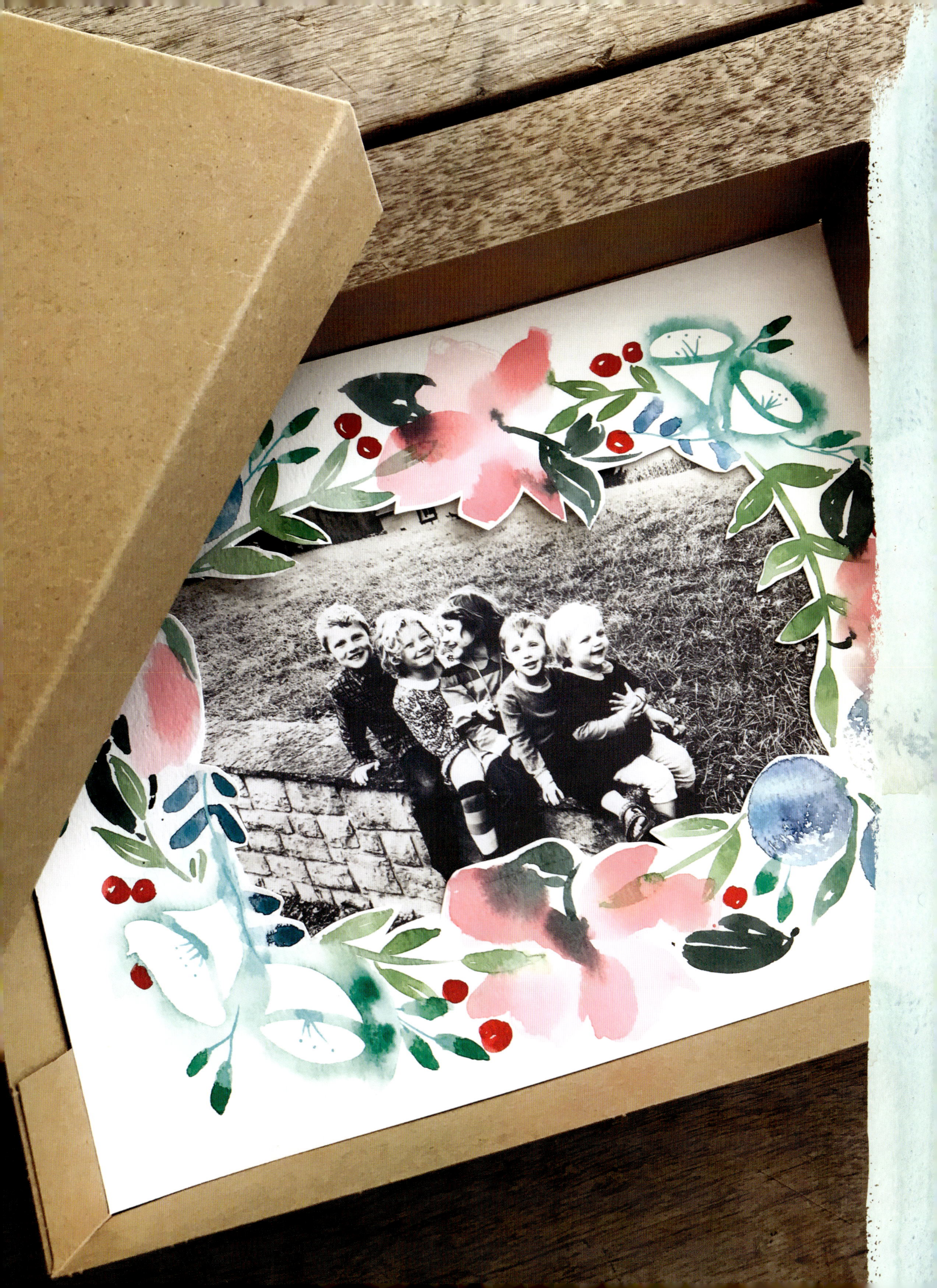

Blossoming Motivation

Here are some examples of other floral frames you might create.

Try varying the colors and types of flowers featured in your frames.

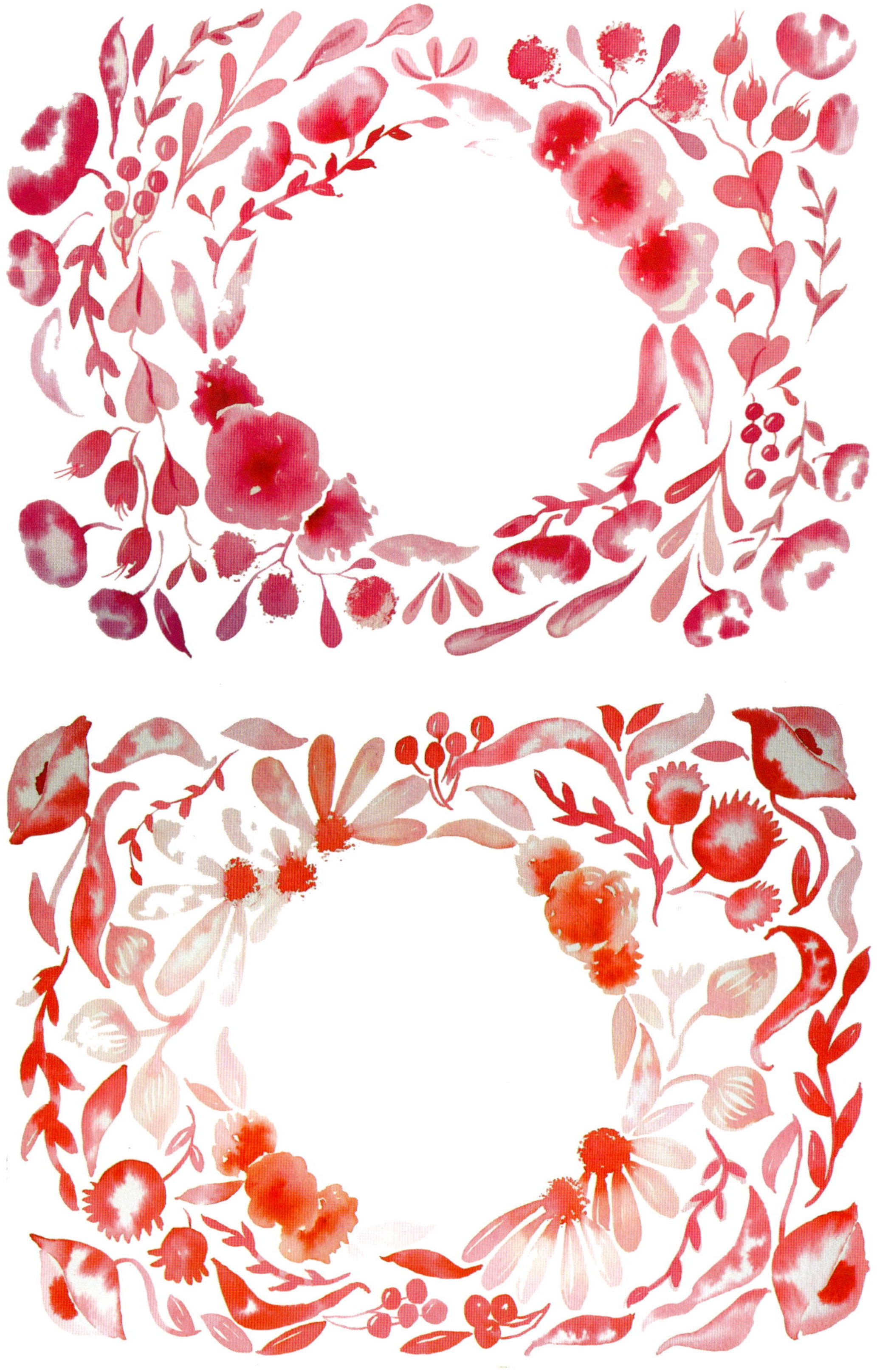

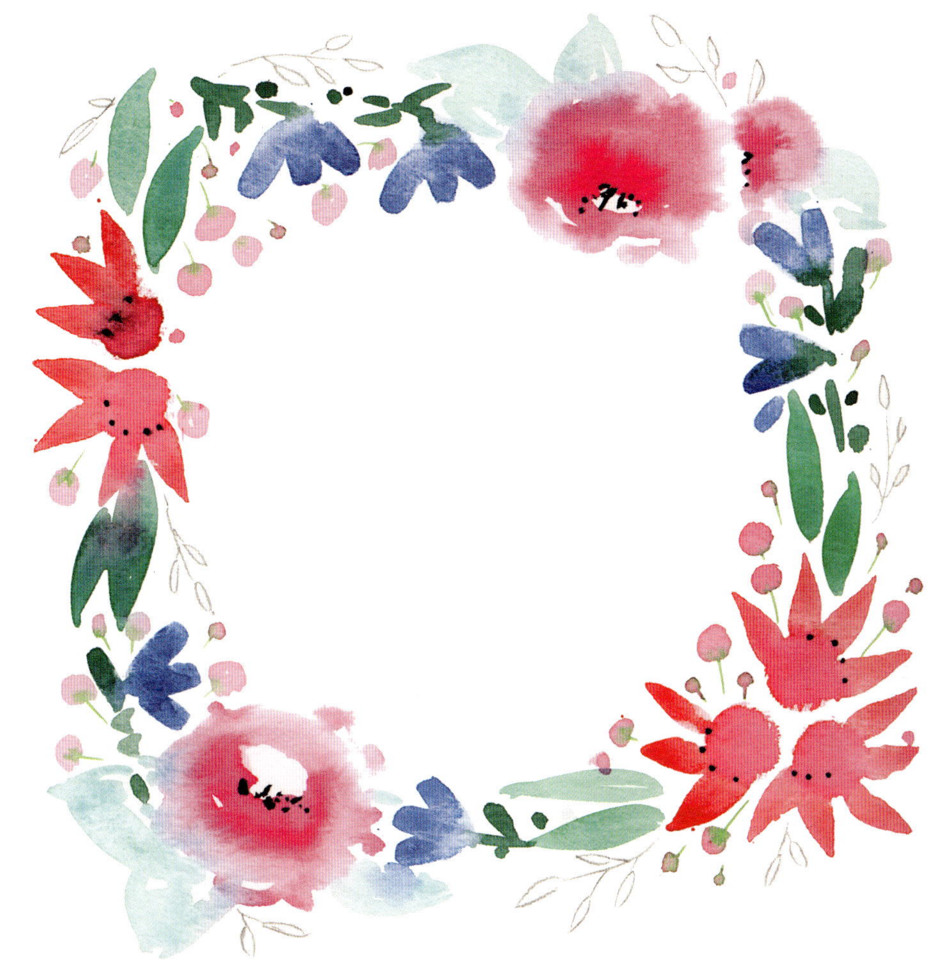

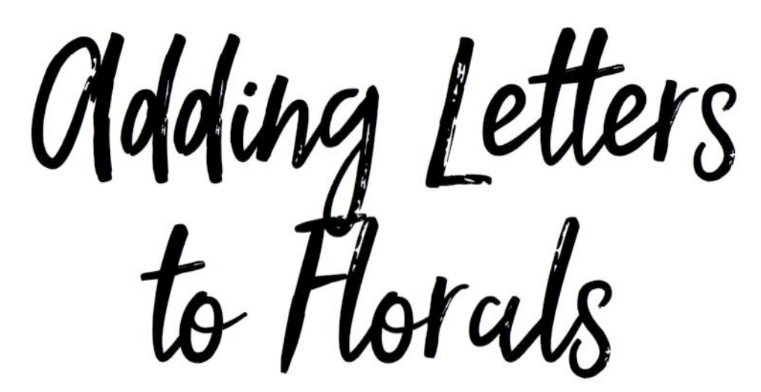

Adding Letters to Florals

Learning how to letter using watercolor and adding letters to your floral paintings will open up a whole new world of creativity for you! You can add lettering to lots of items, including wedding and personal stationery, branding, letters, and wall art. Brush lettering, calligraphy, and hand-drawn fonts are among the many beautiful styles of hand-lettering that are popular today. You can also look to historical lettering styles for inspiration.

If you like to use reference books, find some typeface books at your local library, or go online for ideas. If you prefer just to wing it, like I do, here are a few ways to help you get started.

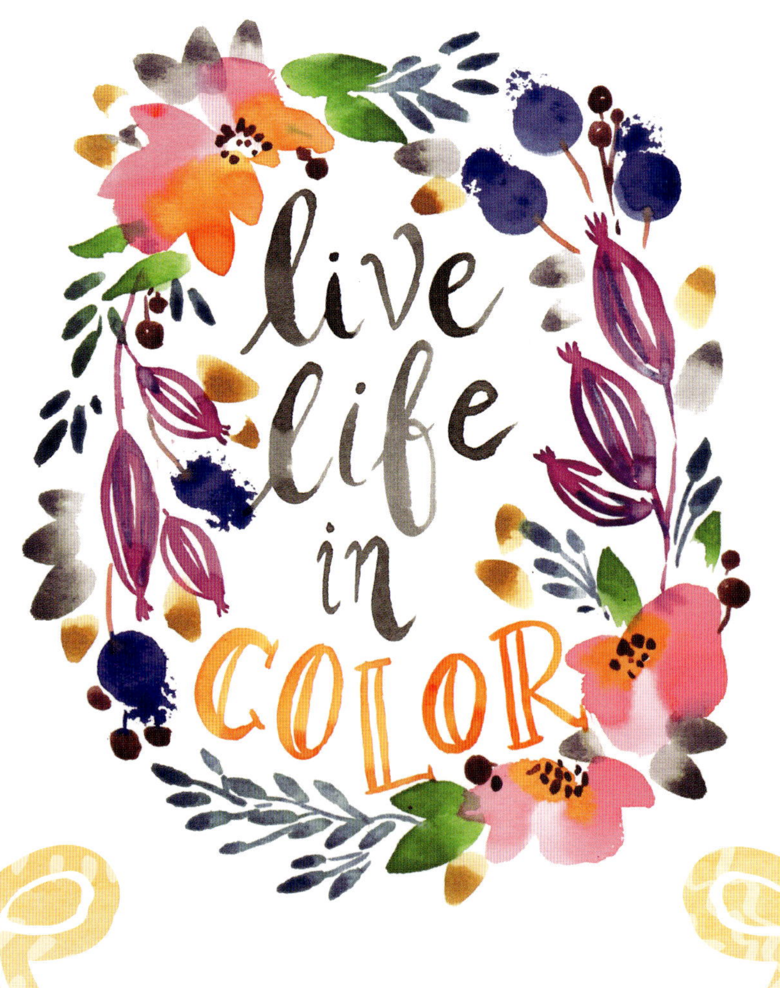

BRUSH LETTERING

With brush lettering, you form letters using a paintbrush. I prefer to use a water brush, which features a handle with a water basin that you fill to moisten the bristles. This makes it perfect for the long strokes required to form letters.

Make sure to apply pressure to the brush on the downward stroke of the letter, creating a thicker line. When you bring the stroke back up, release the pressure to create a thinner line.

I've developed my own style of brush lettering that resembles cursive handwriting. This is a great lettering style for beginners to start with.

Try making your own cursive alphabet with a water brush, focusing on varying your pressure to create different line weights.

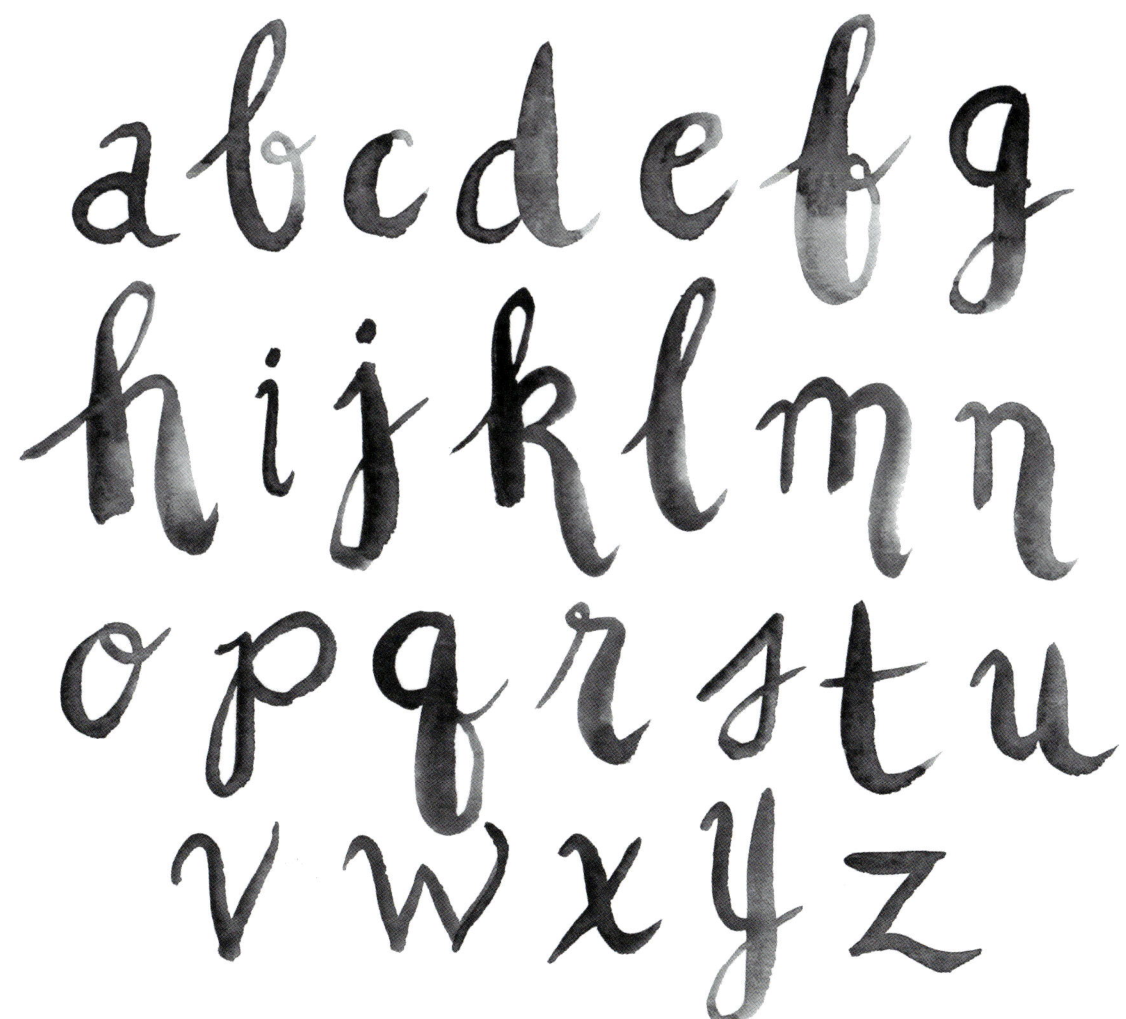

SIMPLE LETTERING

For this type of lettering, I use a small, round detail brush. Using the tip of the brush, I "write" each letter.

ABCDEFGHIJKLM
NOPQRSTUVWXYZ

For these letters, I just added an extra line to the left side of each letter, creating the illusion of a shadow.

ABCDEFGHIJKLM
NOPQRSTUVWXYZ

By now, you've probably noticed that my lettering is not perfect, nor does it look like a font. This is the charm of hand-lettering! Embrace it, and you too will enjoy the process.

LETTERING A QUOTE

Once you've played with a couple of lettering styles, try lettering a quote or a phrase and adding floral decorations to it. Here's how to do it.

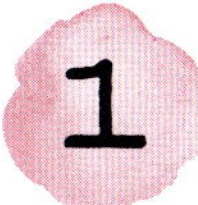

I started by creating a rough pencil outline of where I'll place the lettering. Then I free-formed the letters.

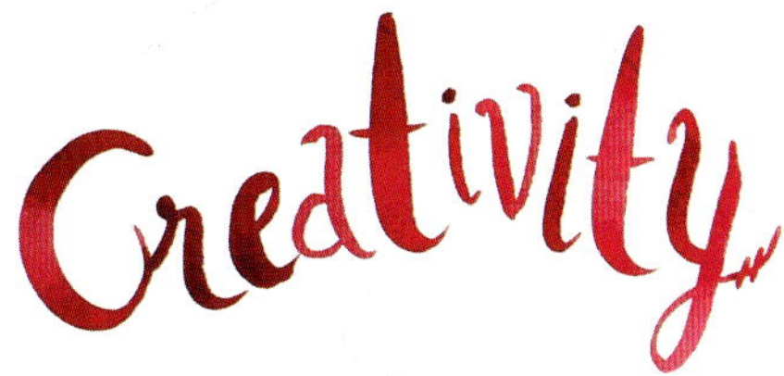

Creativity IS in

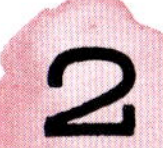

My first word ("creativity") is long, so it got a little cramped on the right side. Don't automatically start over whenever you make a mistake, however. Instead, try to fix what you don't like about your piece.

To balance my artwork, I drew a light circle where I wanted to place my next word. Then I used a different lettering style for the next word ("is") to add variety and interest. I also varied the colors.

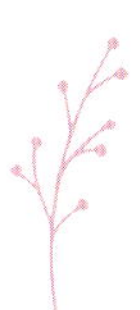

As long as your quote is relatively short, I suggest painting the final lettering without using a pencil first. Free-formed letters will lend spontaneity to your finished piece.

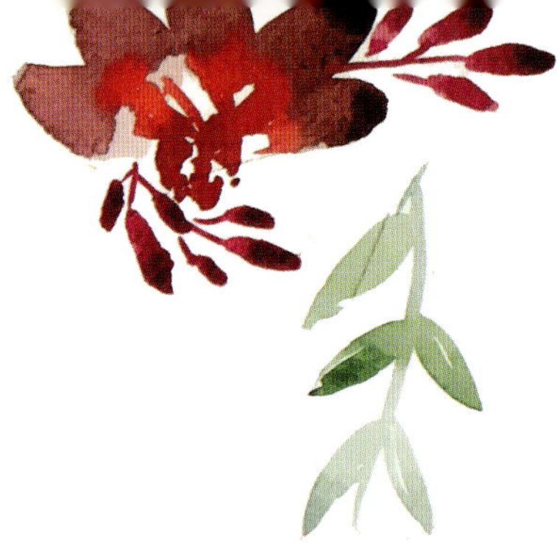

Creativity IS intelligence

3

I like to "bounce" my letters around a bit, rather than placing them on an imaginary line. Everything remains relatively centered, and I can always balance out the piece later through the placement of my florals.

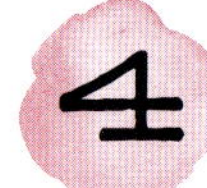

Always consider which words you wish to emphasize. I wanted to communicate the feeling of fun, so I made that word slightly larger than the rest.

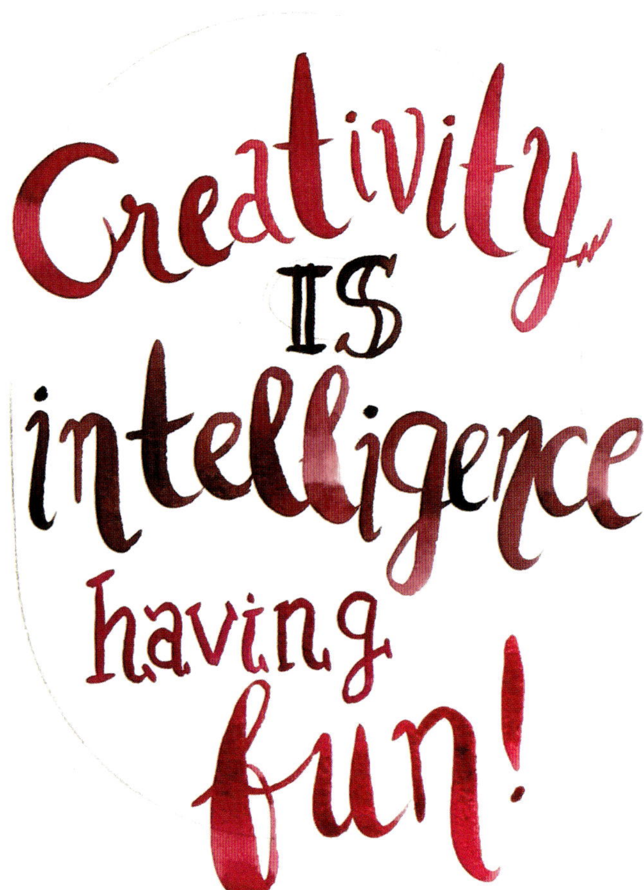

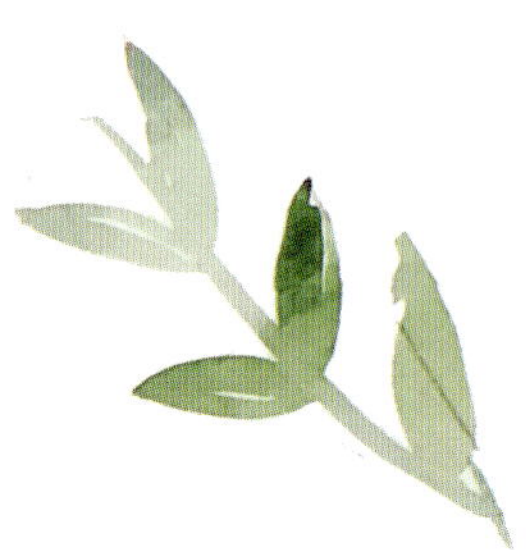

Now, using the skills you learned in the floral frames project (see pages 60-67), add floral details around the edges of the paper to complement your quote.

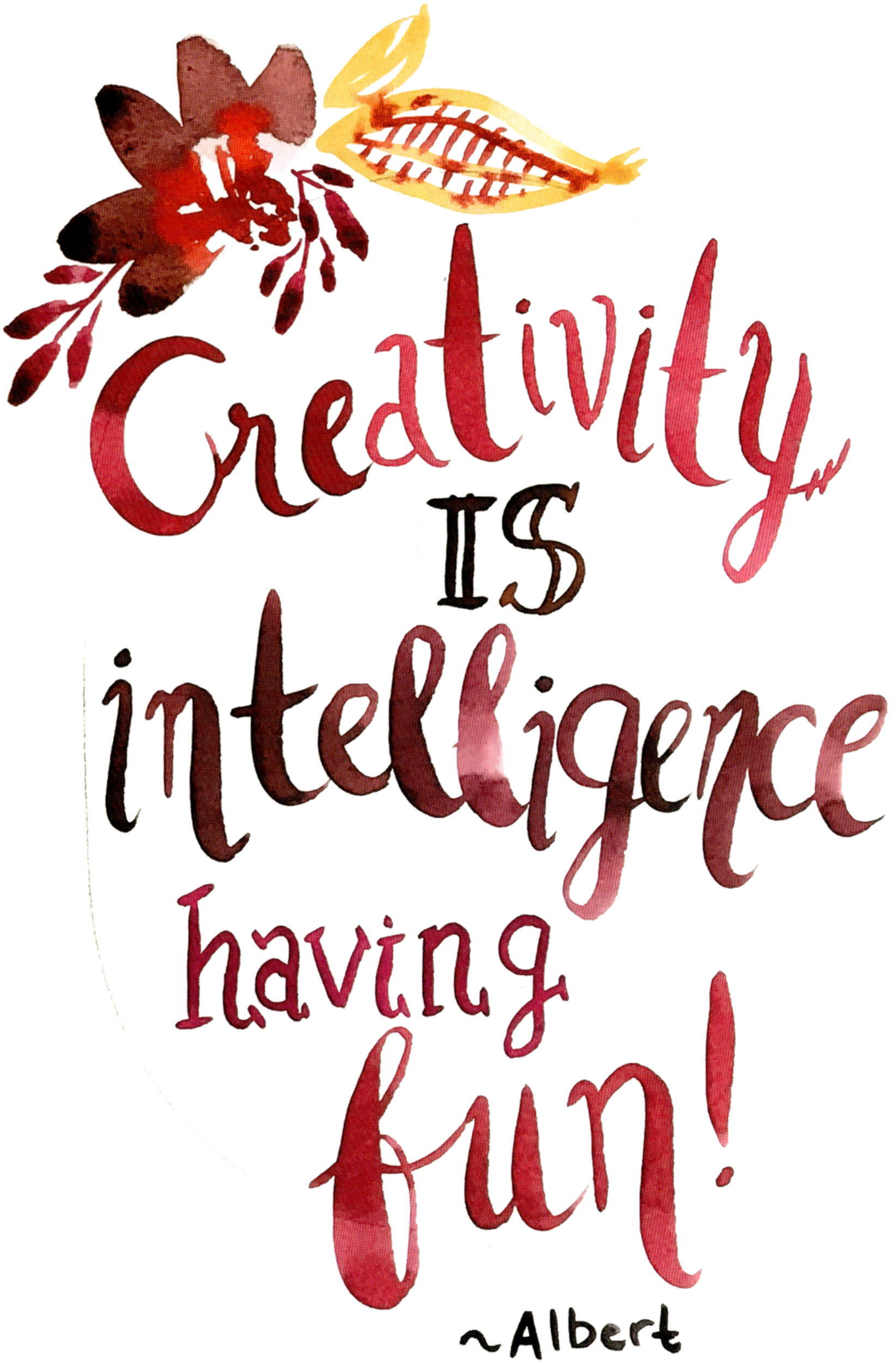

Creativity
IS
intelligence
having
fun!
~Albert

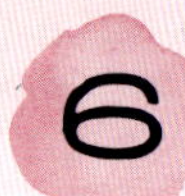

Erase your pencil guidelines to finish up your floral-decorated hand-lettering piece.

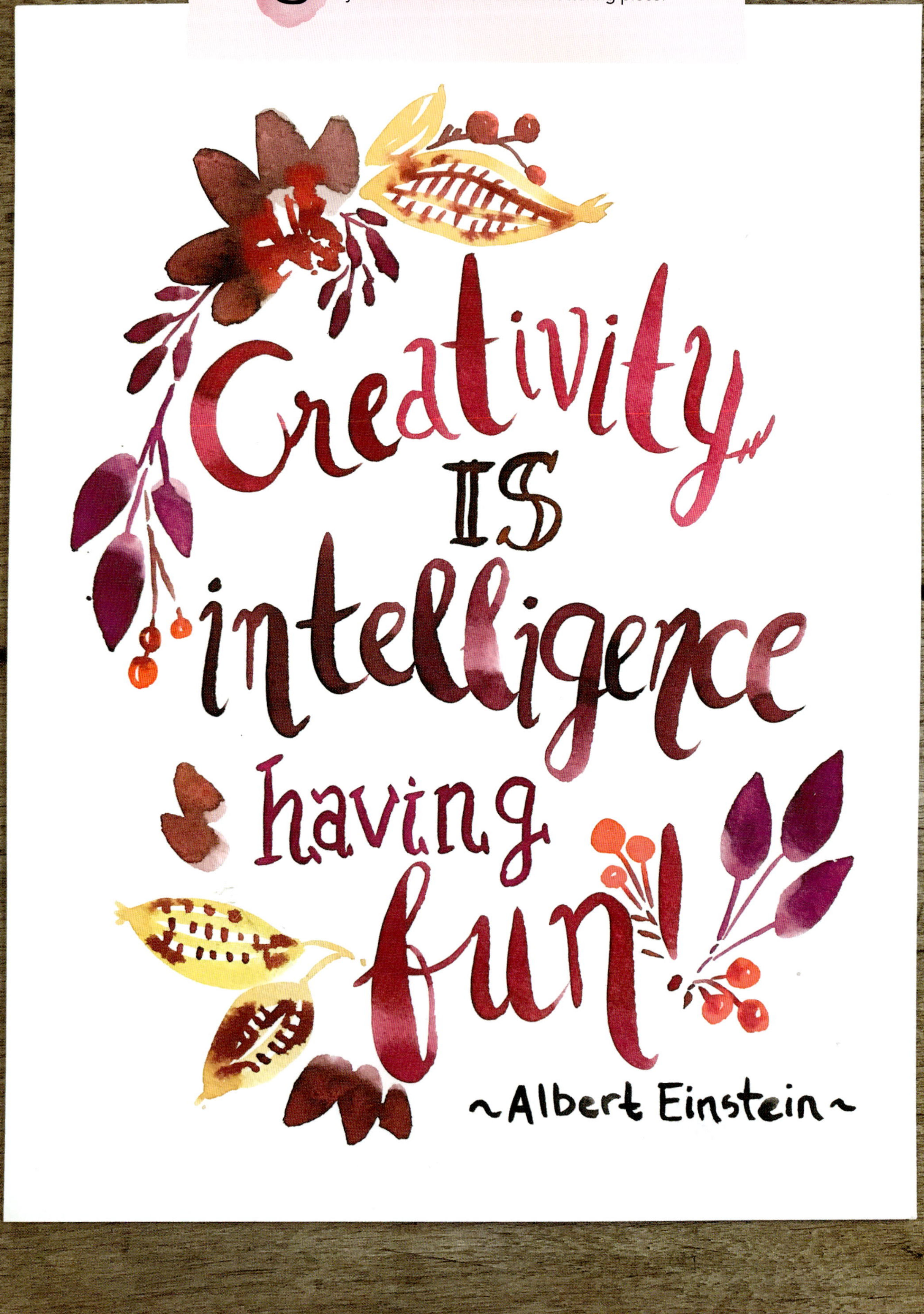

Creativity
IS
intelligence
having
fun!
~Albert Einstein~

Gallery Wall

Don't forget to display your finished artwork! A gallery wall is a great way to show off your masterpieces and provide inspiration for future floral compositions.

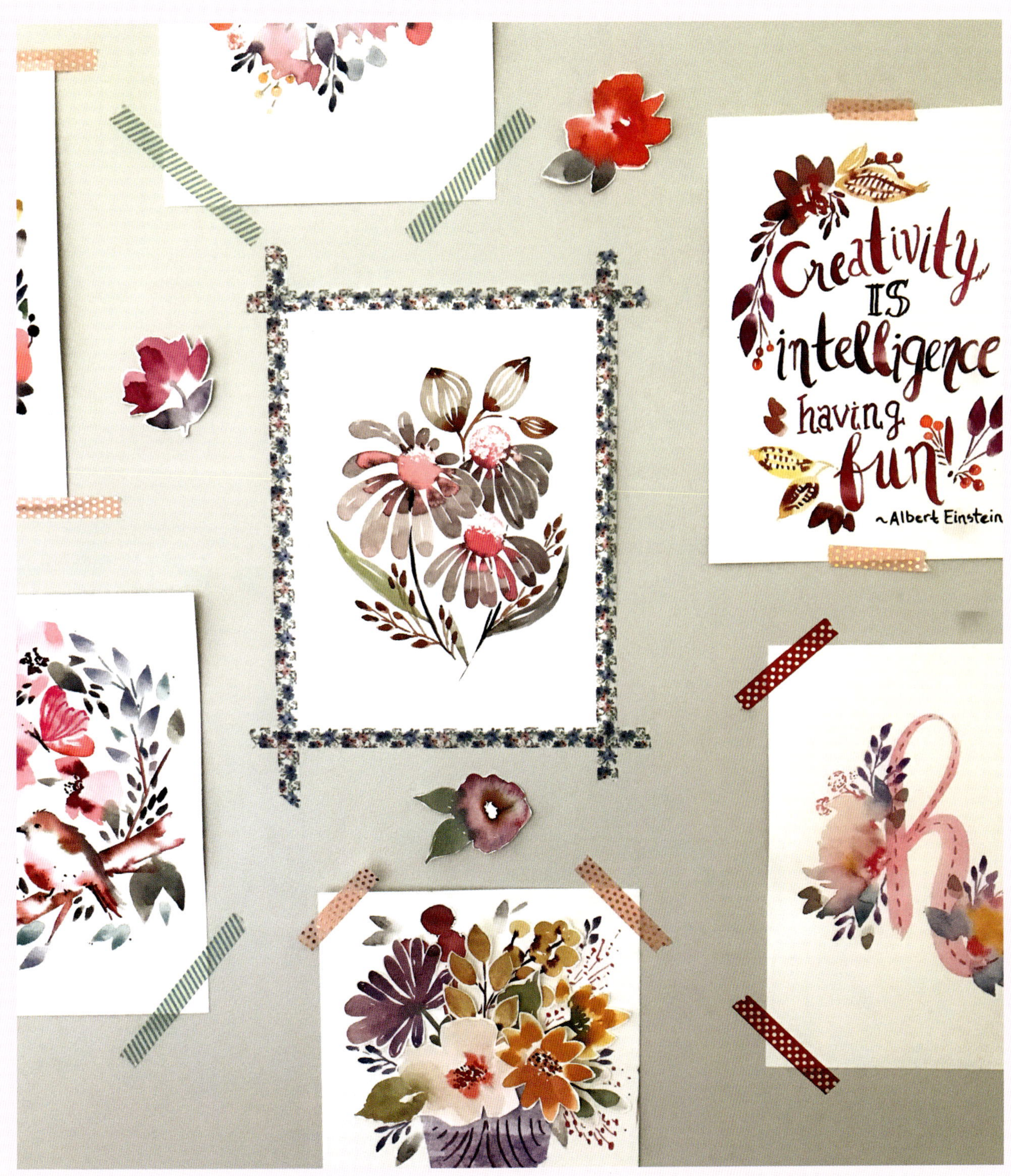

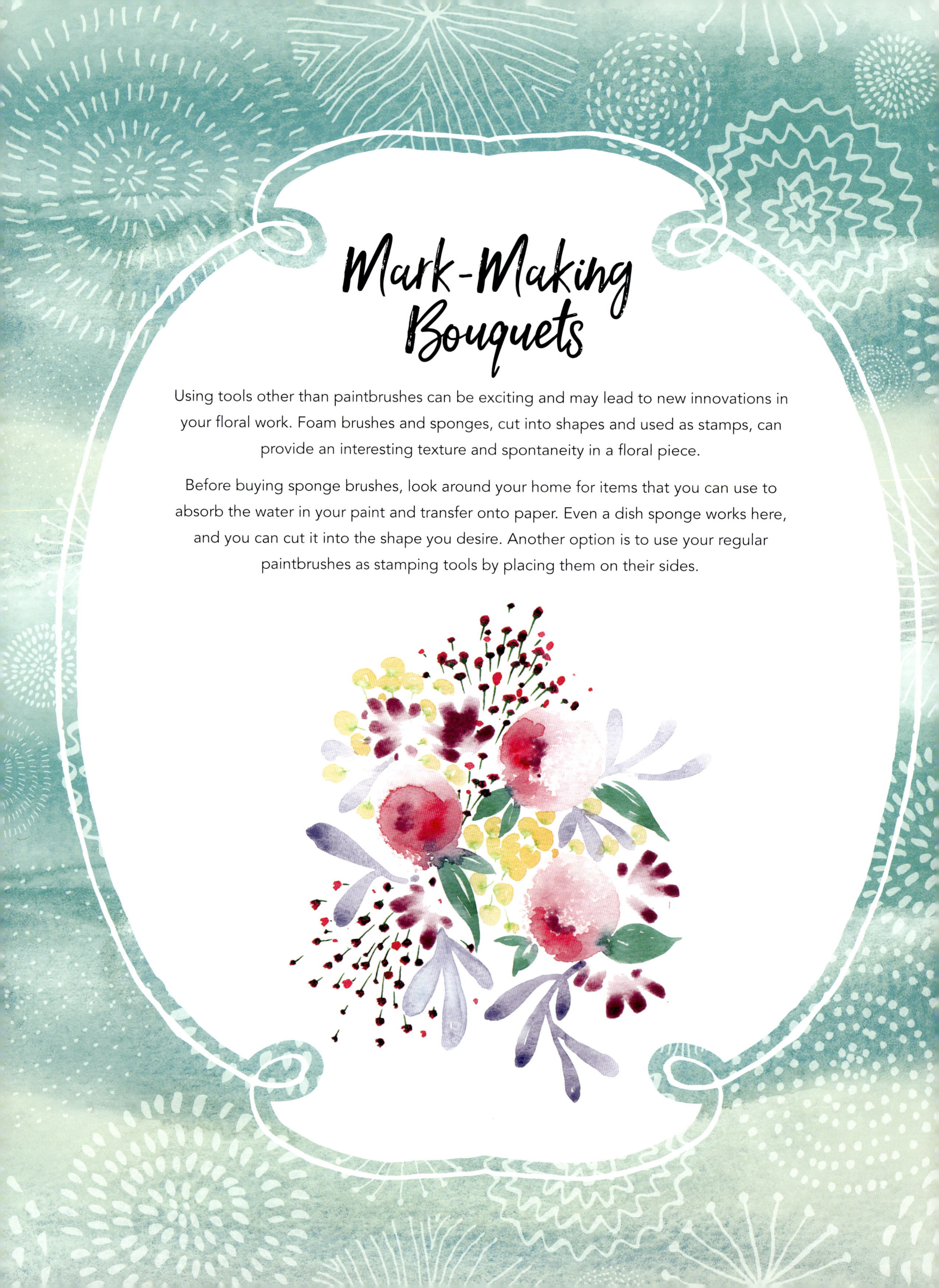

Mark-Making Bouquets

Using tools other than paintbrushes can be exciting and may lead to new innovations in your floral work. Foam brushes and sponges, cut into shapes and used as stamps, can provide an interesting texture and spontaneity in a floral piece.

Before buying sponge brushes, look around your home for items that you can use to absorb the water in your paint and transfer onto paper. Even a dish sponge works here, and you can cut it into the shape you desire. Another option is to use your regular paintbrushes as stamping tools by placing them on their sides.

Here is a fun exercise: Using your brushes as stamps, explore how many ways you can repeat their shapes to create flowers.

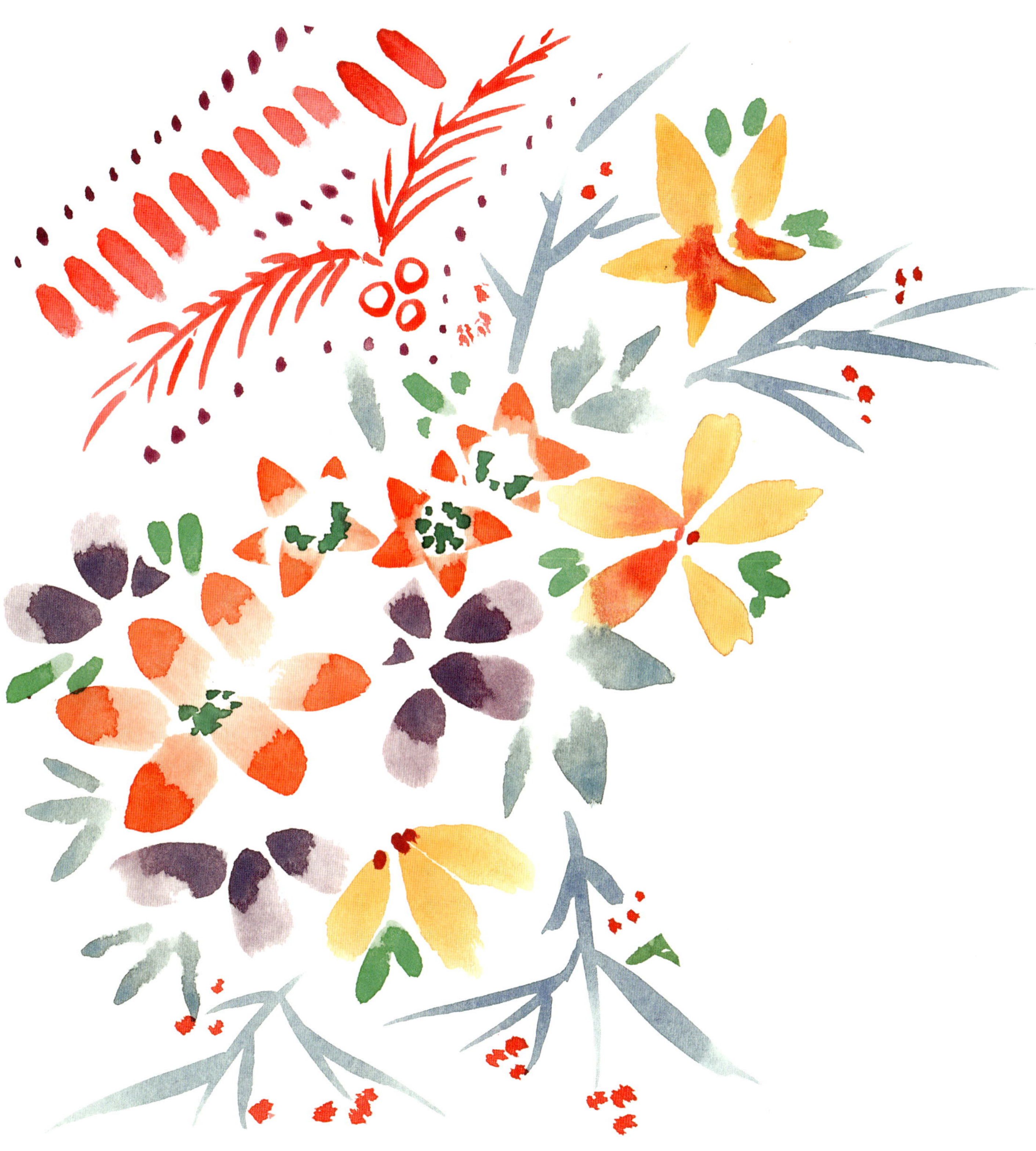

Years ago, I purchased round stamps in several sizes, and I've used them many times. The flat foam brush can be found in many different stores; hardware-supply stores usually carry different widths in their paint section.

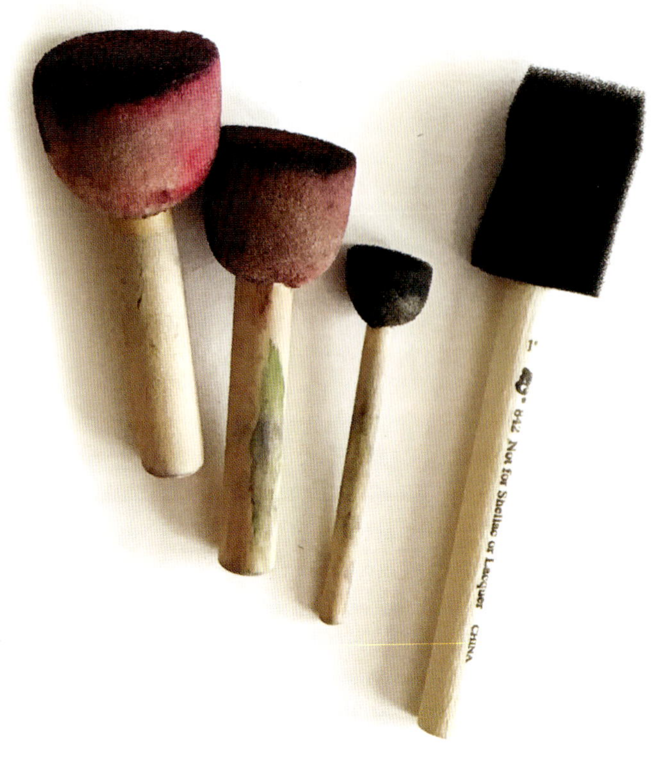

You can use scissors to cut the flat sponge into a cute new shape.

1 Starting with your largest round sponge, begin by placing three big focal flowers near the center of the page.

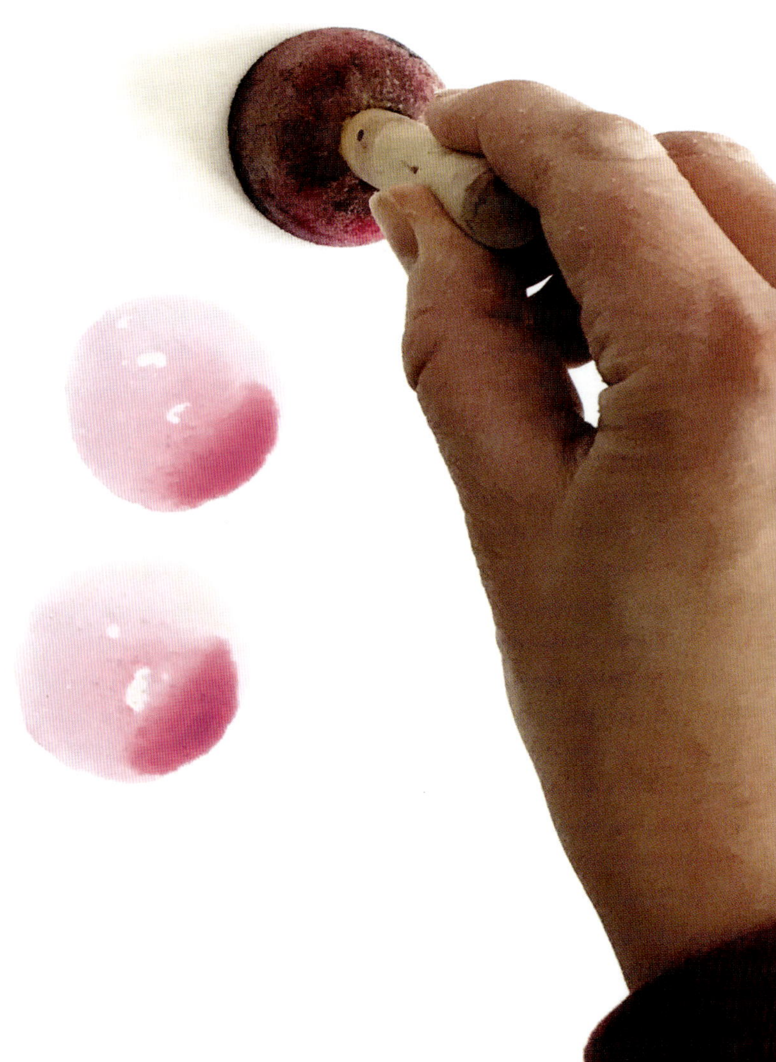

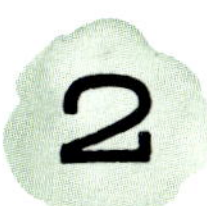

Using a large round brush on its side, stamp petals around the focal flowers.

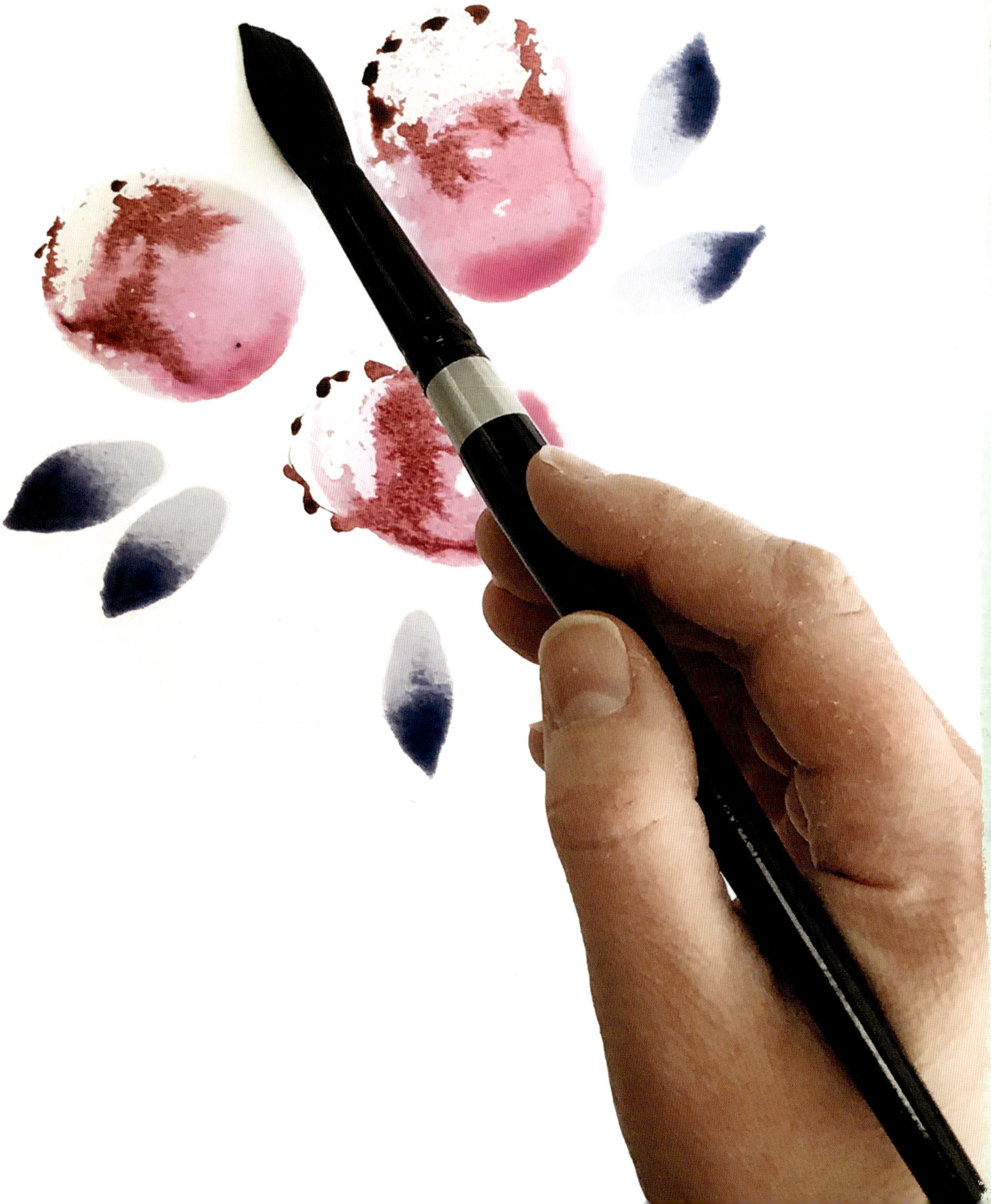

3 With the flat sponge stamp and another paint color, stamp some secondary buds.

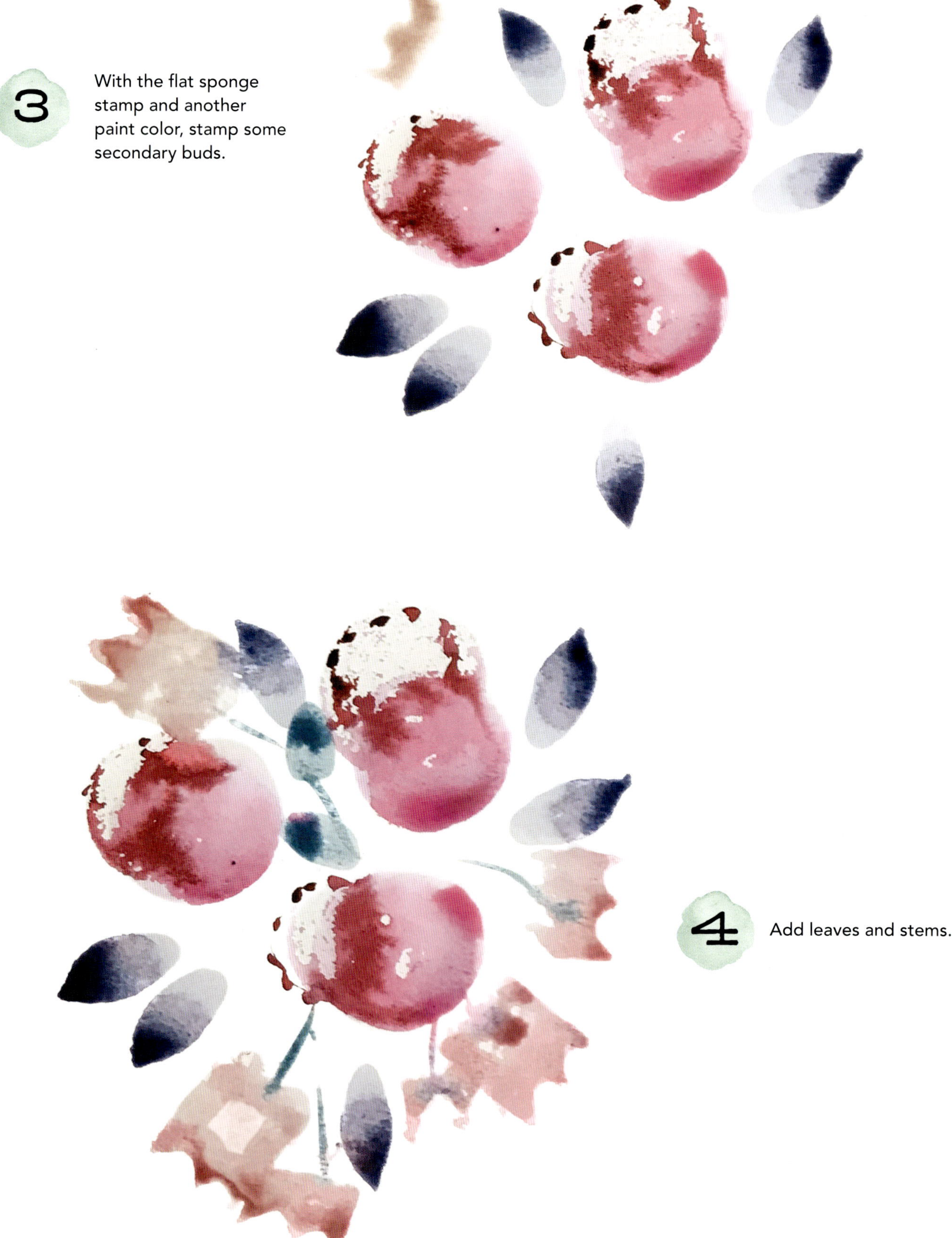

4 Add leaves and stems.

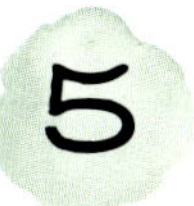

5 With the smallest round sponge, stamp several small blooms extending from the central bouquet.

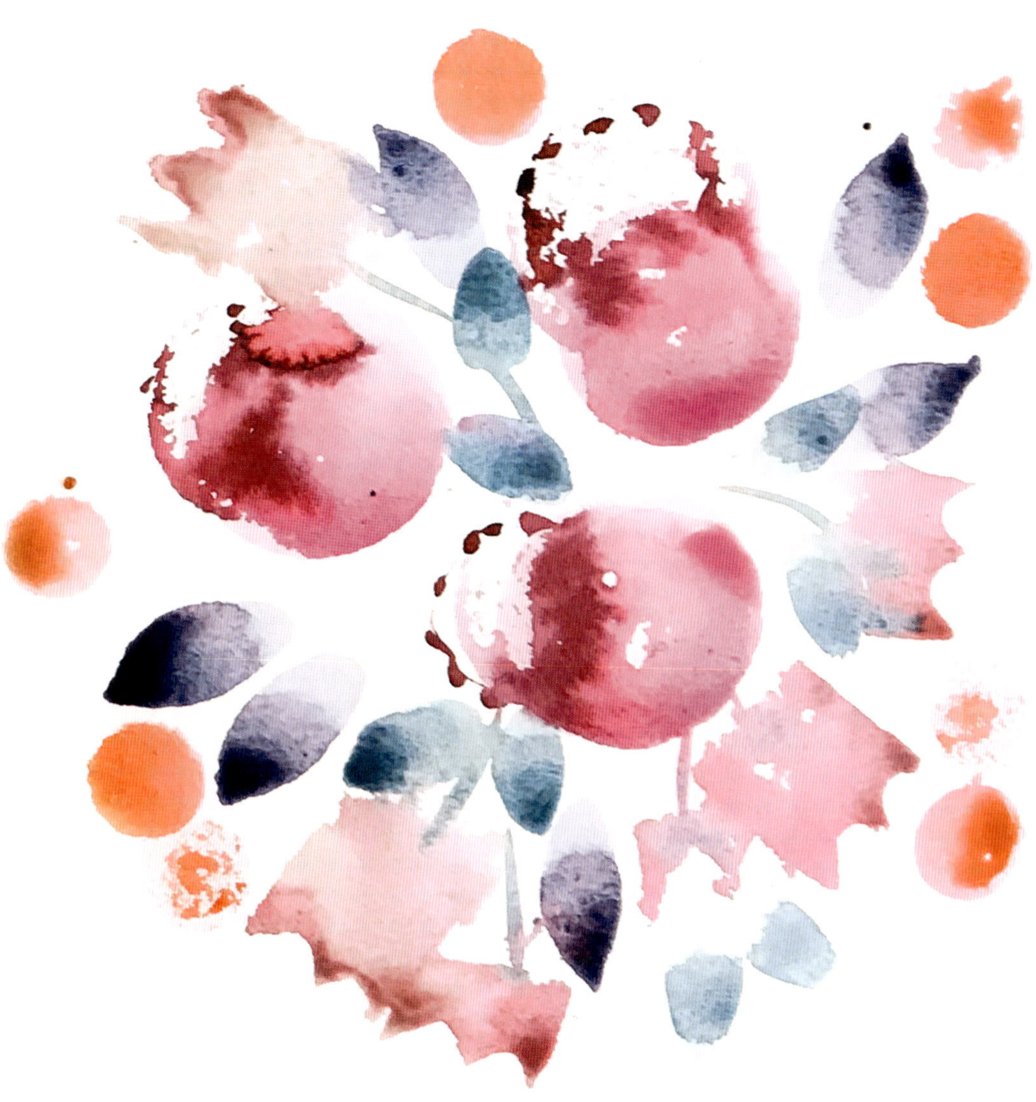

Sponge brushes hold a lot of water, which can lead to a beautiful and serendipitous blending of colors.

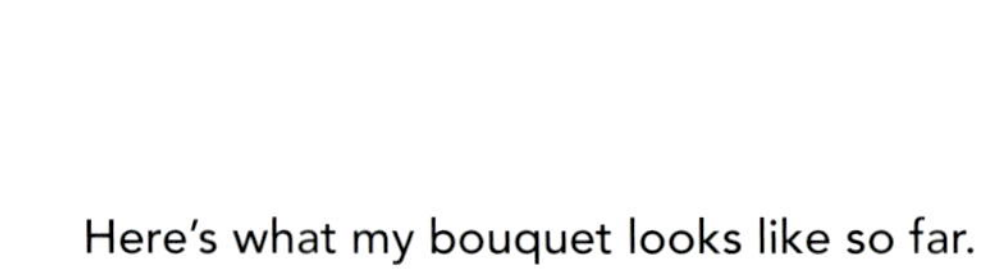

Here's what my bouquet looks like so far.

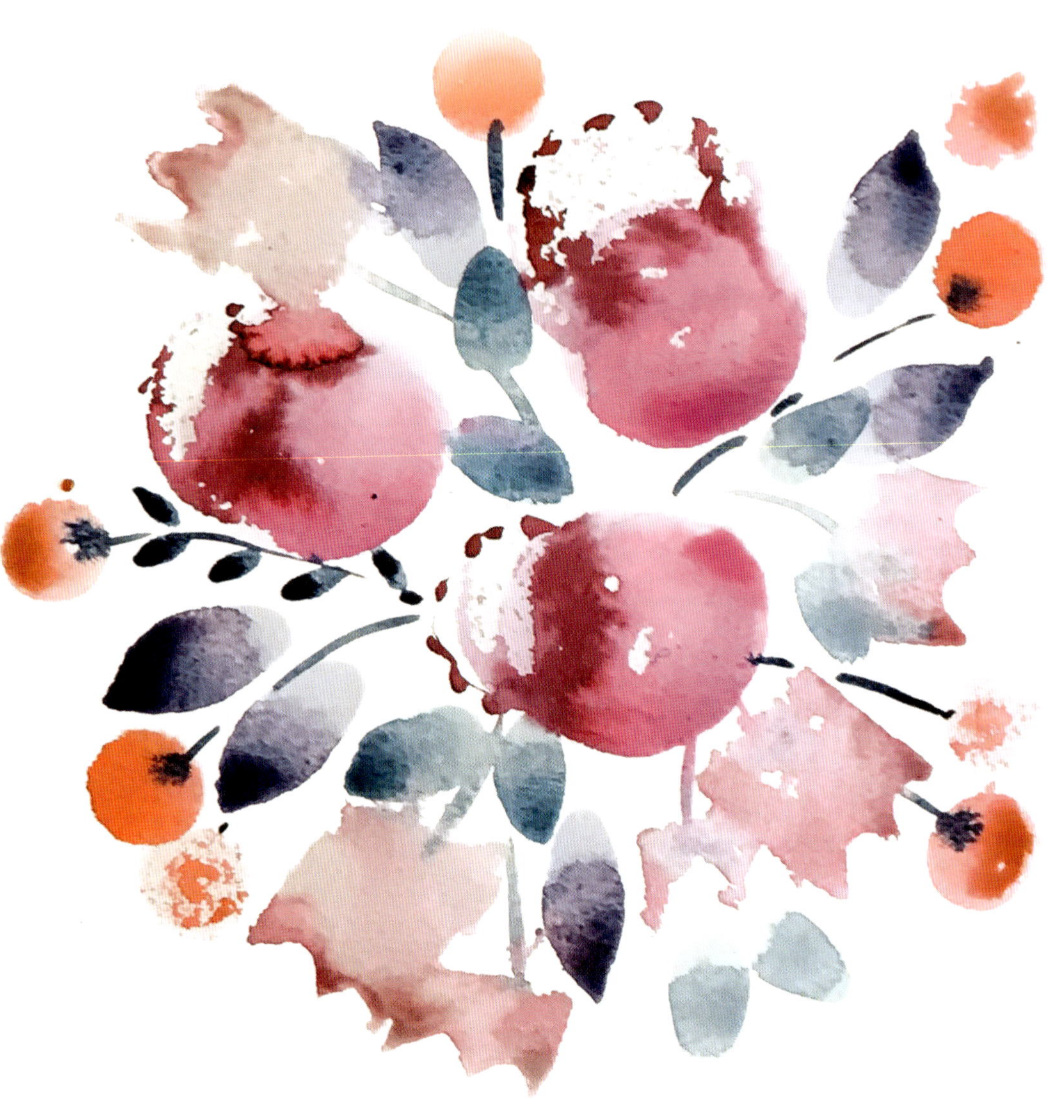

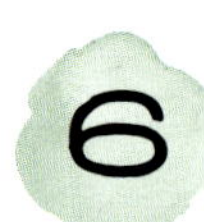

6 All that remains is to fill in the white spaces to create a full, lush-looking bouquet. Stems and small leaves extending and branching out of the small gaps will add interesting details and put the finishing touches on your floral piece.

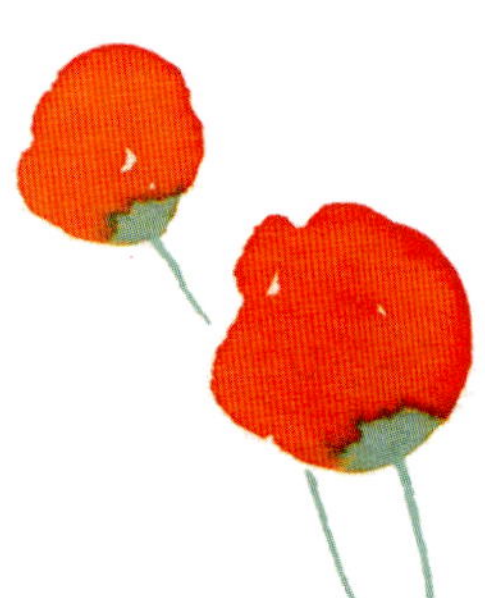

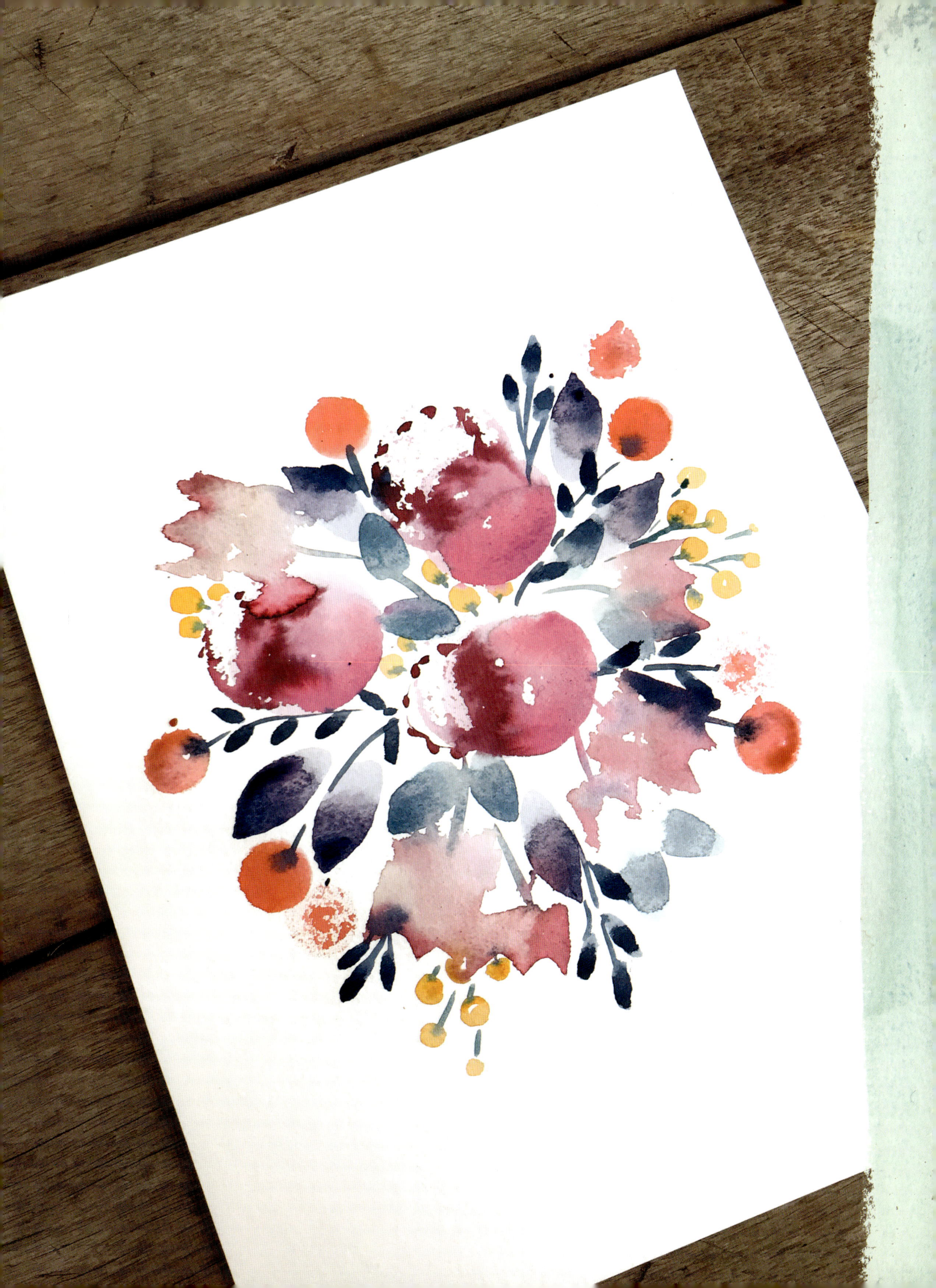

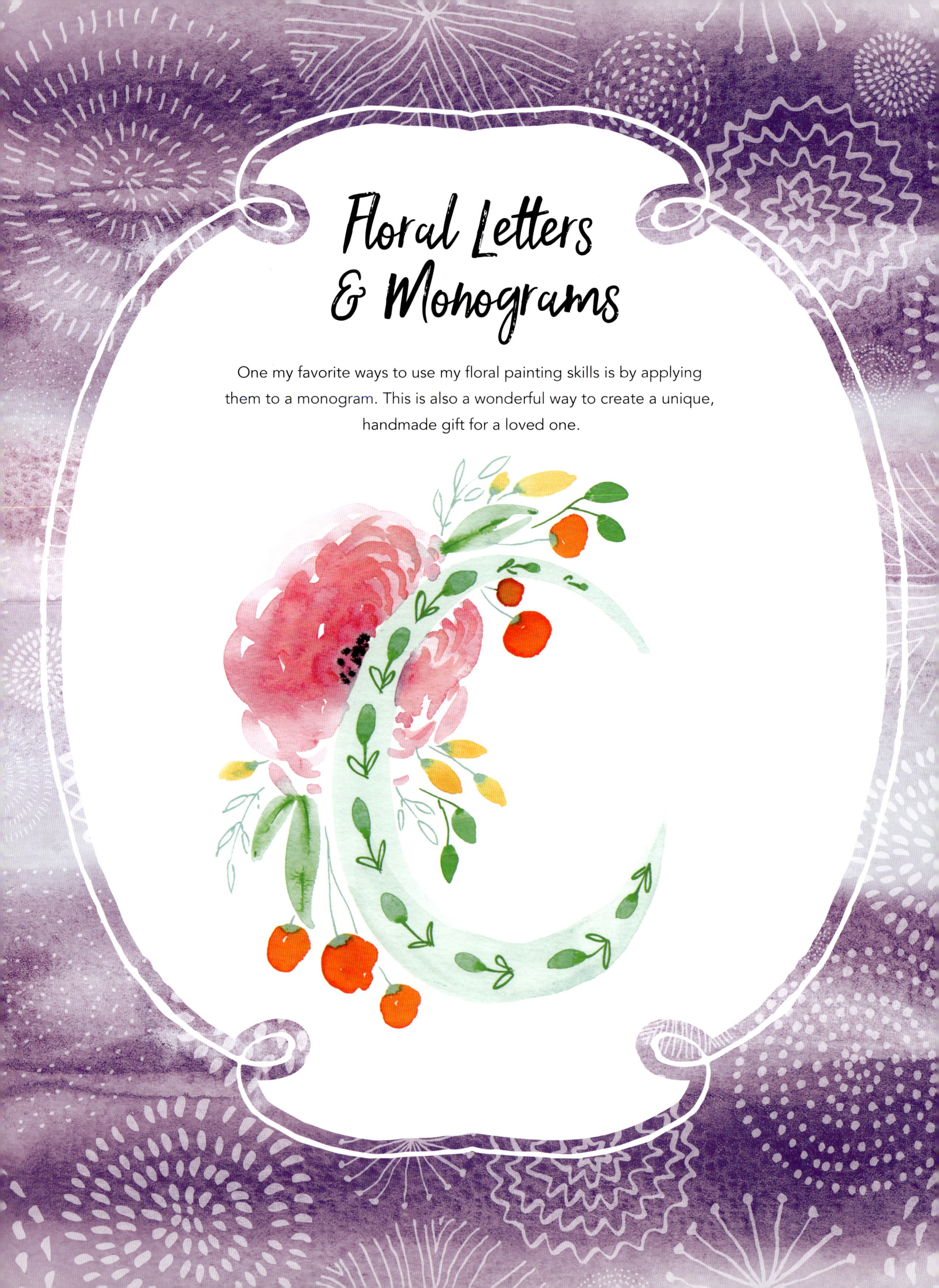

Floral Letters & Monograms

One my favorite ways to use my floral painting skills is by applying them to a monogram. This is also a wonderful way to create a unique, handmade gift for a loved one.

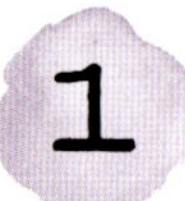

Start by using your largest round brush according to the principles of brush lettering (see page 69), and paint the letter of your choice.

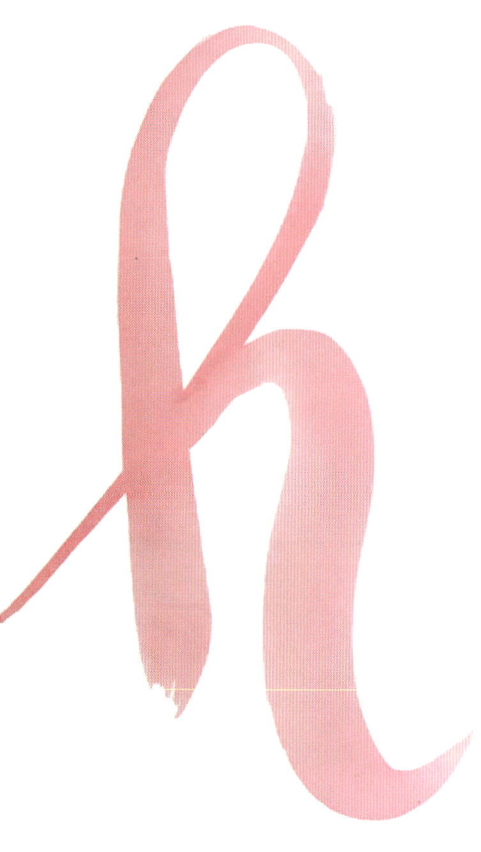

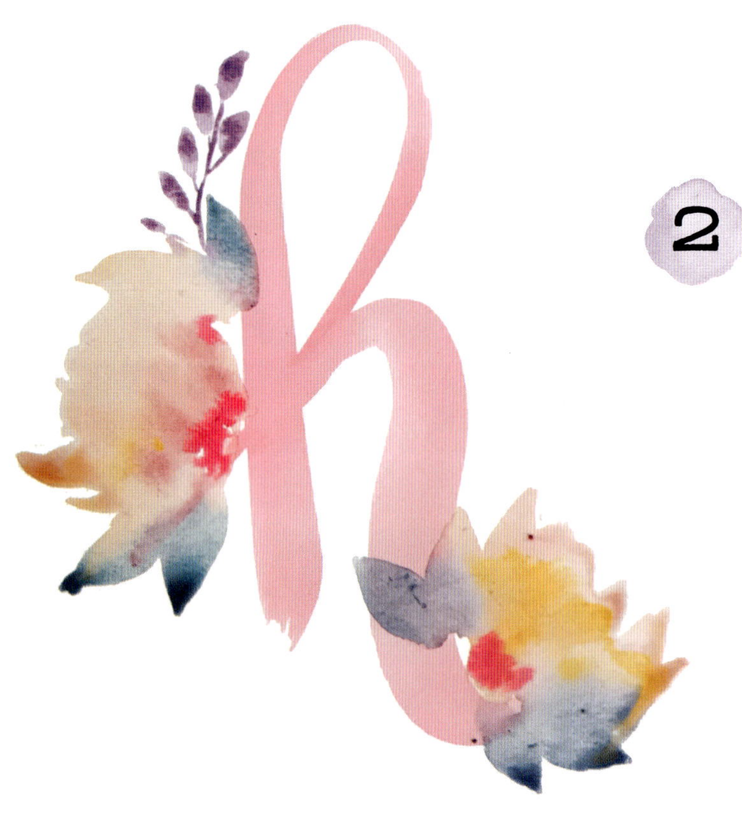

2 And now for some fun! Using all of the floral painting skills you have learned thus far, decorate your letter with blooms, buds, and leaves.

Try to evaluate where on your letter blooms would look most natural or pleasing to you, and go from there.

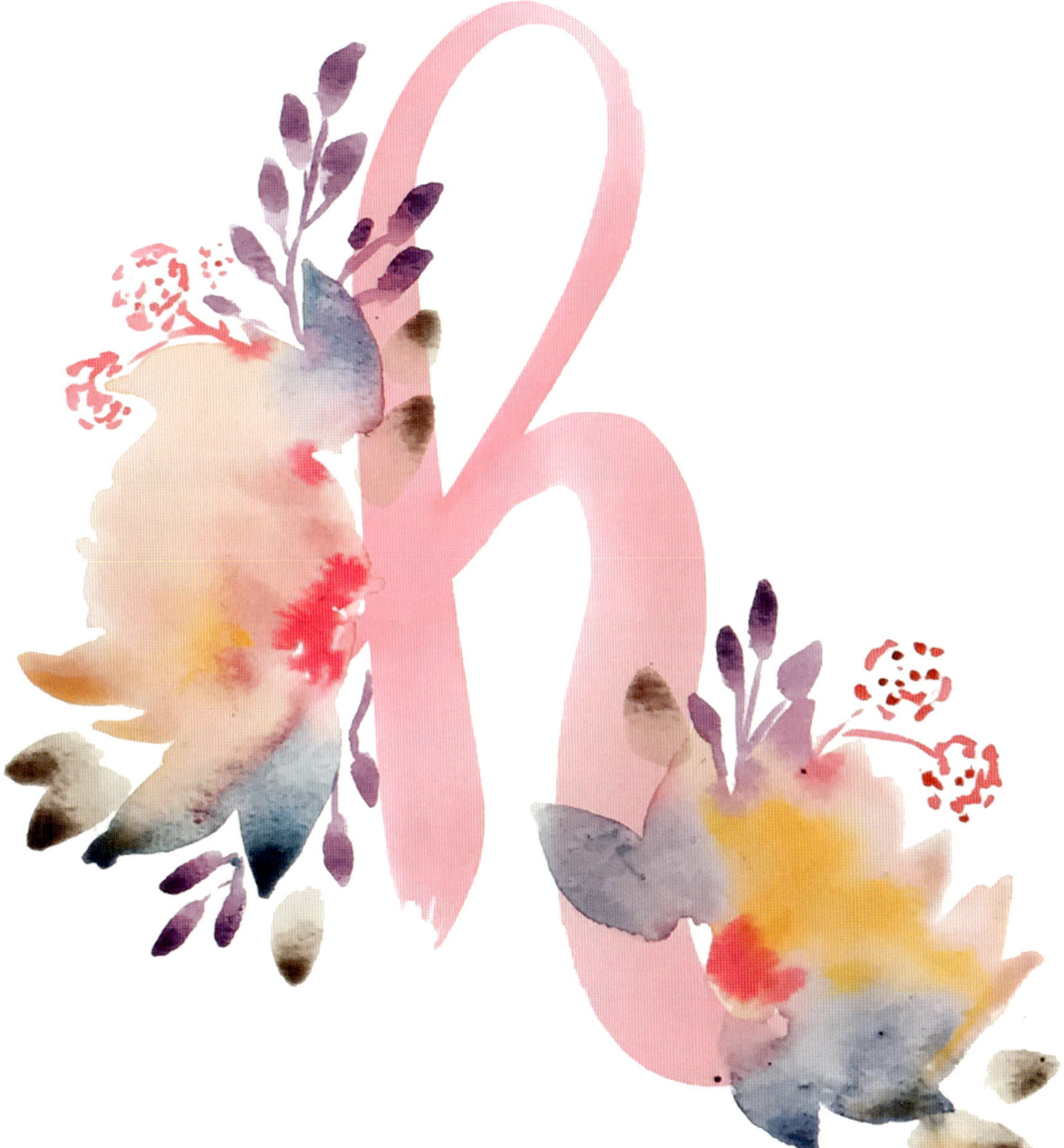

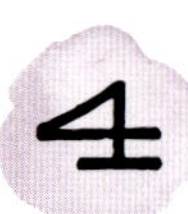

To really jazz up your floral monogram and finish your piece, add details on the letter too!

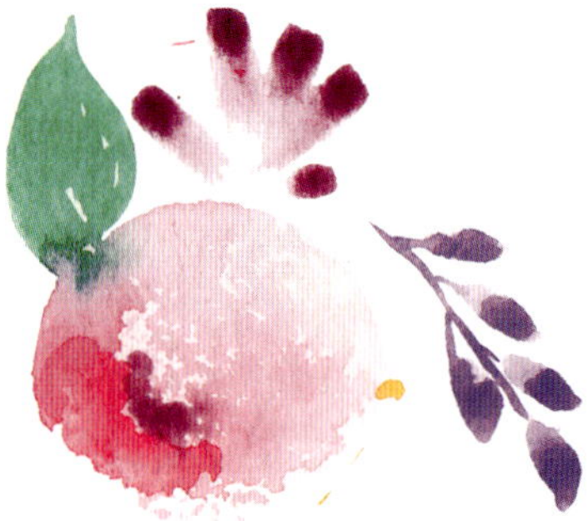

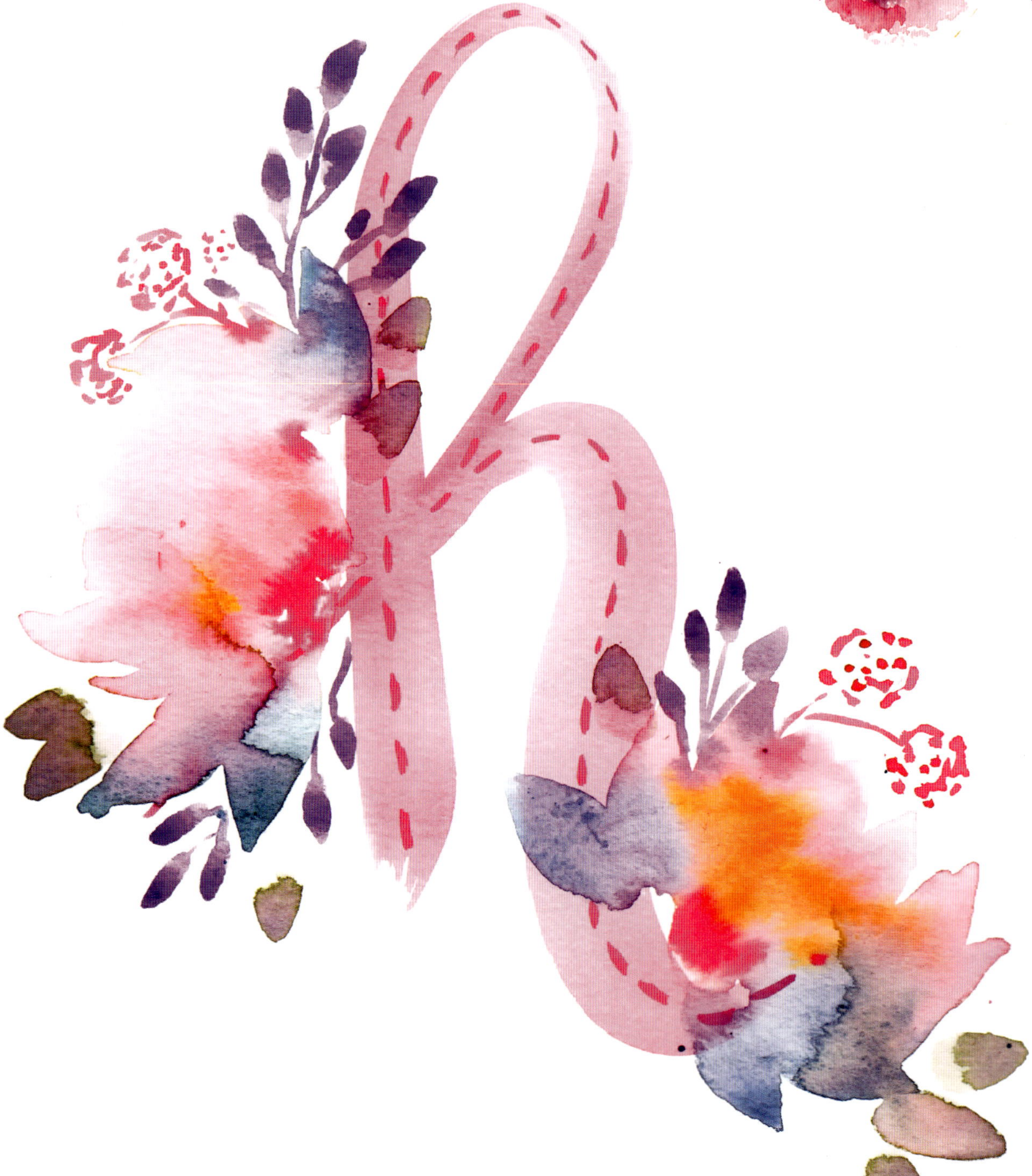

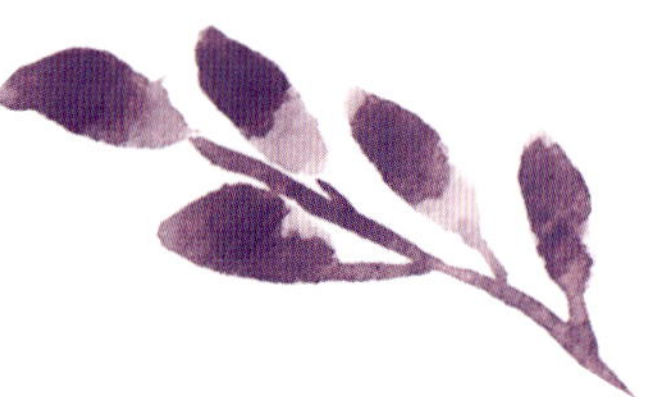

Are you looking for some ideas on how to use your gorgeous monograms? Here is a notebook I made using an initial that I painted and then cut out and sewed onto a blank journal.

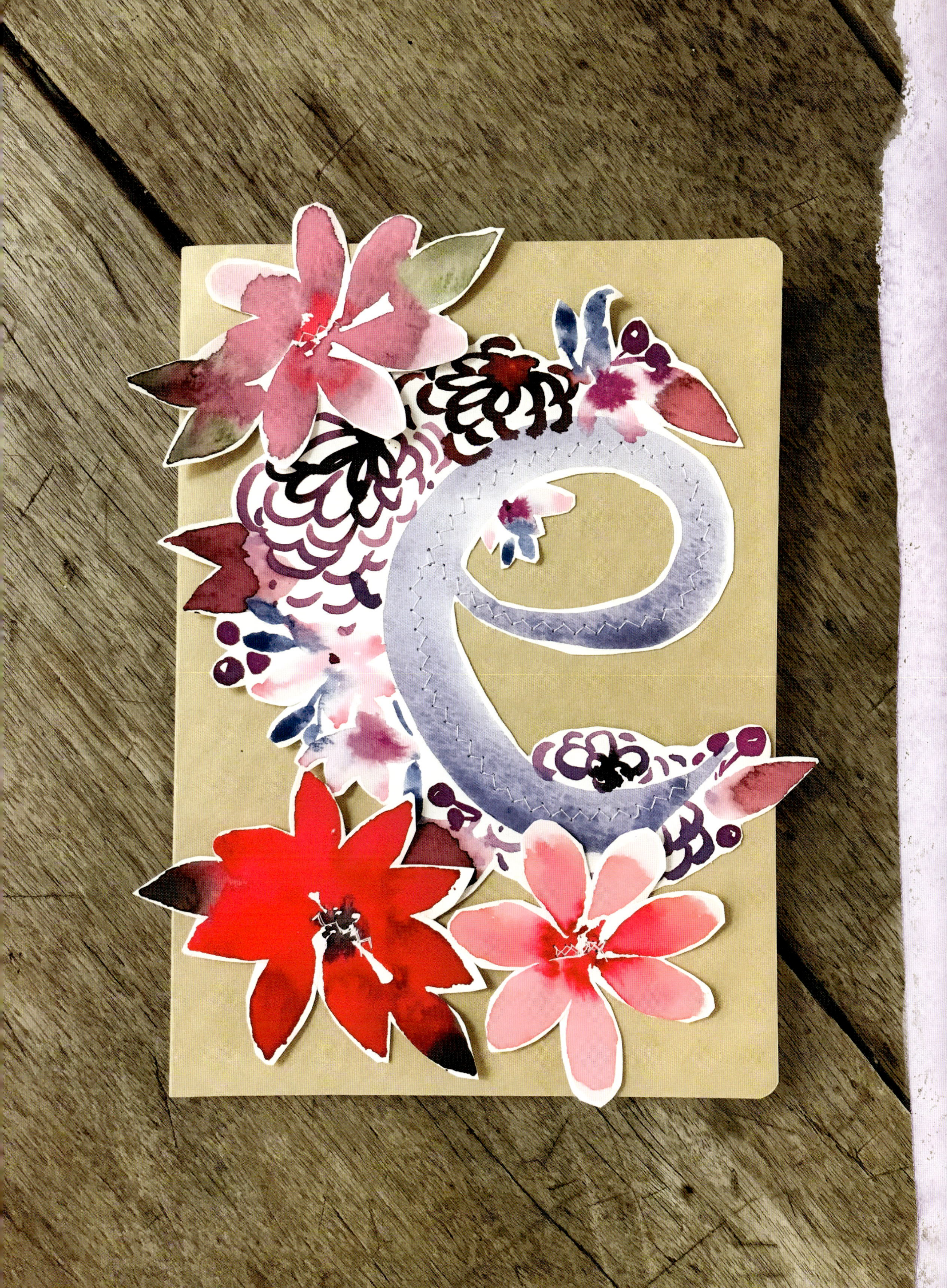

Modern Seed Packet Painting

If you love vintage gardening ephemera as much as I do, then this project is for you! Antique seed packets and catalogs are a huge source of floral inspiration for me. Of course, so are the modern seed catalogs that arrive in the mailbox every late winter, just in time to stave off the March doldrums with the promise of spring flowers.

If you do an online search for vintage seed packets, you will notice that they have two things in common: gorgeous lettering and lush illustrations. Let's incorporate those elements into a beautiful modern seed packet painting of your own.

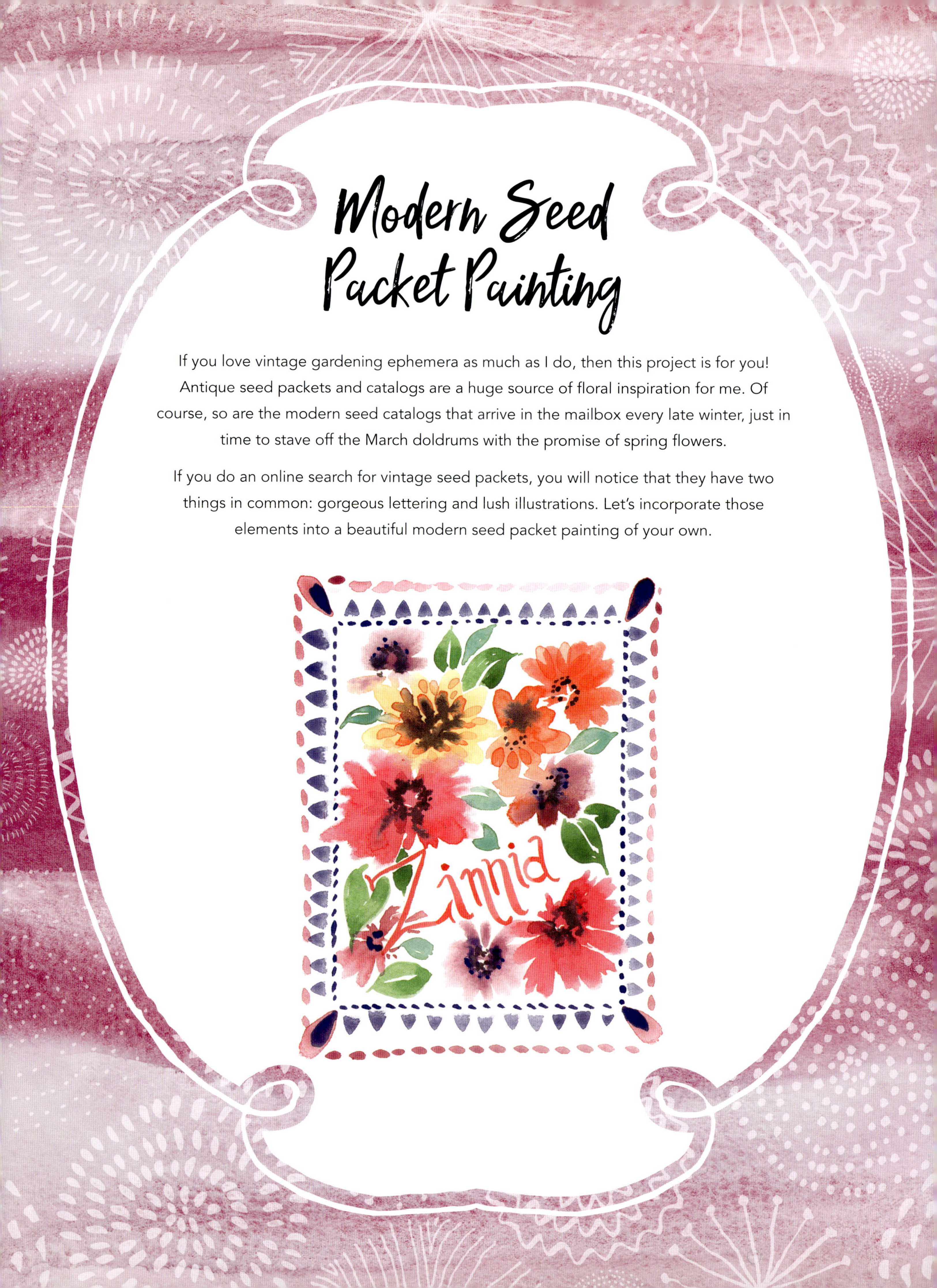

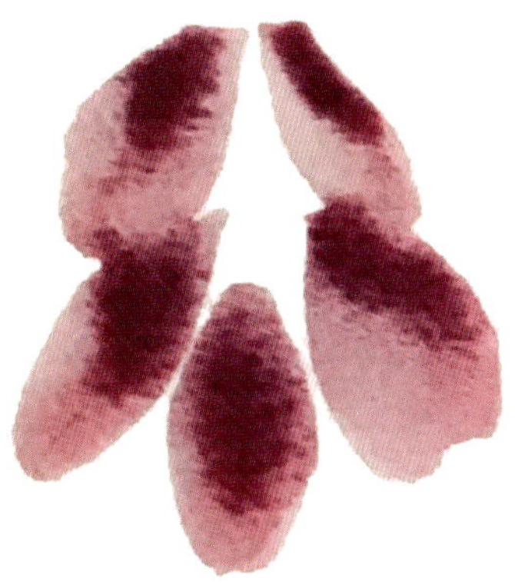

1 Roughly draw a rectangle in pencil to use as a guideline for your painting. Observe the essential shape of your chosen flower, and mimic it with your brush. This takes experience and practice, so you may have to do it a few times! Try to place your florals inside the rectangle and leave space around it for a decorative border.

I'm painting foxgloves onto my modern seed packet. Any kind of flower will work just as well, however!

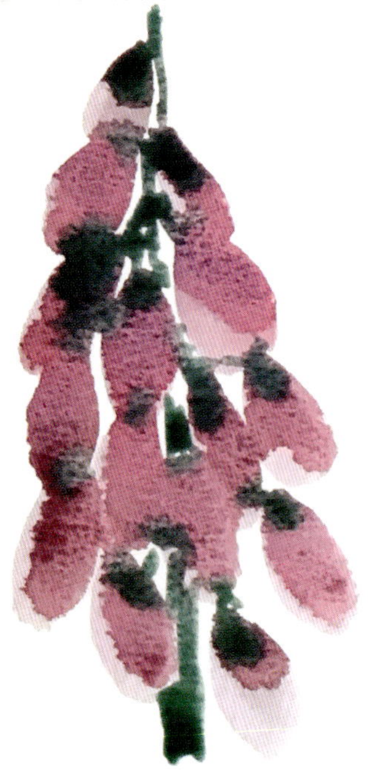

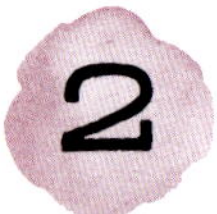

Let the colors bleed into each other, creating a lovely effect.

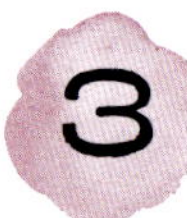

Once you've painted the basic shape of your flower, consider where the lettering should go. Is there a place in the composition where it fits most naturally? Using your lettering skills, add the flower's name.

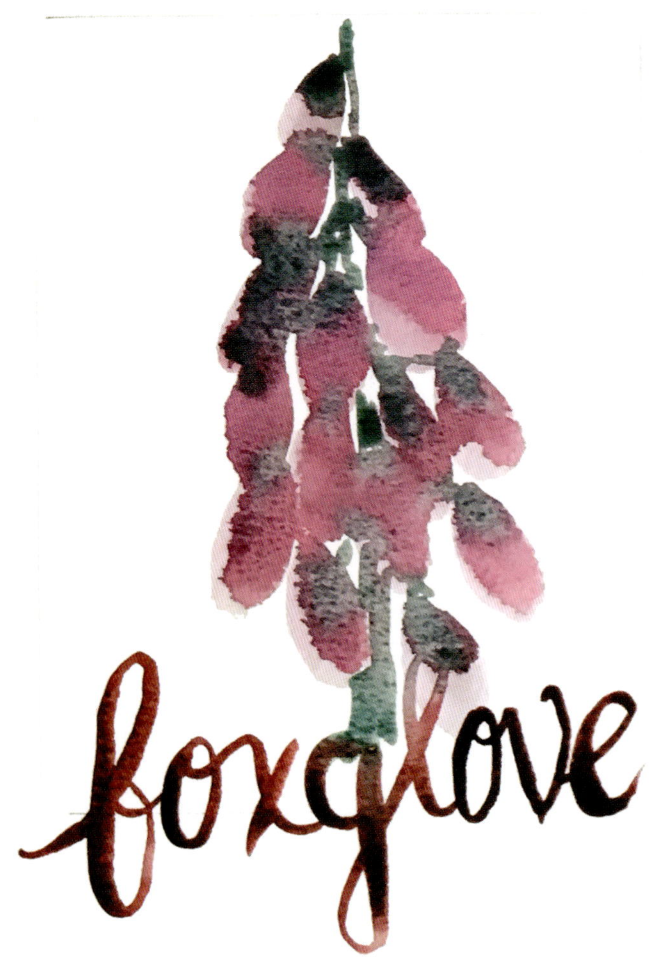

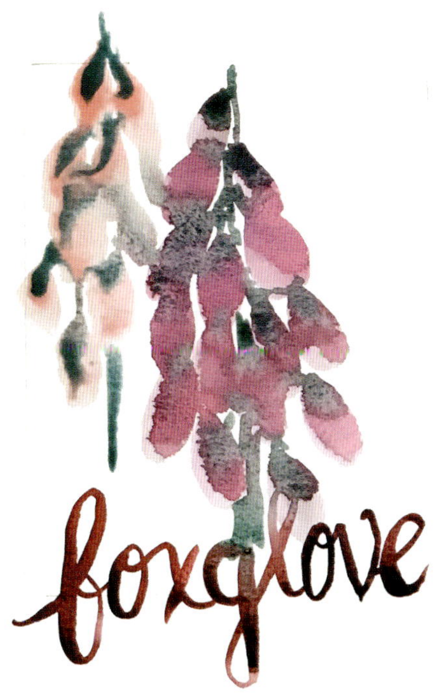

Try including three or five flowers in your painting. According to the Rule of Odds, an image is more visually appealing if it features an odd number of objects.

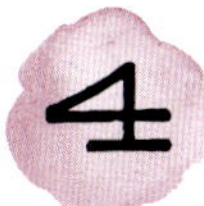

4 Continue to fill in the guideline area with flowers.

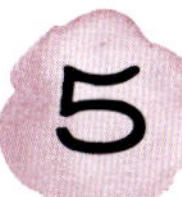

5 Now, think about the border. You can utilize your brushes' natural shapes as "stamps" to create a patterned border around your painting. A small decoration in each corner would also look beautiful.

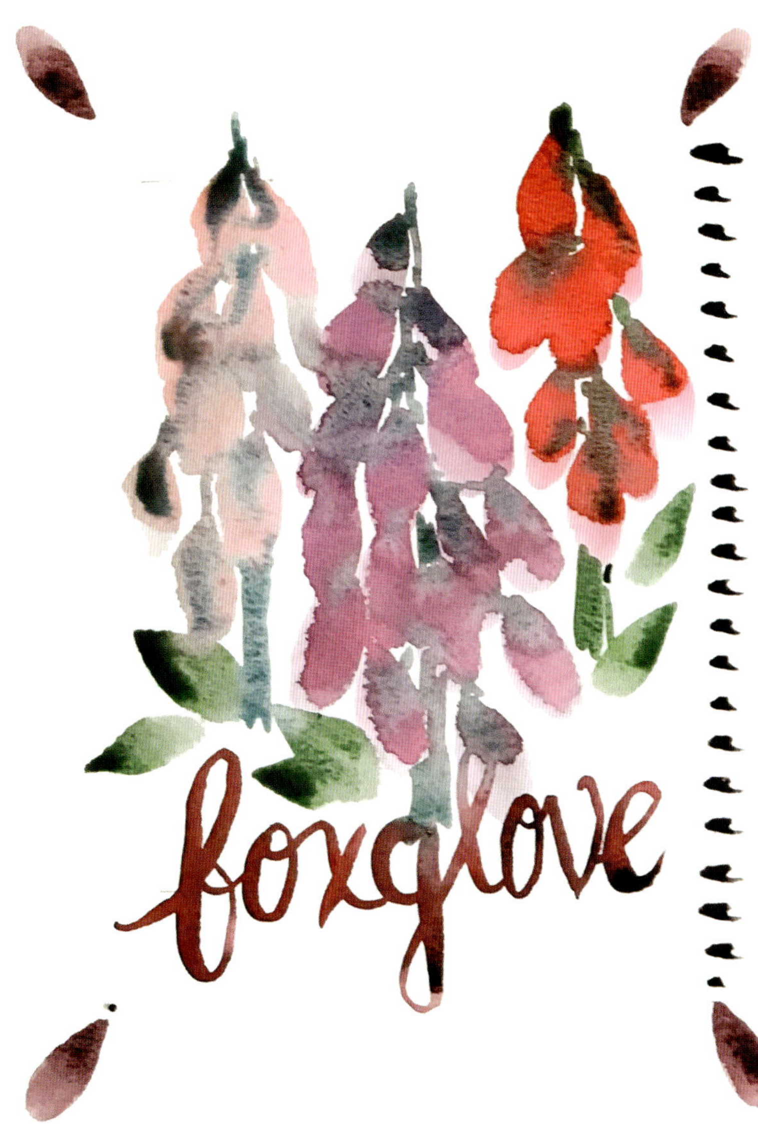

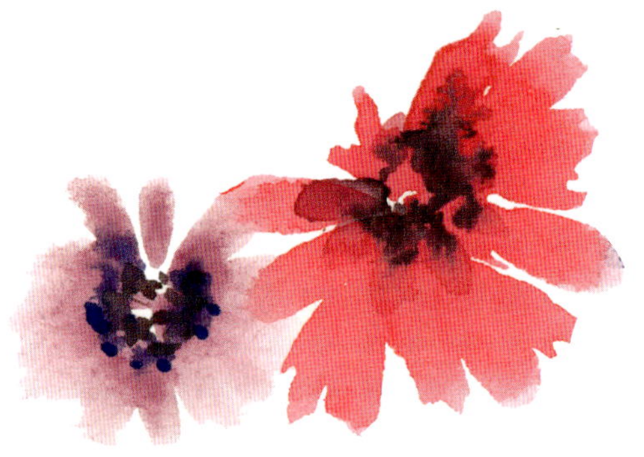

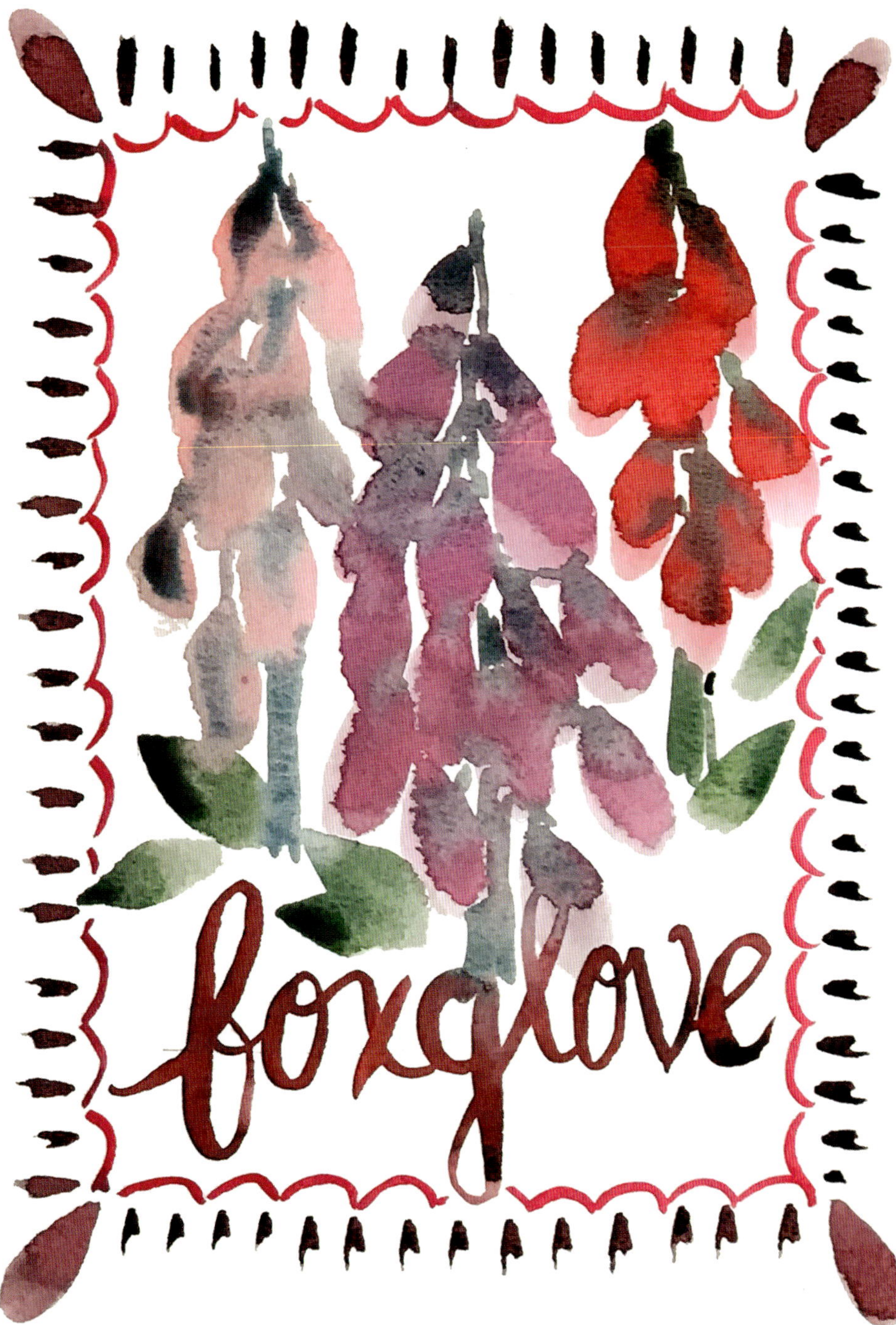

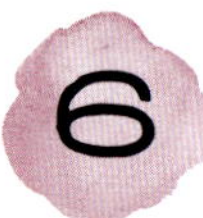

6 Continue adding to your border until you are satisfied with it.

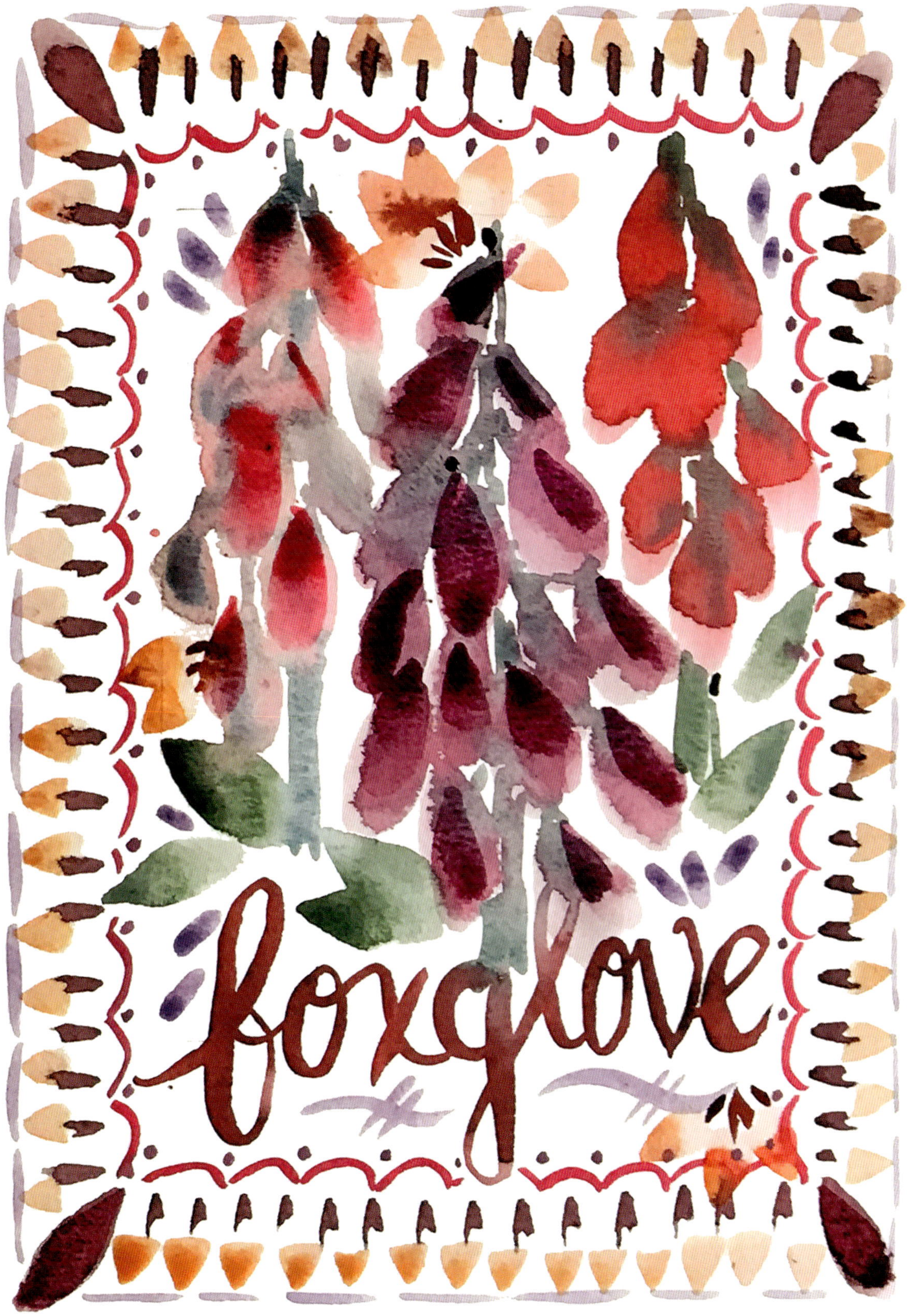

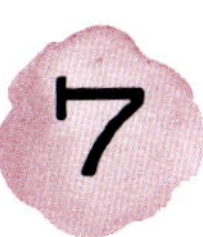

Add any finishing touches, such as a pop of a contrast color to warm things up or cool them down, according to your liking. Add details with a drybrushing technique (see page 12), if you desire.

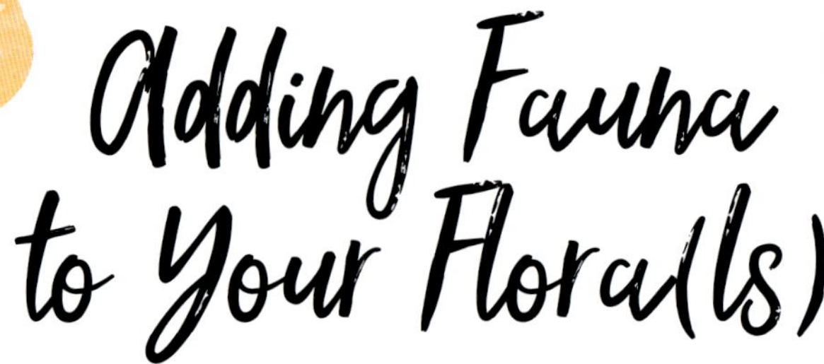

Adding Fauna to Your Floral(s)

You can add interest and energy to your floral paintings by including an animal. My favorite animals to mix with florals are birds and butterflies. They naturally complement each other, and you can have lots of fun with the colors and combinations. The following painting project features both birds *and* butterflies!

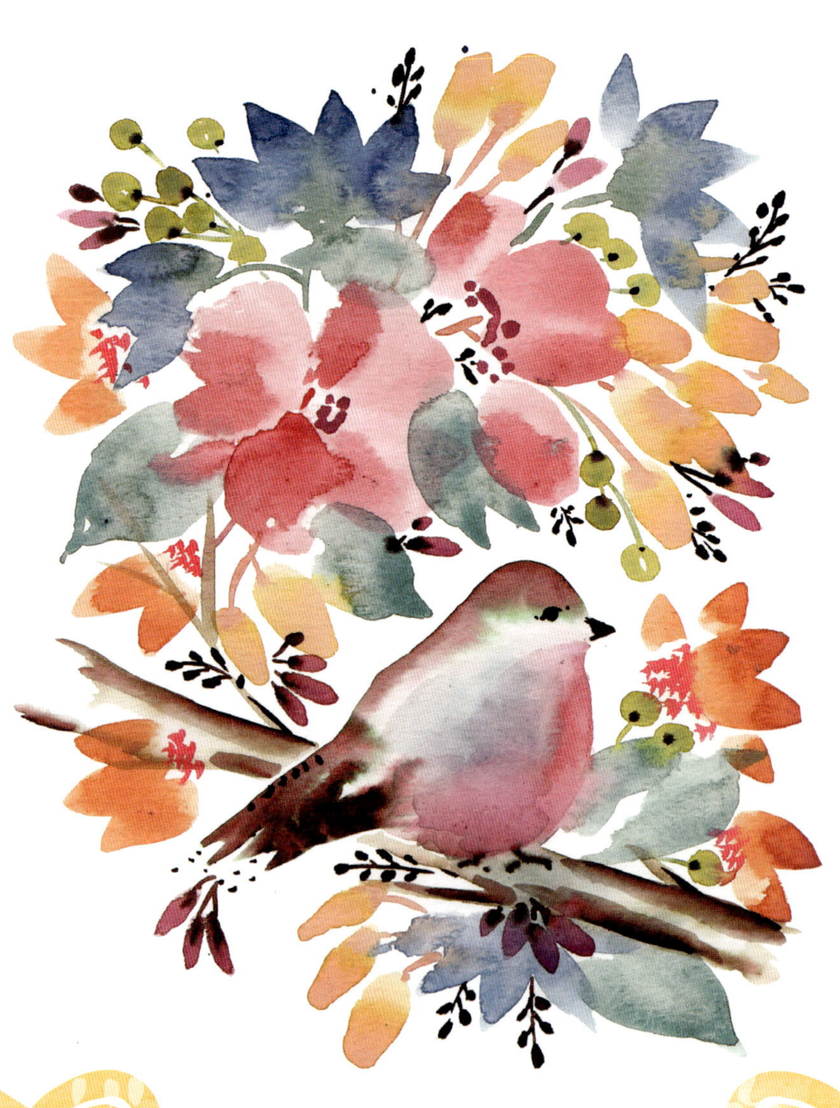

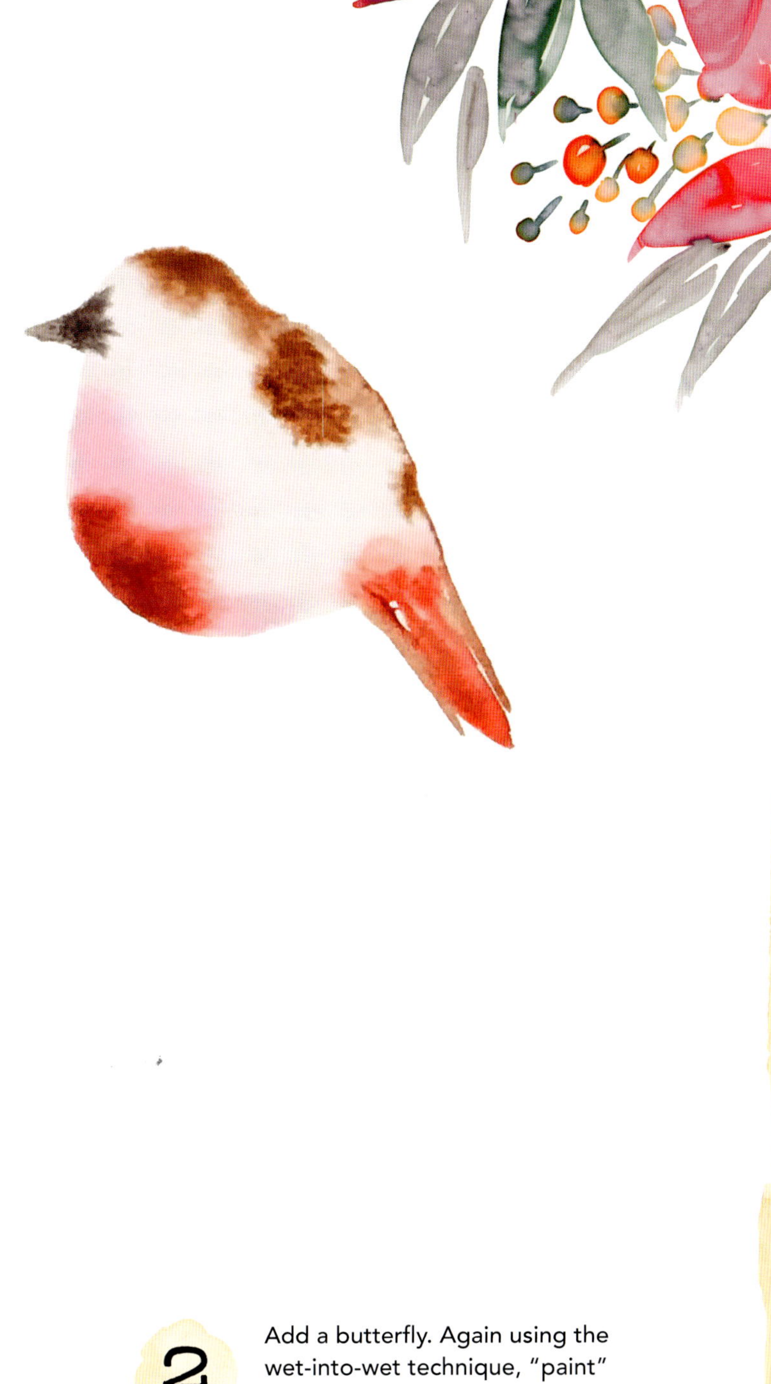

1 To paint this bird, begin by using a wet-into-wet technique (see page 11). With clean water, "paint" the silhouetted shape of the bird. Drop in a color for the bird's belly, and use a contrasting color for its back and head.

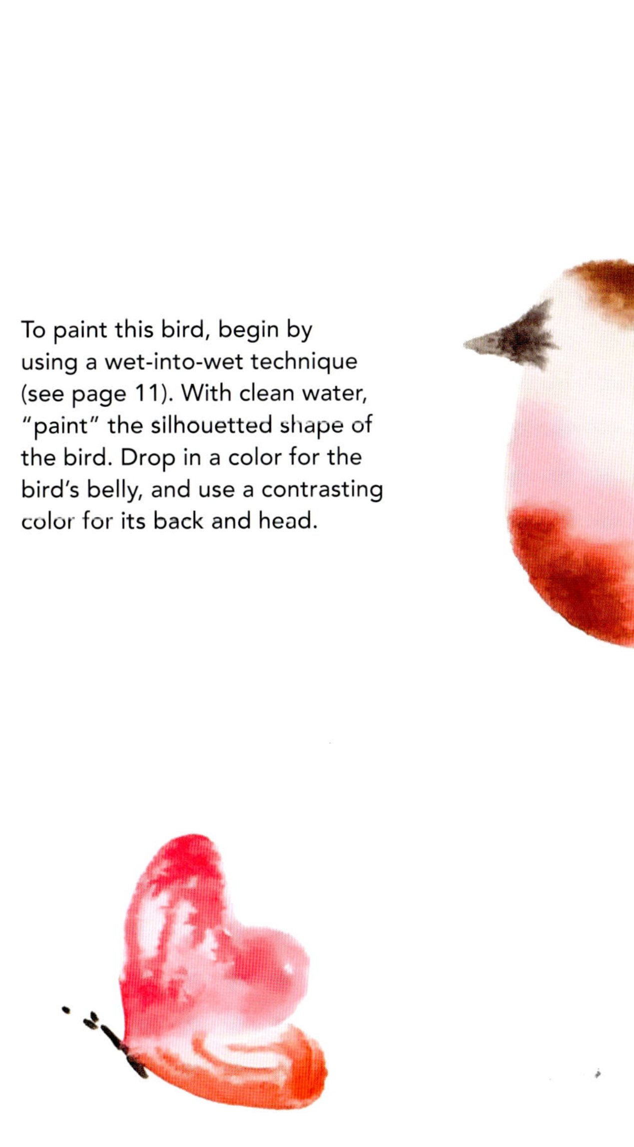

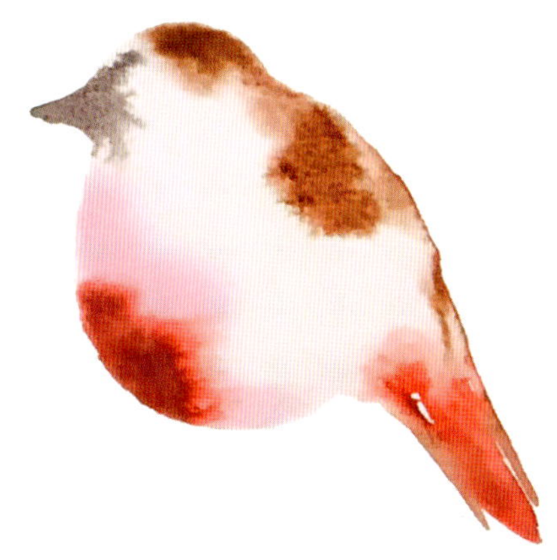

2 Add a butterfly. Again using the wet-into-wet technique, "paint" the silhouette of a butterfly and drop in your color. Wait until the wings are fully dry to add the body and antennae.

I like to wait until the bird dries a bit to add color for its beak.

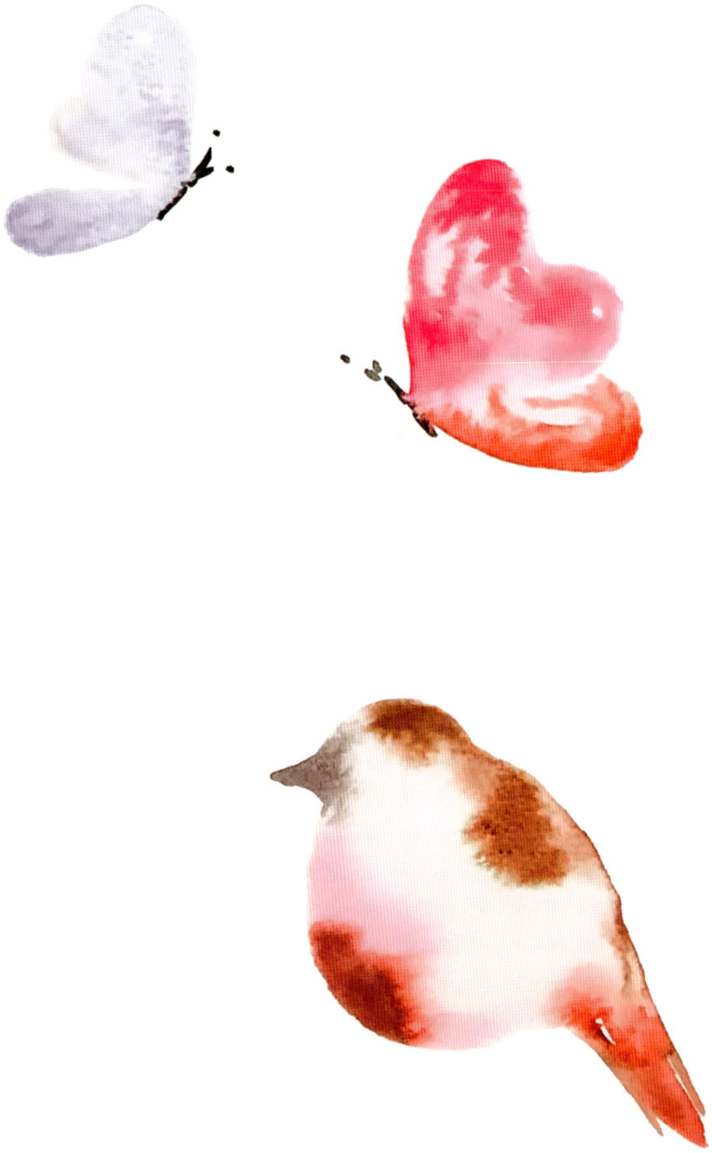

Add a second butterfly. This one can face the opposite direction to create variety.

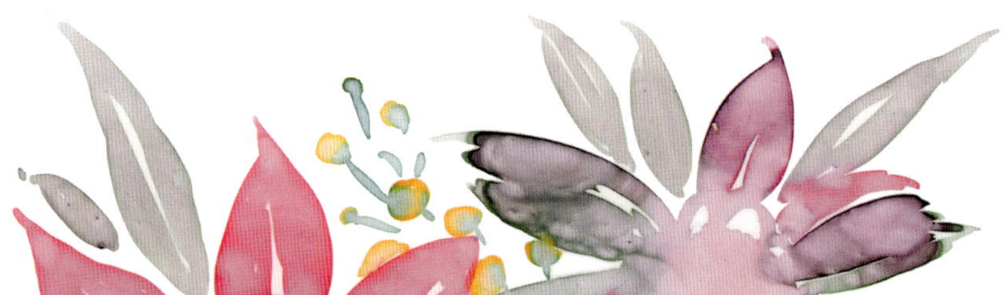

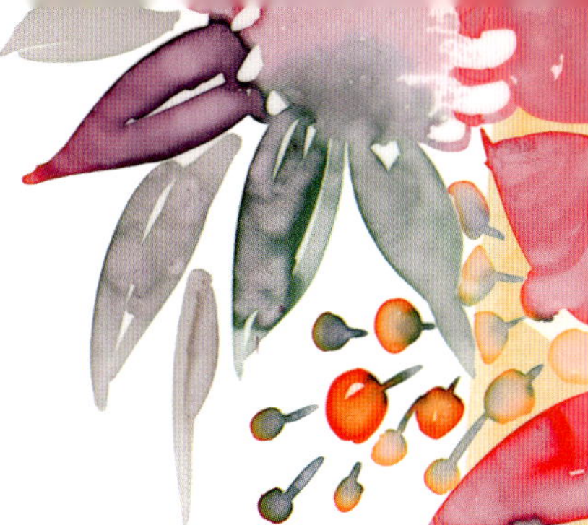

It's often best to ground your animal. This ties it in with the rest of the painting.

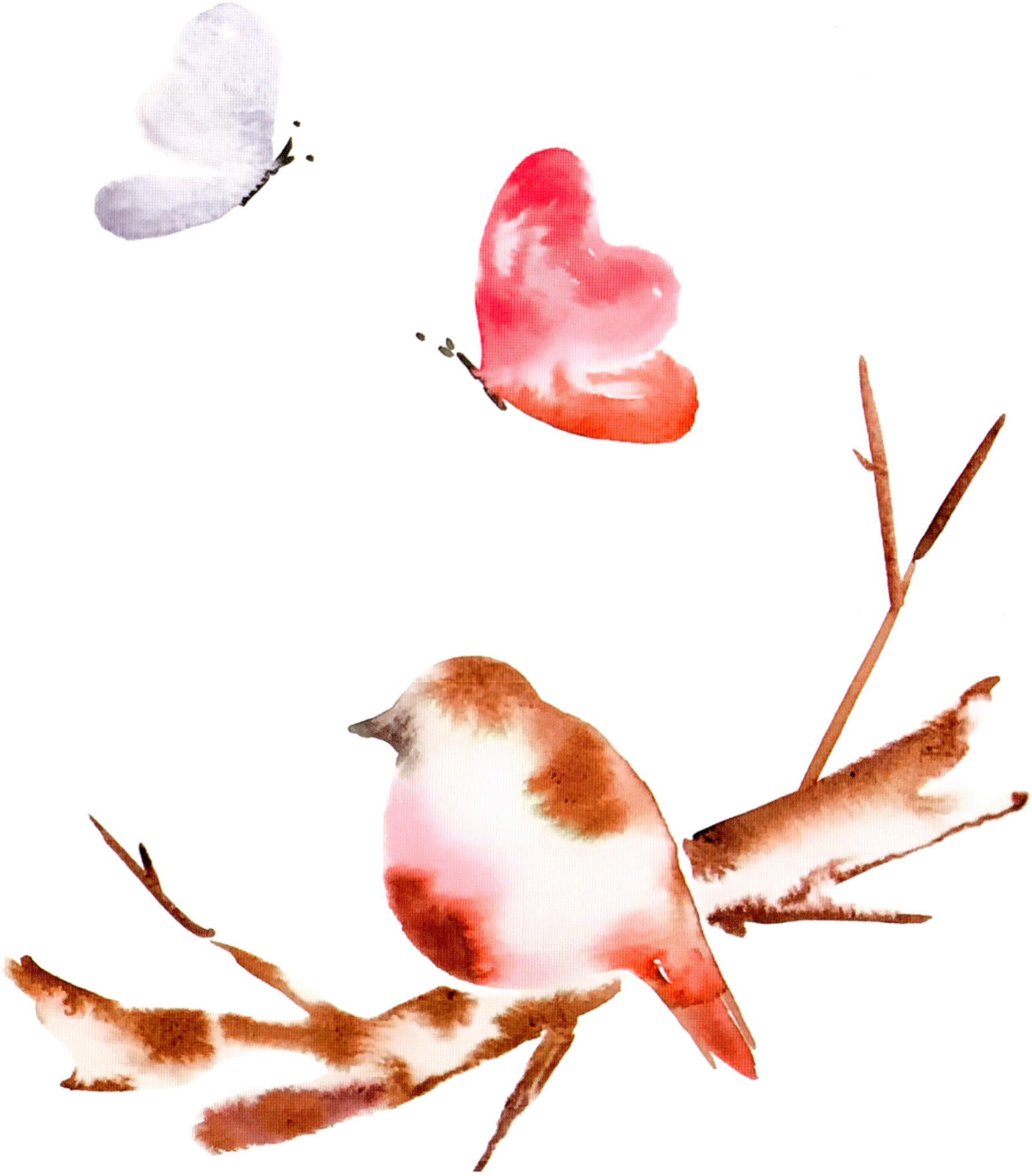

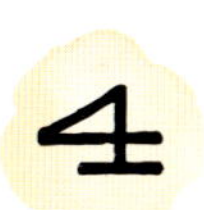

4 Adding a branch using the same wet-into-wet technique gives the bird a place to rest, as well as some form for you to fill with florals.

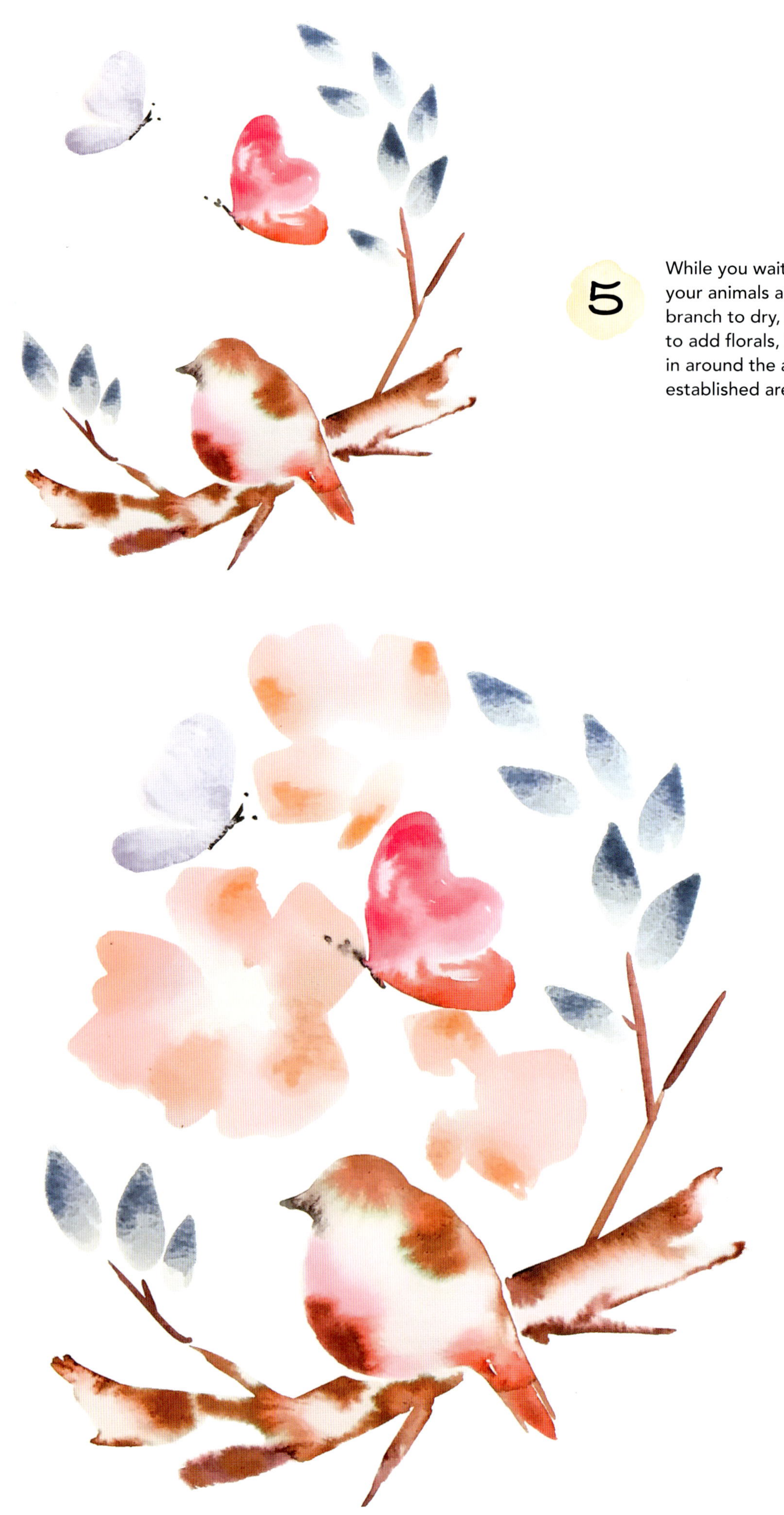

5

While you wait for your animals and branch to dry, begin to add florals, filling in around the already-established areas.

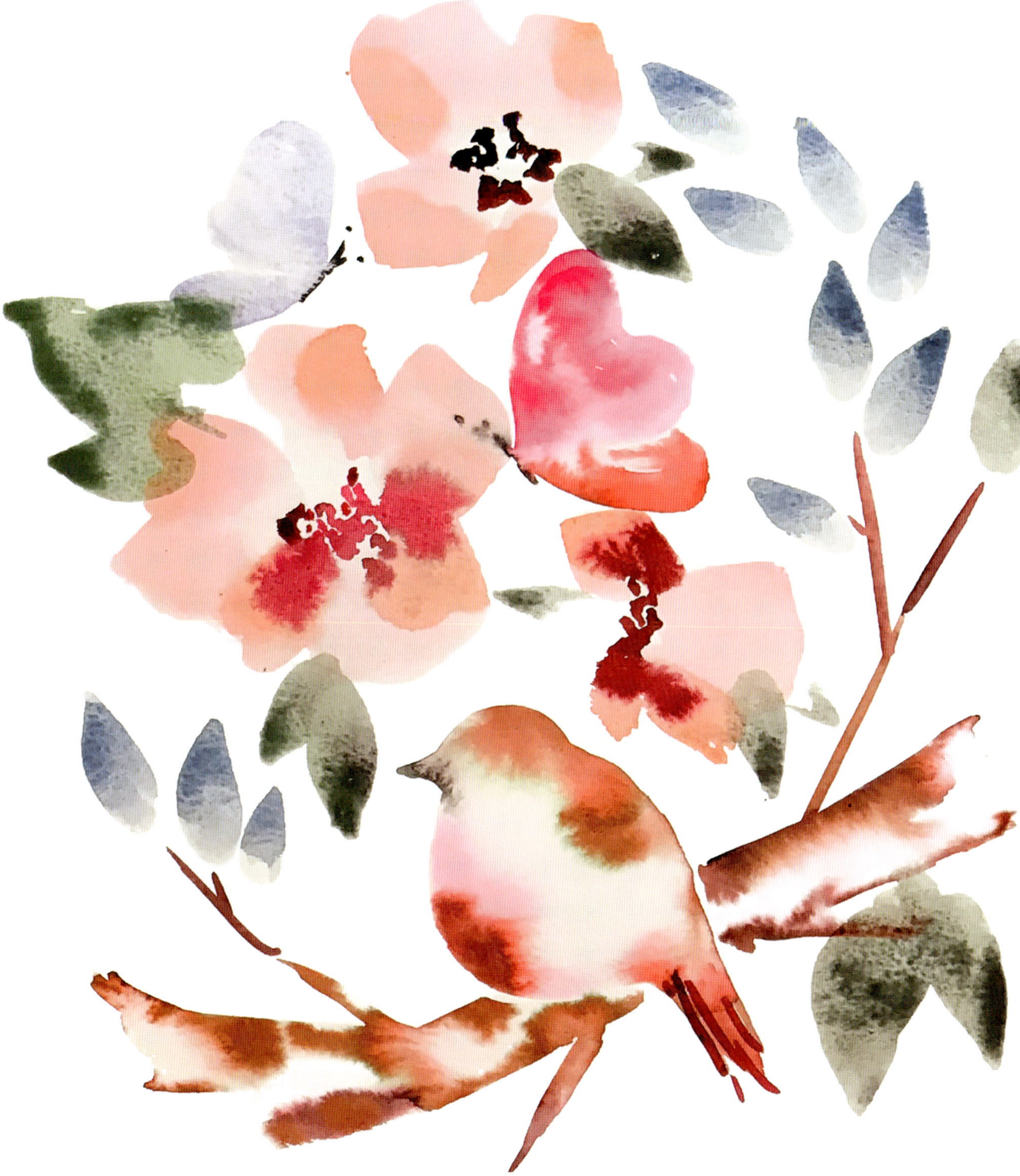

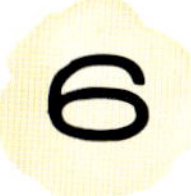

Use a variety of blooms, buds, and leaves to add interest in your painting.

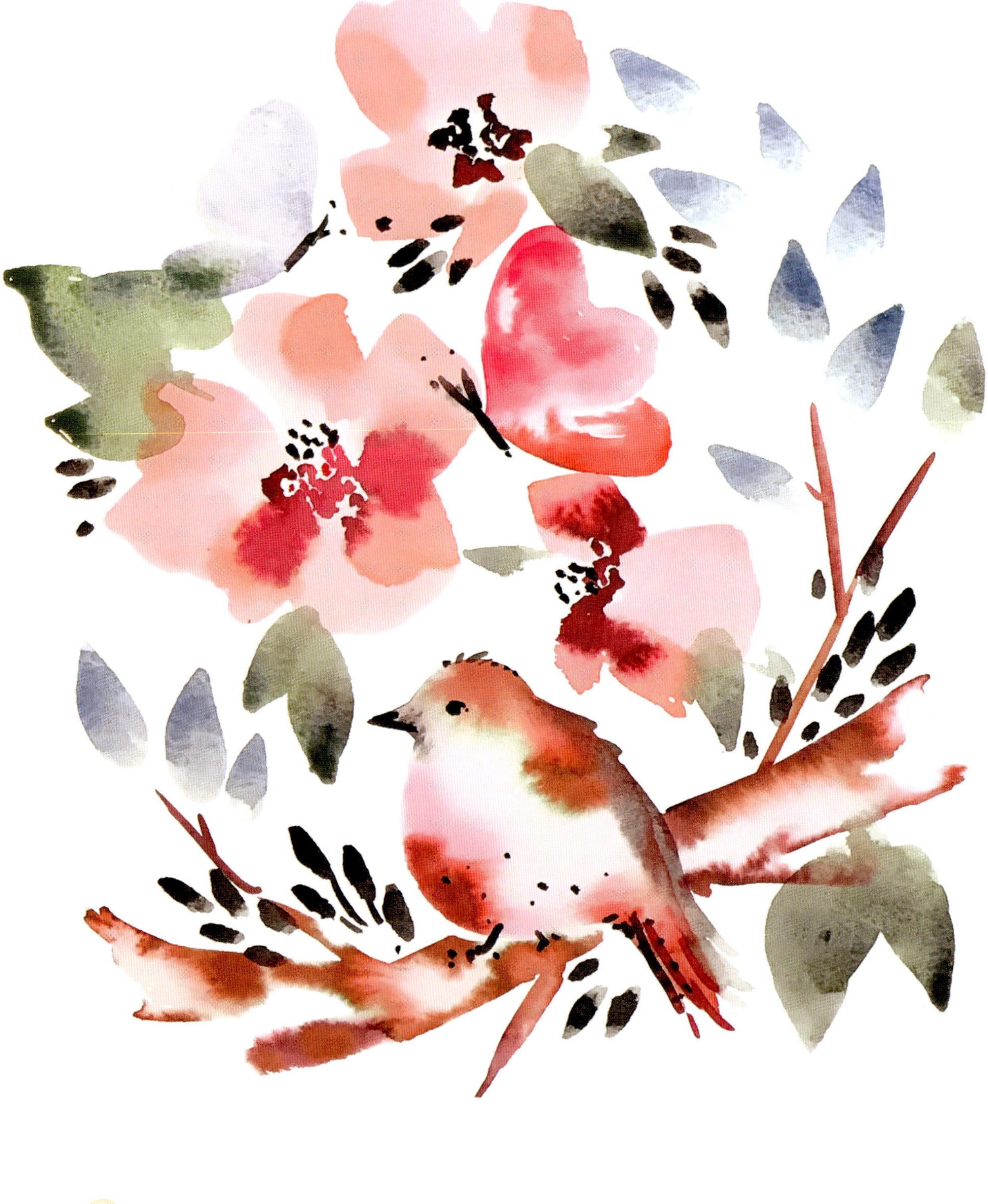

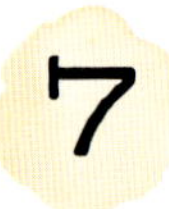

Let the bird and butterflies dry, and then begin to add details using the drybrushing technique (see page 12). Create featherlike markings on the bird's tail, head, and wings.

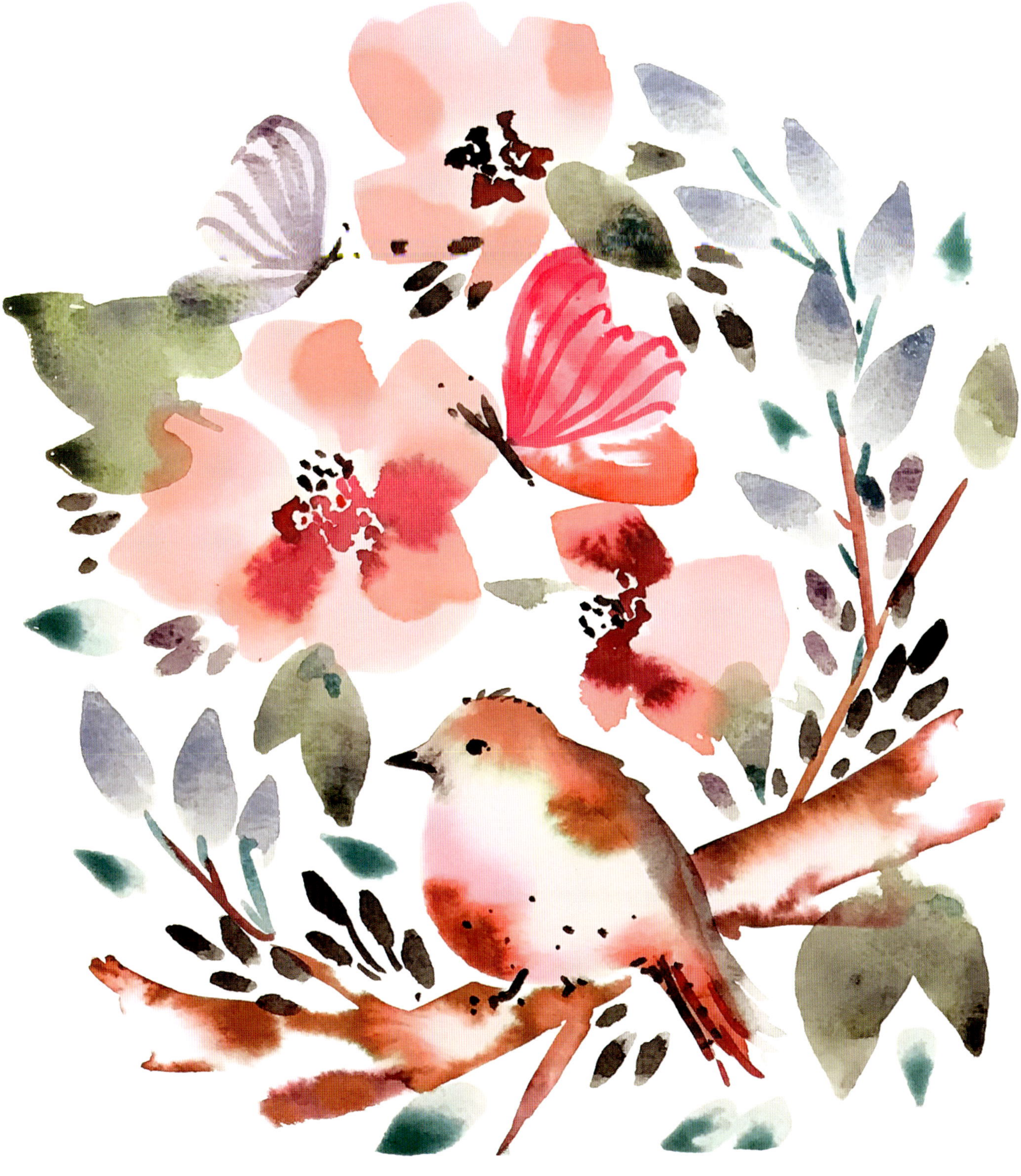

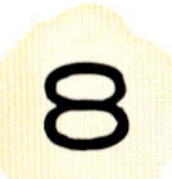

Make line or dot markings on the butterflies. Use your imagination, and add details in your own style.

Adding an unexpected pop of color at the very end keeps your painting fresh and inspires you to experiment with new color combinations.

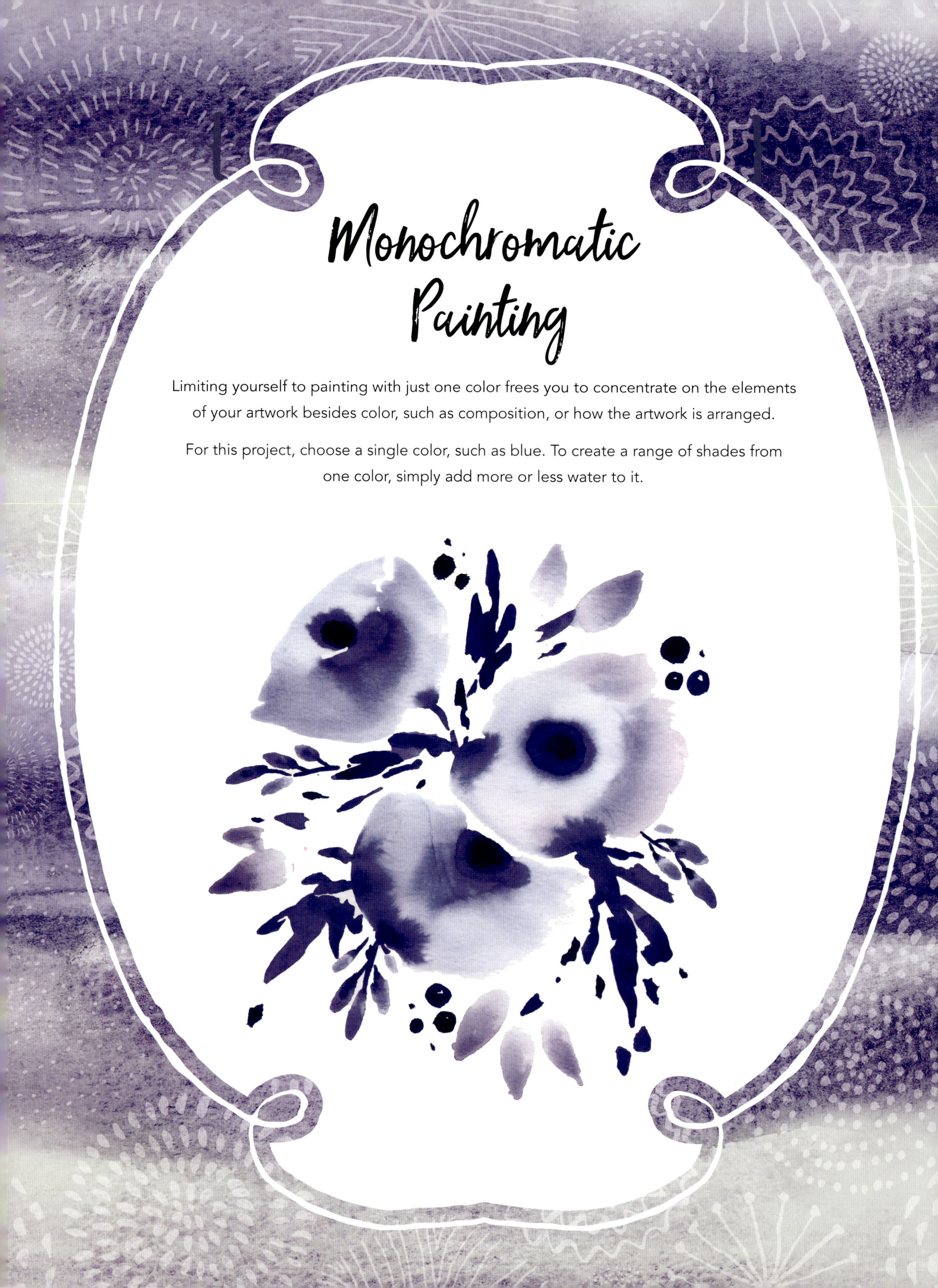

Monochromatic Painting

Limiting yourself to painting with just one color frees you to concentrate on the elements of your artwork besides color, such as composition, or how the artwork is arranged.

For this project, choose a single color, such as blue. To create a range of shades from one color, simply add more or less water to it.

Dropping in a lighter shade around one side of your bloom creates additional dimension.

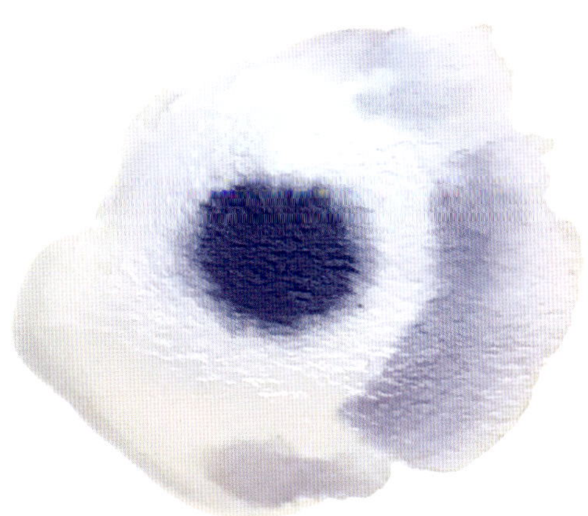

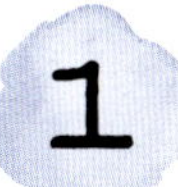

1 Using the wet-into-wet technique (see page 11), paint one large bloom. Apply the darkest saturation of color in the center, and let it bleed out toward the edges.

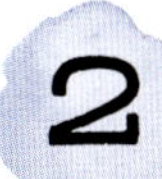

2 Using the same method, add a second bloom slightly behind the first. You can continue to drop dark color into the centers of the blooms as they dry to ensure vibrant color in the middle.

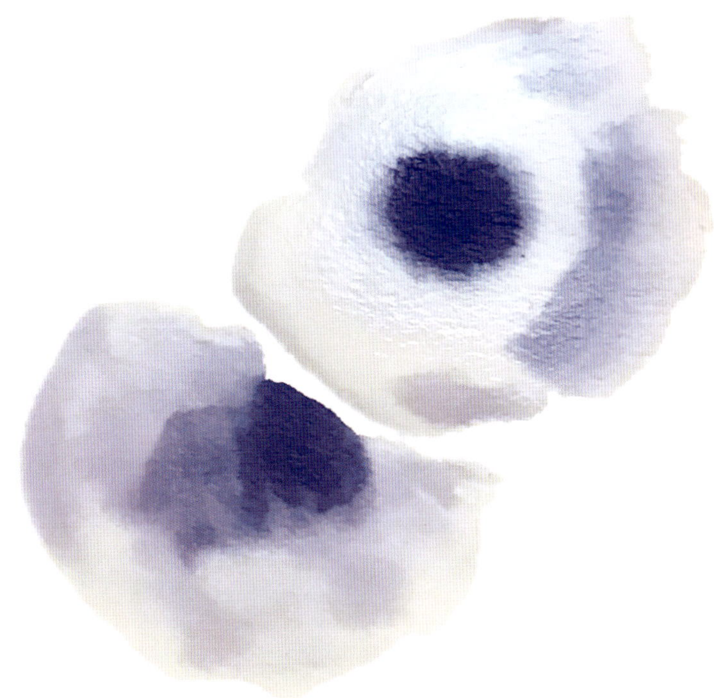

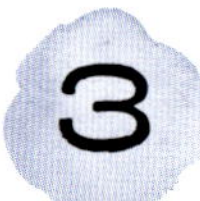

Add a third bloom on one side, creating an asymmetrical composition. Try to use your observational skills to paint this bloom from a different angle. Here, the third bloom is seen from the side, with a bit of its center peeking out.

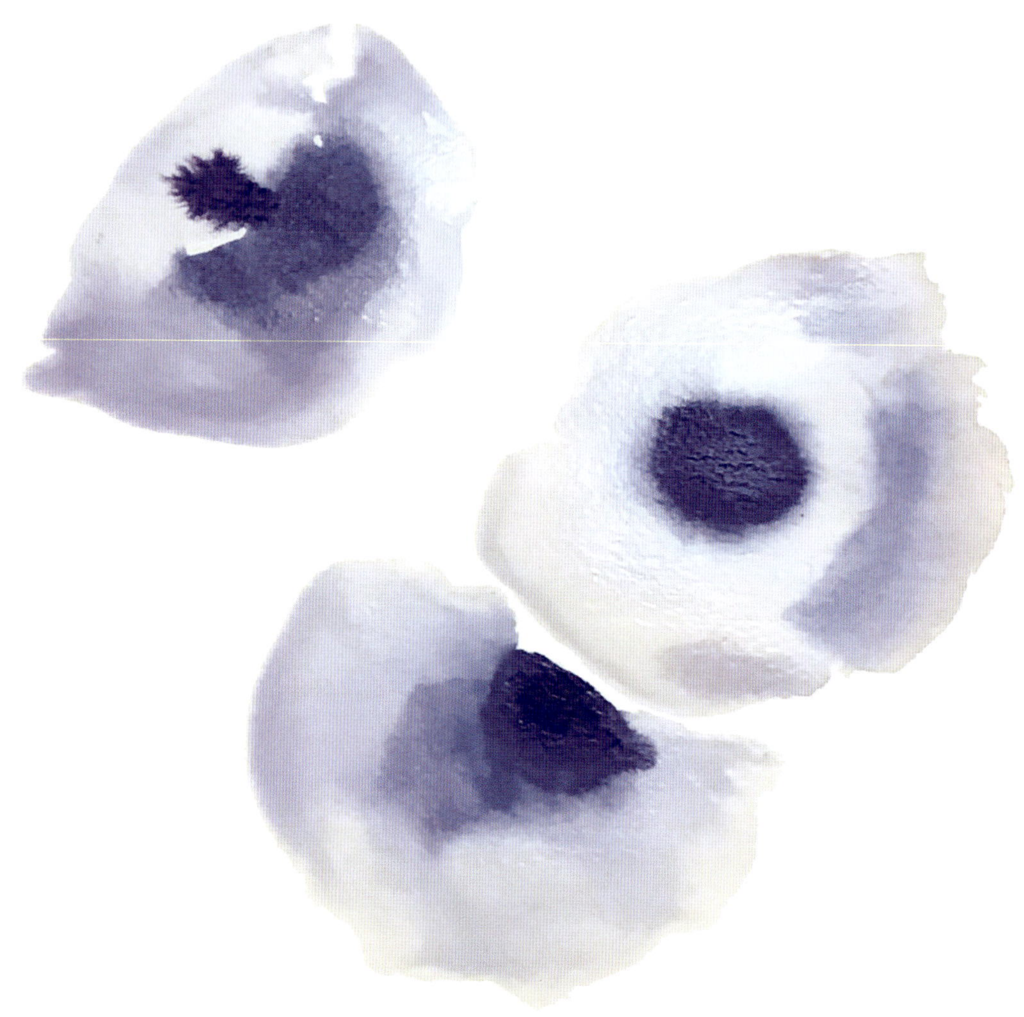

Varying the directions of the flowers will add interest to your painting.

Now, in a dark shade, add some foliage around the blooms to ground them.

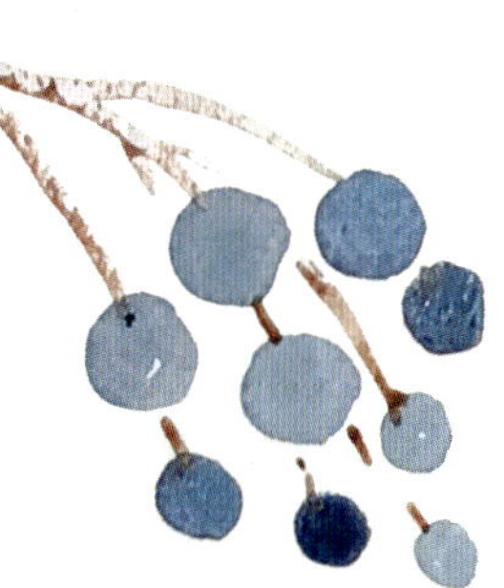

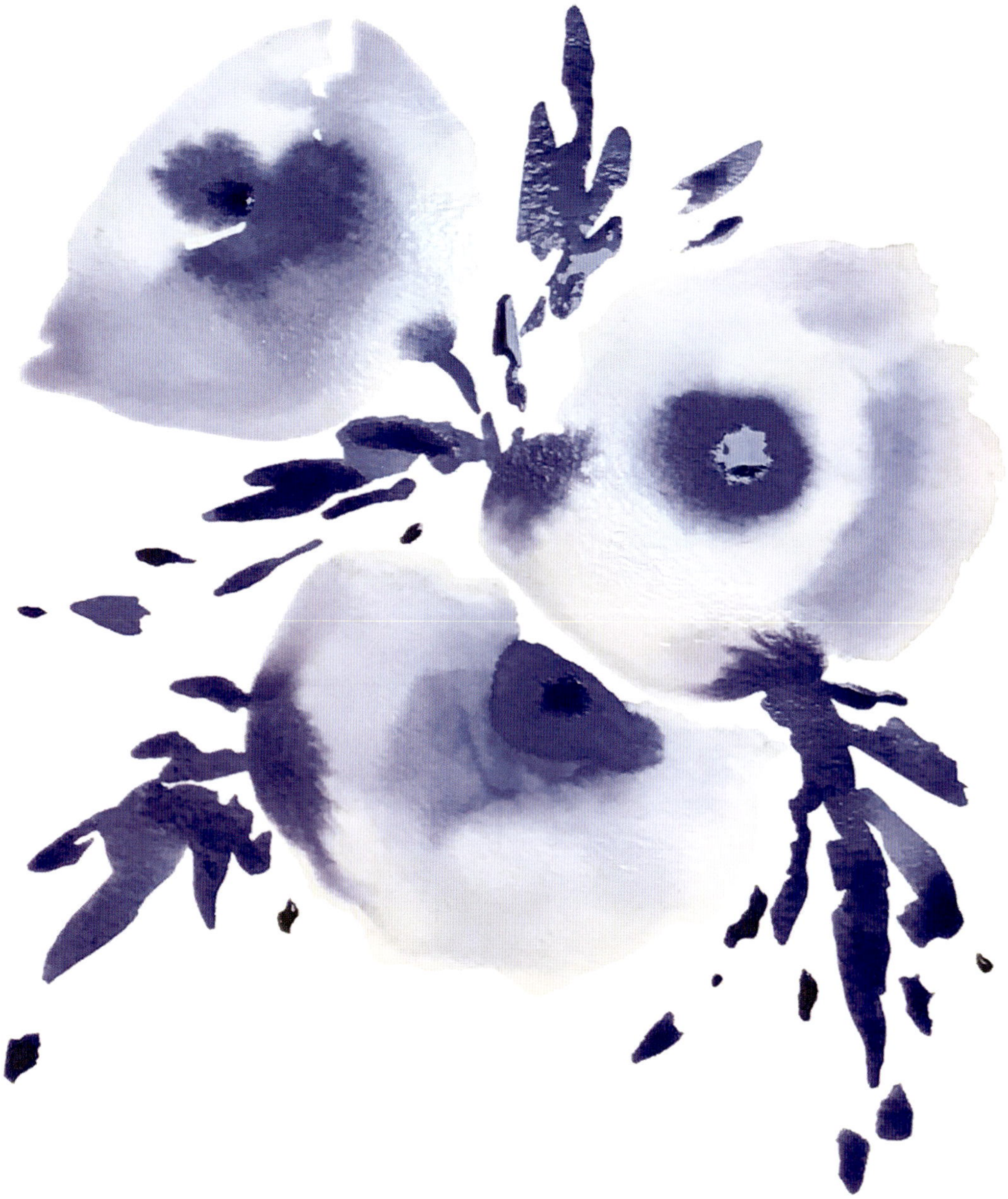

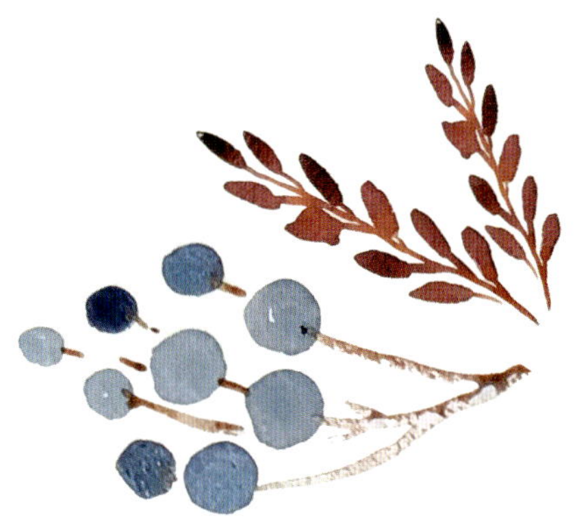

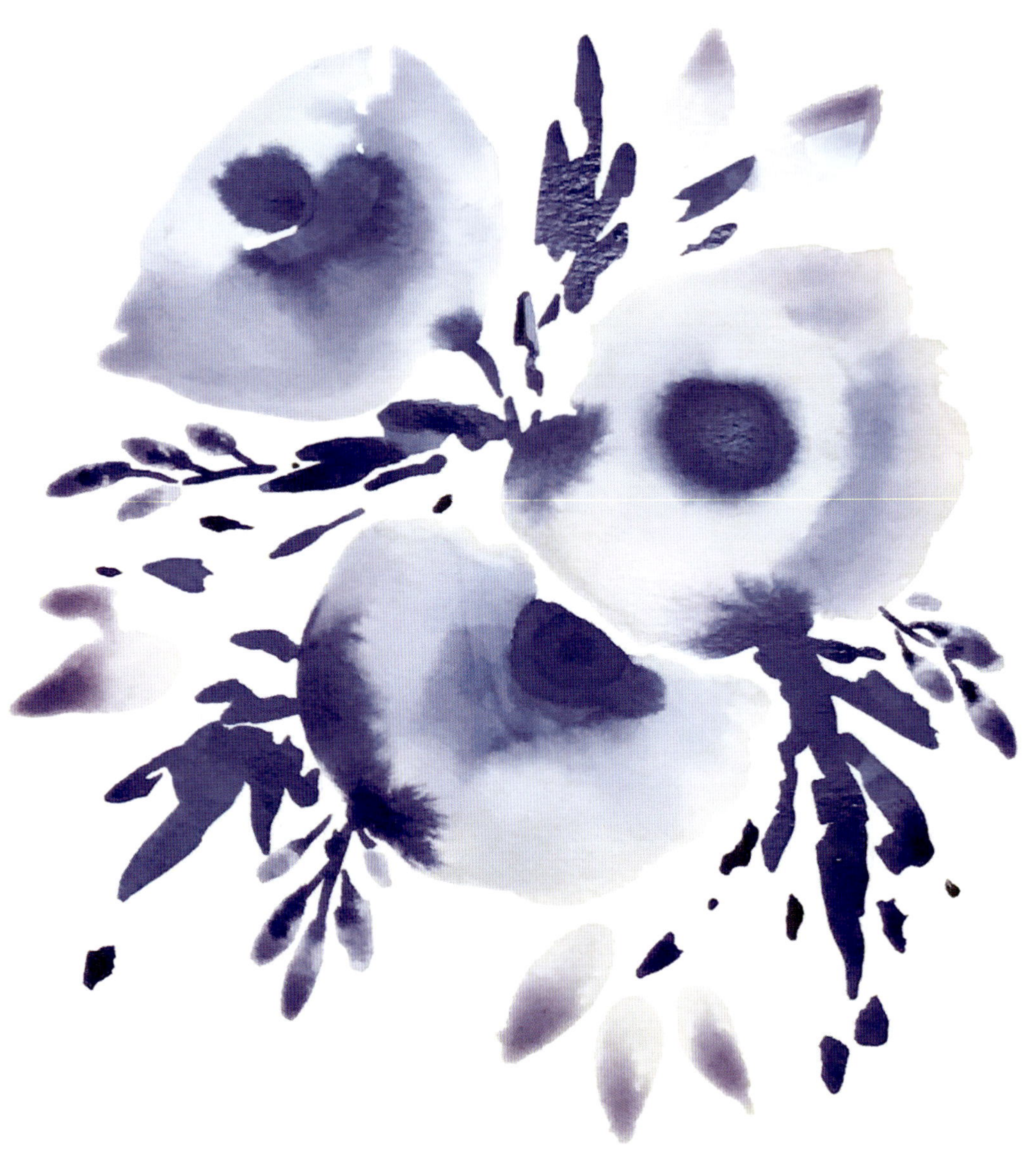

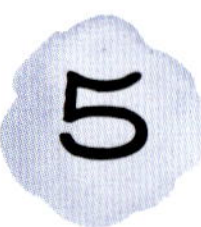

By adding varying amounts of water to the pigment, you can achieve a range of shades of a single color. Using this principle, add a second type of foliage in a lighter or darker shade.

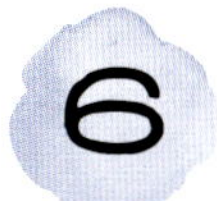

6

To finish your painting and fill out the composition, use a very dark shade to add a few buds or berries.

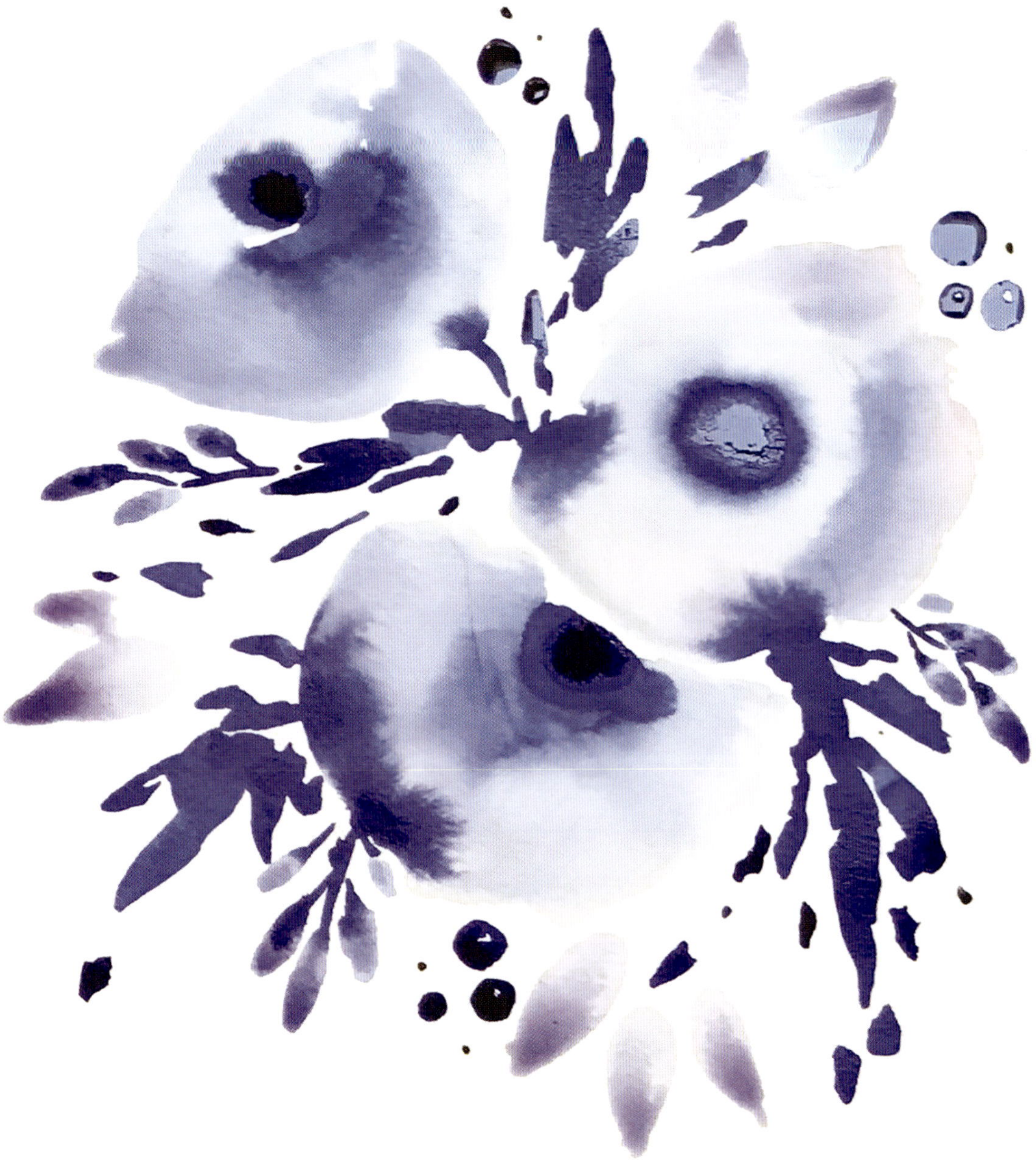

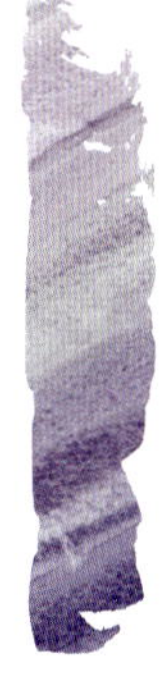

Now that you've learned how to paint a monochromatic painting, try using other colors. Orange would make a beautiful color for a monochromatic painting, as would purple!

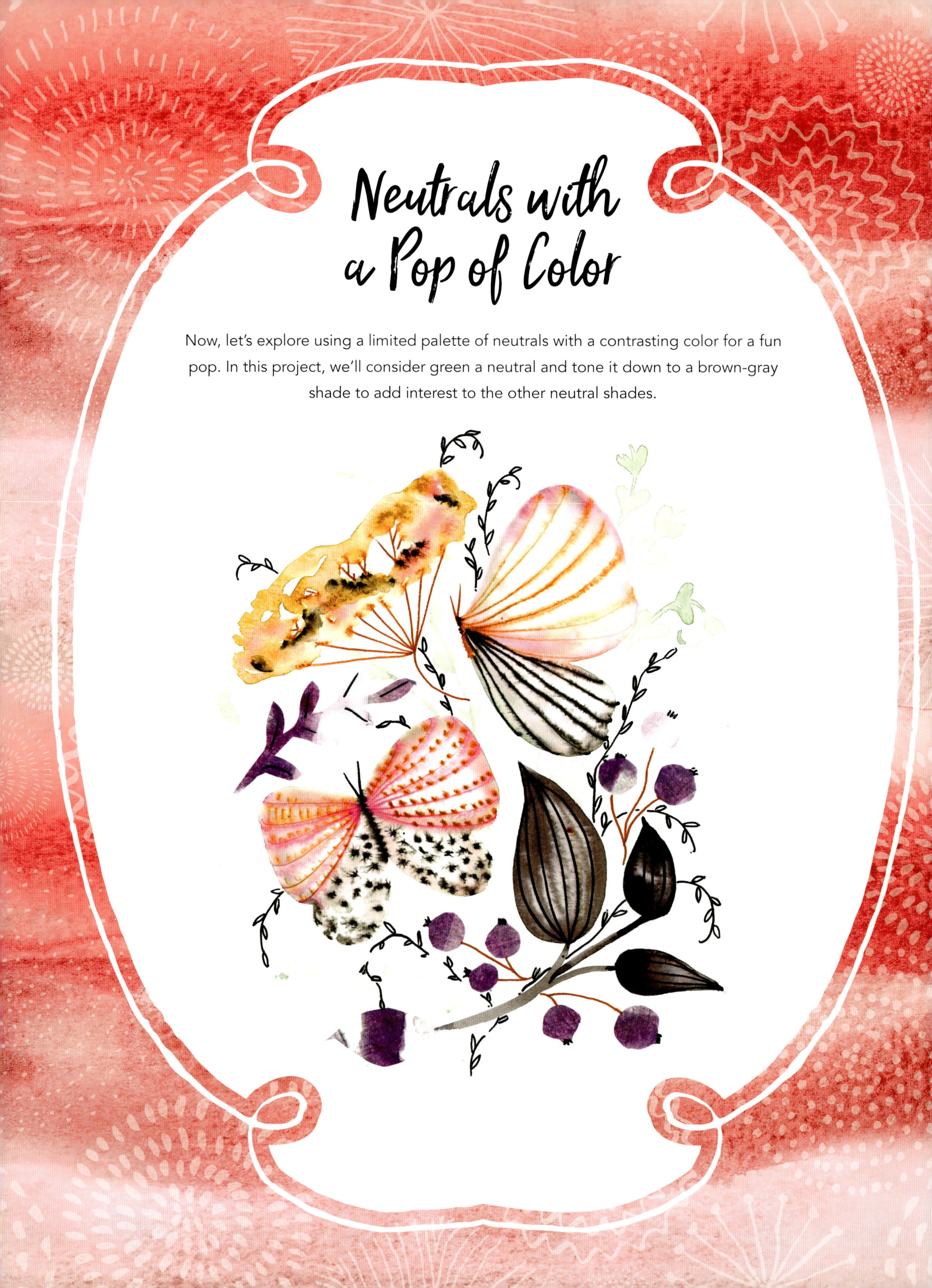

Neutrals with a Pop of Color

Now, let's explore using a limited palette of neutrals with a contrasting color for a fun pop. In this project, we'll consider green a neutral and tone it down to a brown-gray shade to add interest to the other neutral shades.

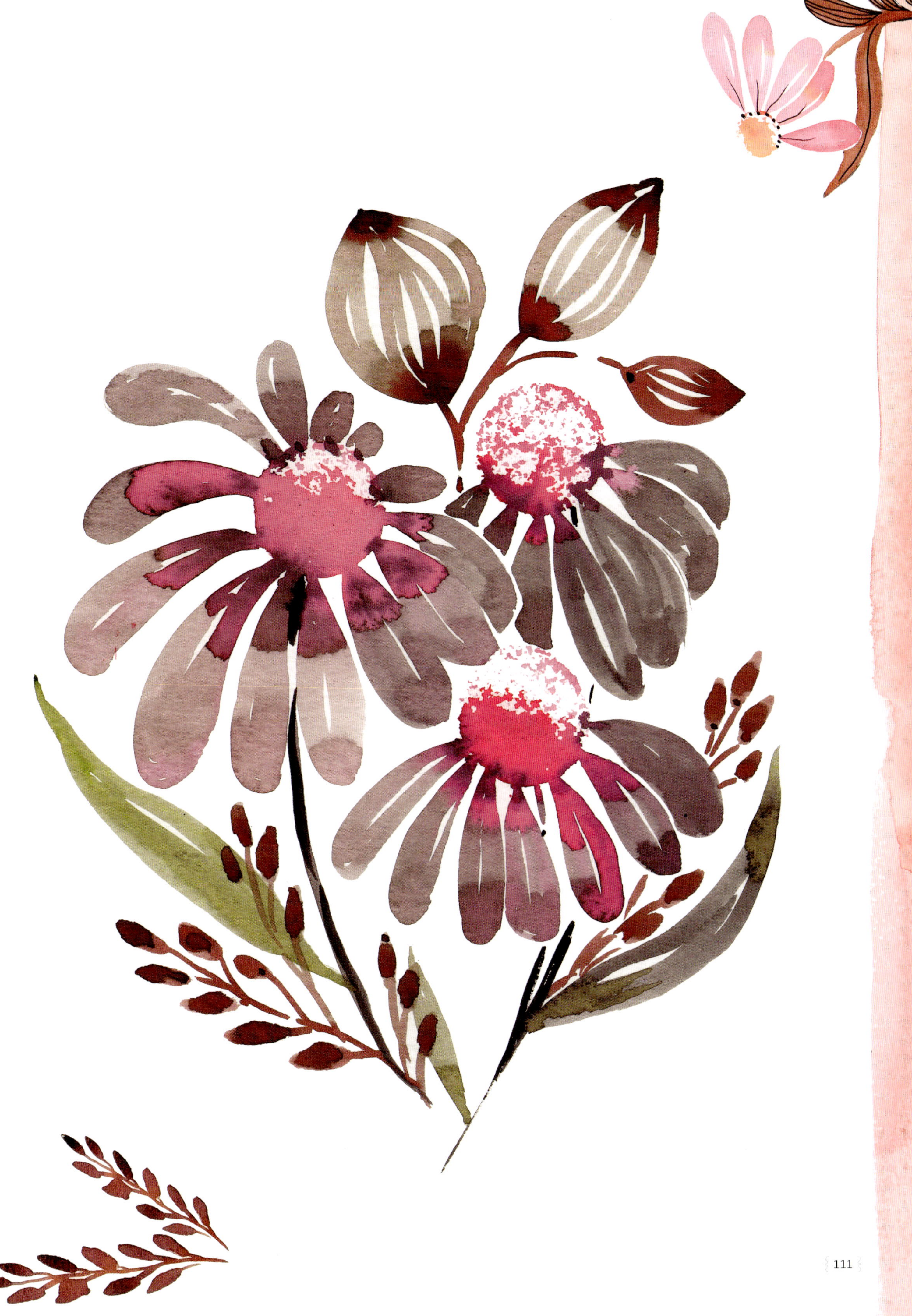

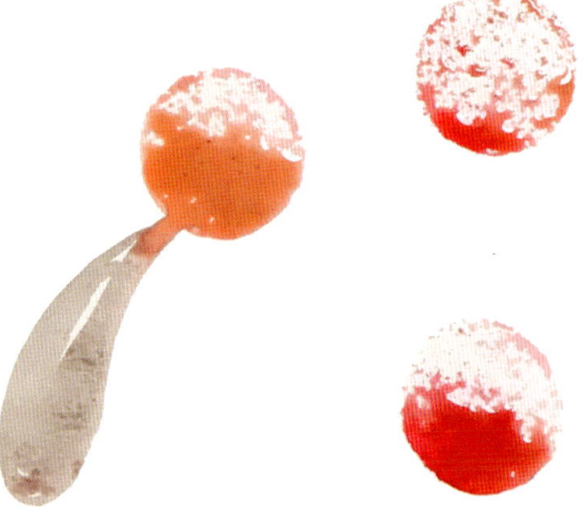

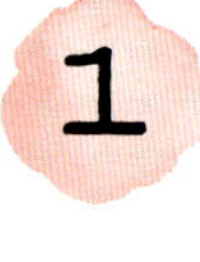

Start with a pop of color to establish the centers of the flowers. I used a round sponge brush to add an additional element of texture. (For more on using sponges, see pages 76-83.)

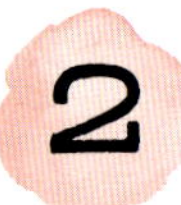

With the bright floral centers defined, add petals in a neutral color (black, gray, or brown) coming down and overlapping each other. If the centers of your flowers are still wet, this will create an interesting bleeding effect on the petals.

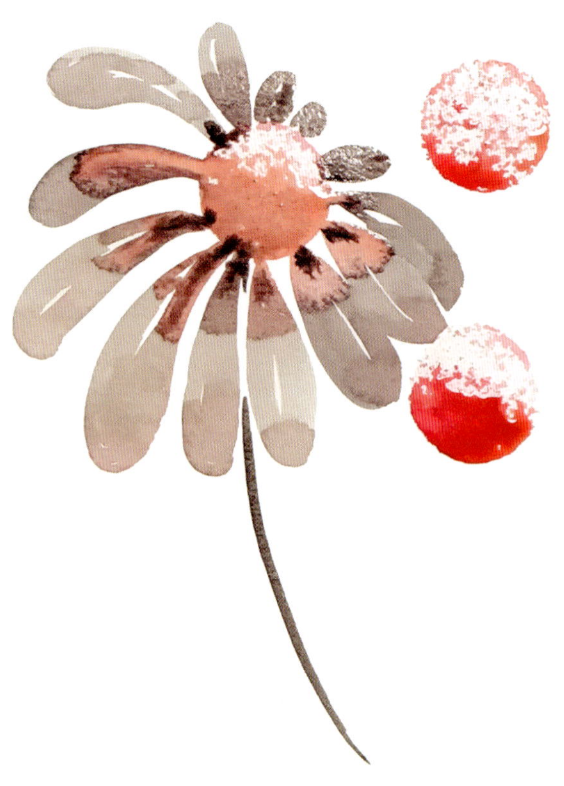

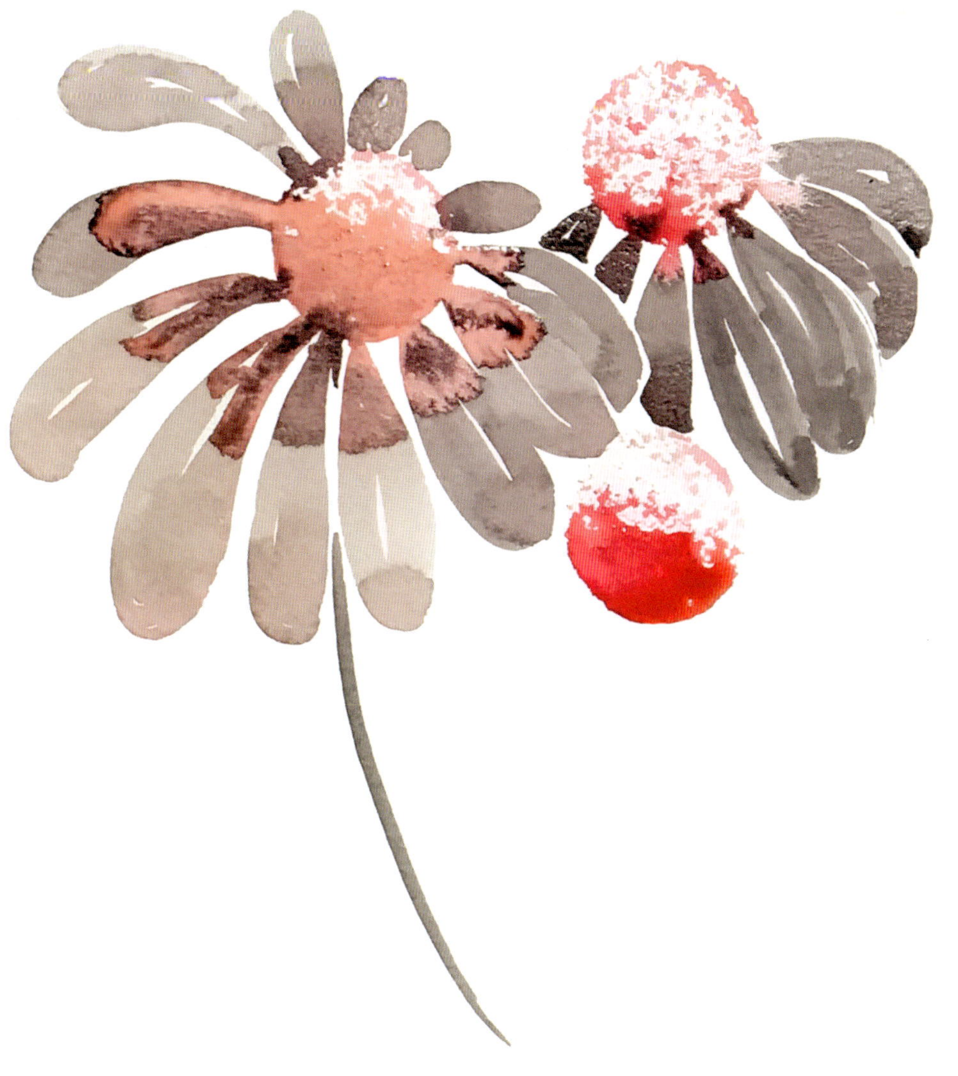

3 Continue adding petals.

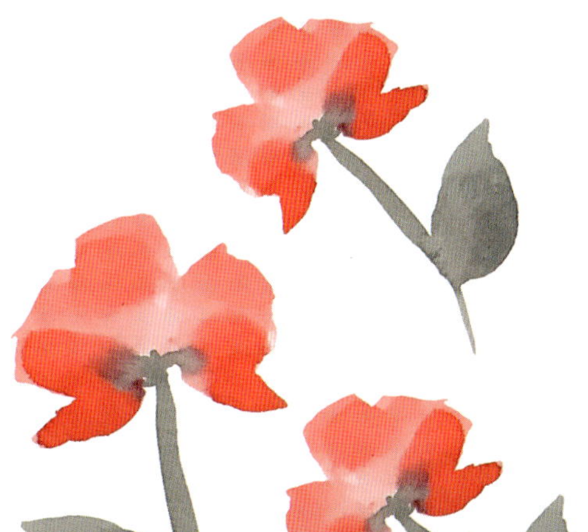

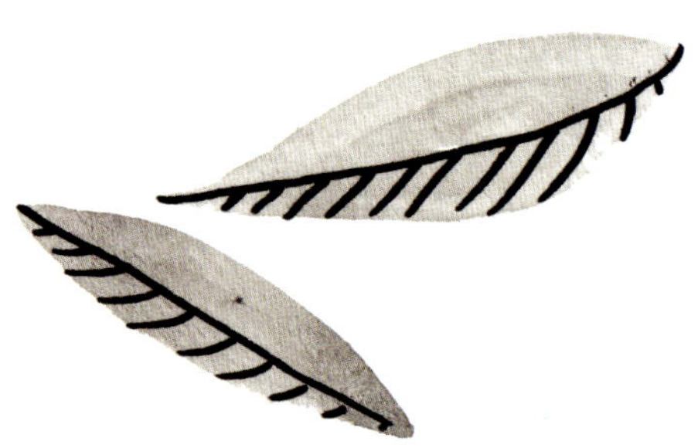

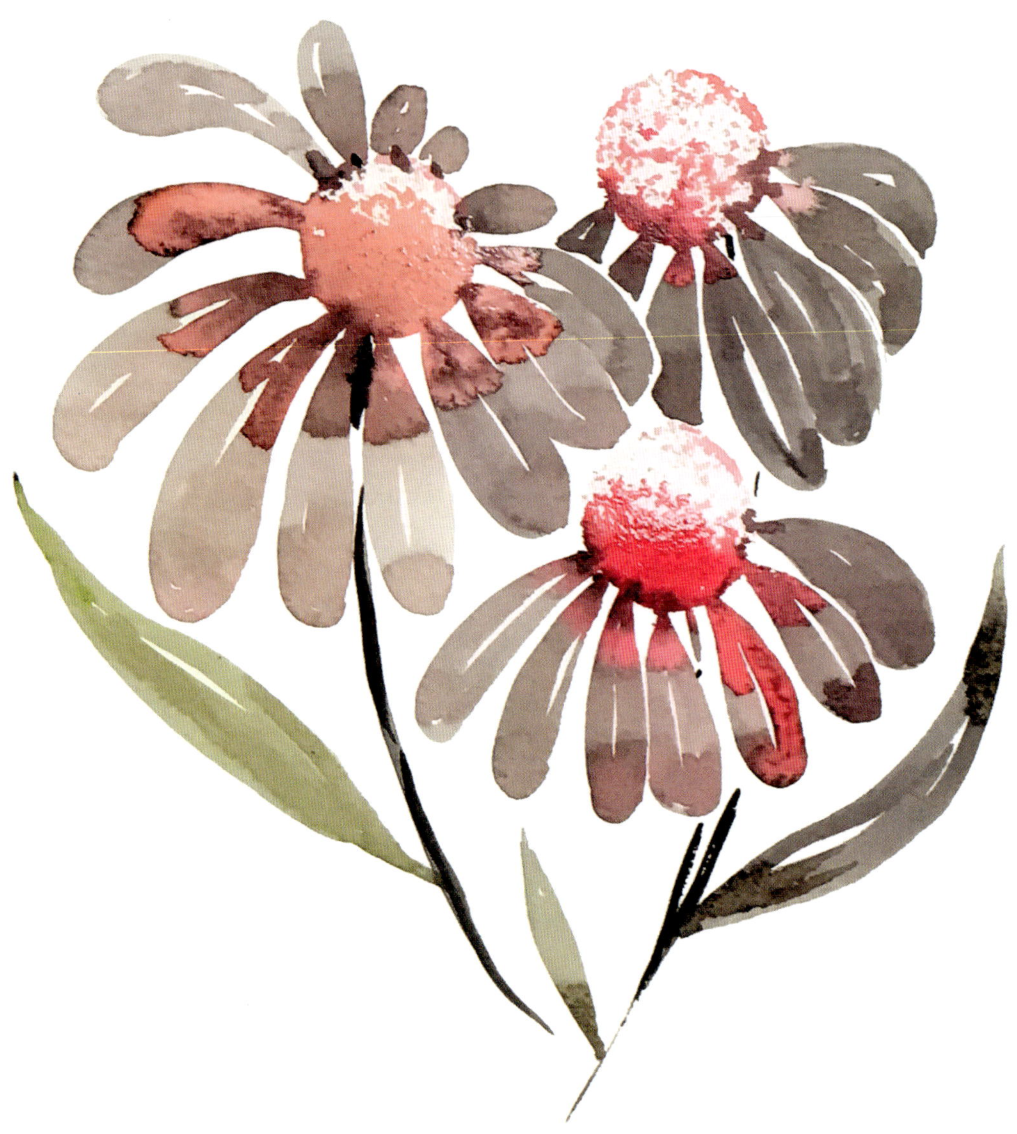

Add more petals. Then paint a few leaves using a neutral green color, created by mixing green with black, gray, or brown. Pull a fine-tipped paintbrush downward to add stems to the flowers.

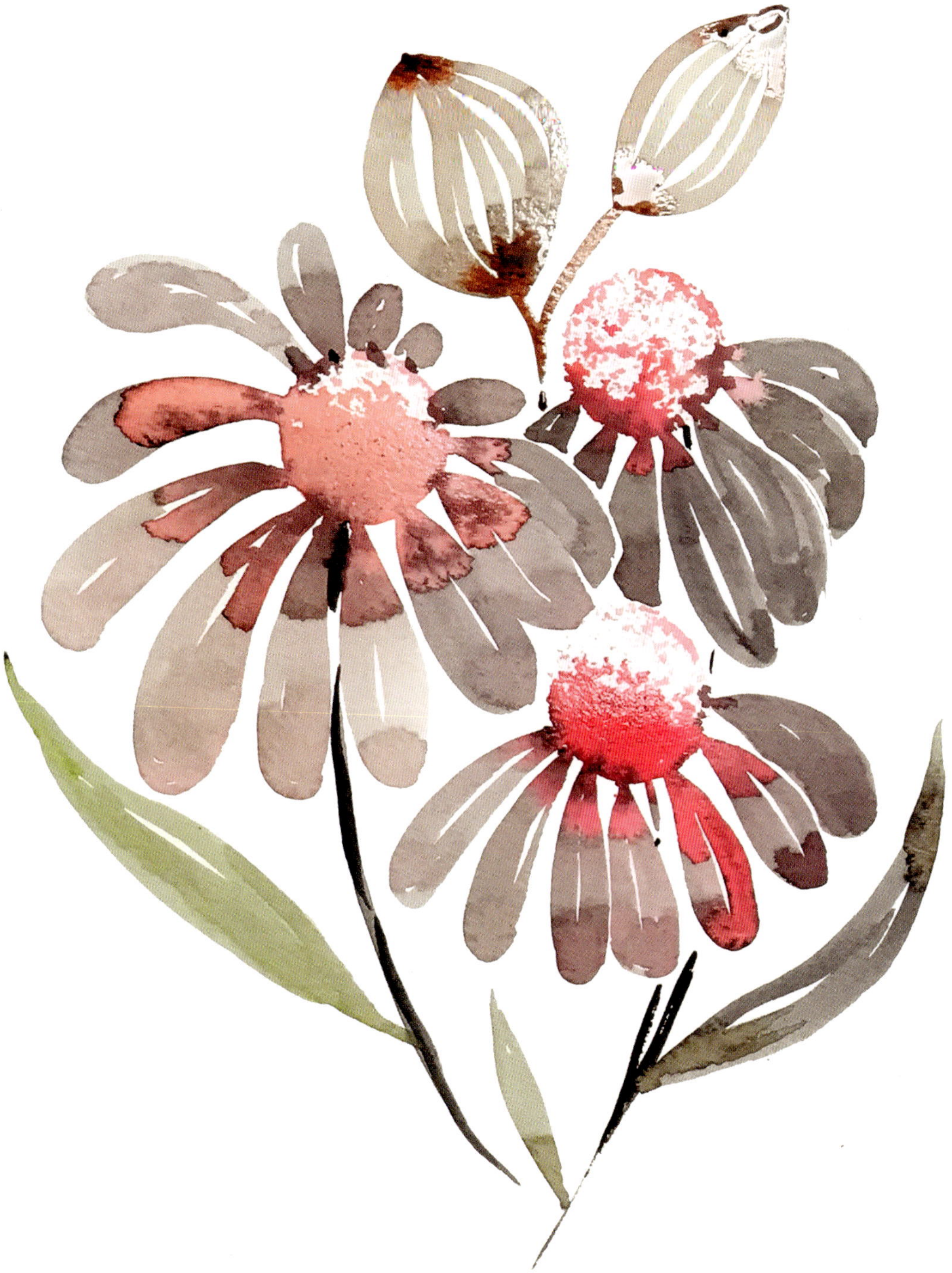

5 With another neutral color, add a second type of bud or bloom to your piece. Use "A Library of Flowers" (pages 30-41) for inspiration.

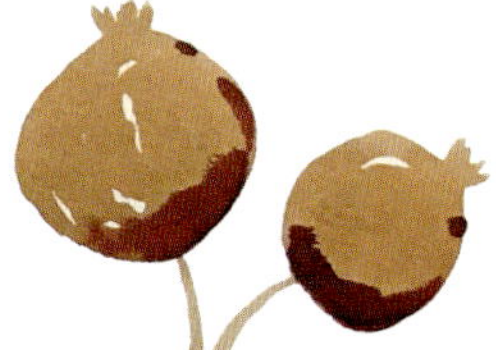

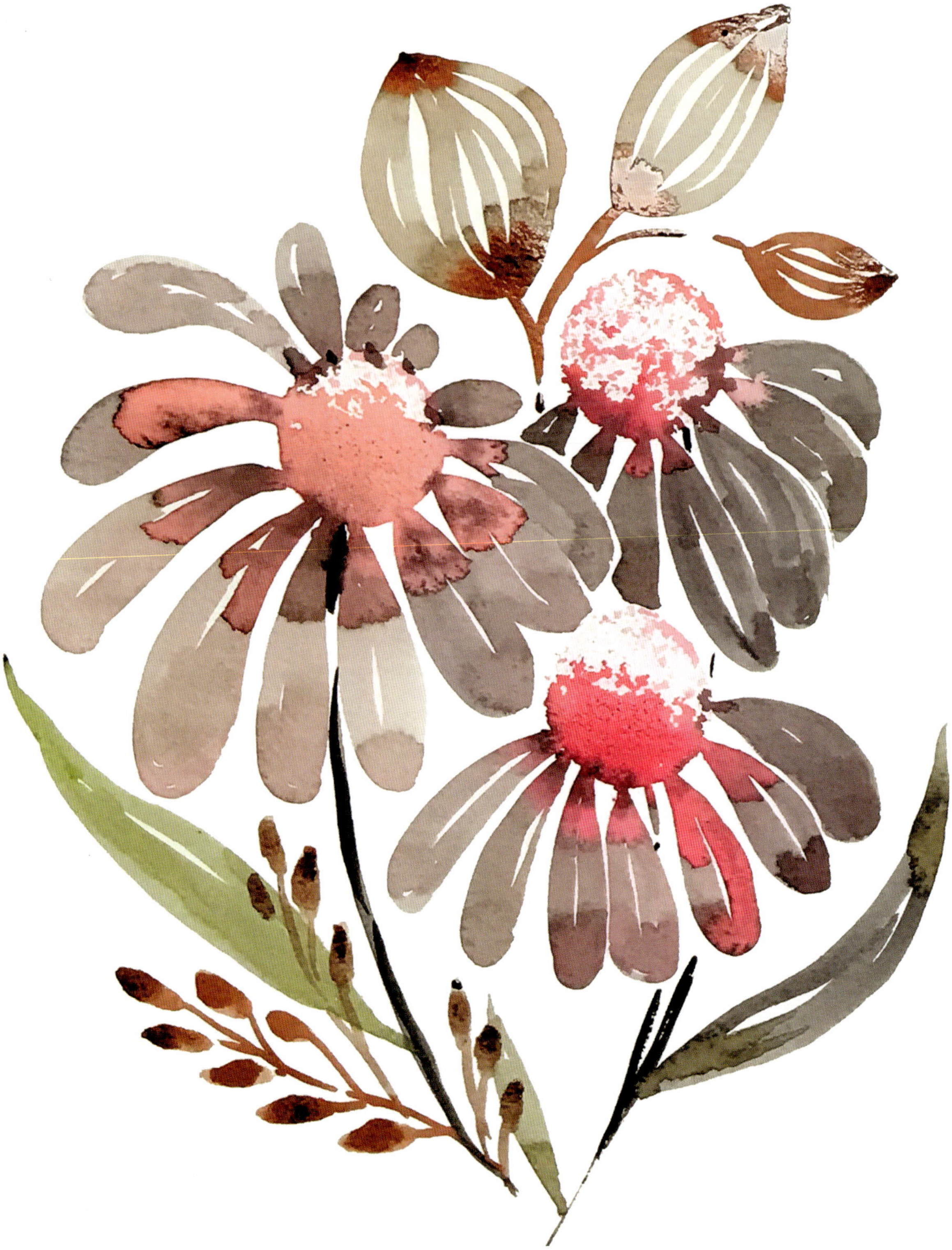

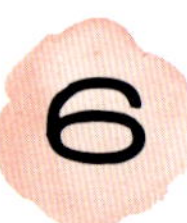

With a darker shade of a neutral already in your piece, add some smaller buds for a final touch.

Varying sizes and shapes creates an interesting floral composition.

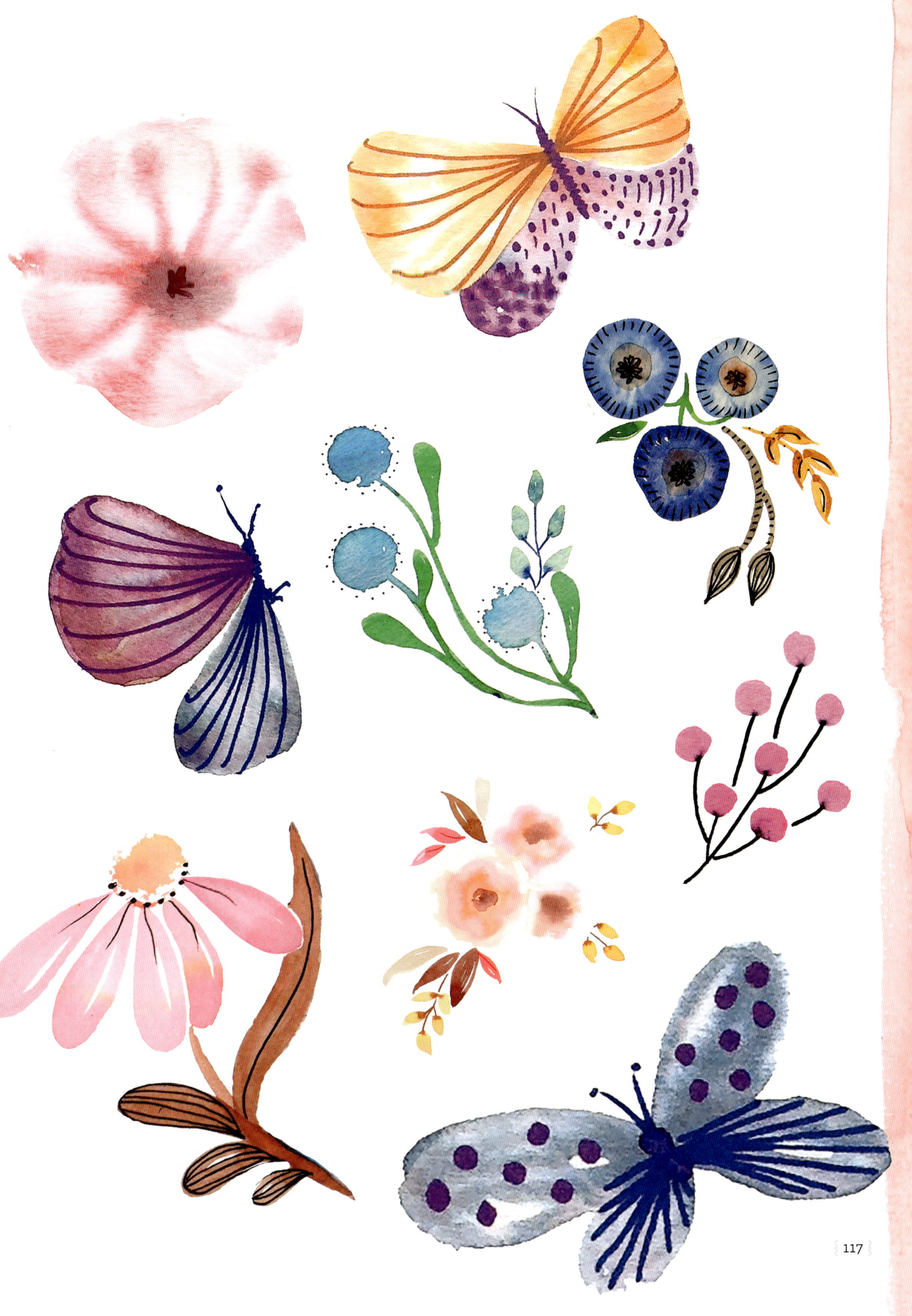

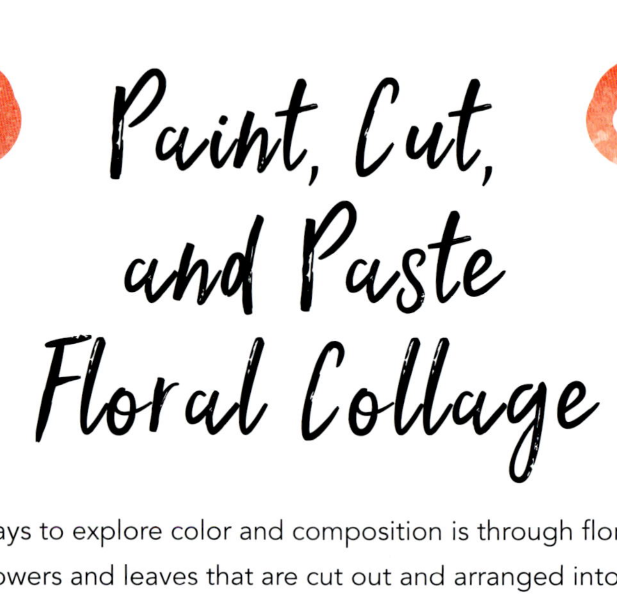

Paint, Cut, and Paste Floral Collage

One of my favorite ways to explore color and composition is through floral collage. This uses individually painted flowers and leaves that are cut out and arranged into a pleasing bouquet. I find successfully composing a piece easier when I can move the elements around on paper before committing to a final version. Being able to move things around and add or subtract from my composition is also great in case I make a mistake. That way, I haven't ruined the whole picture!

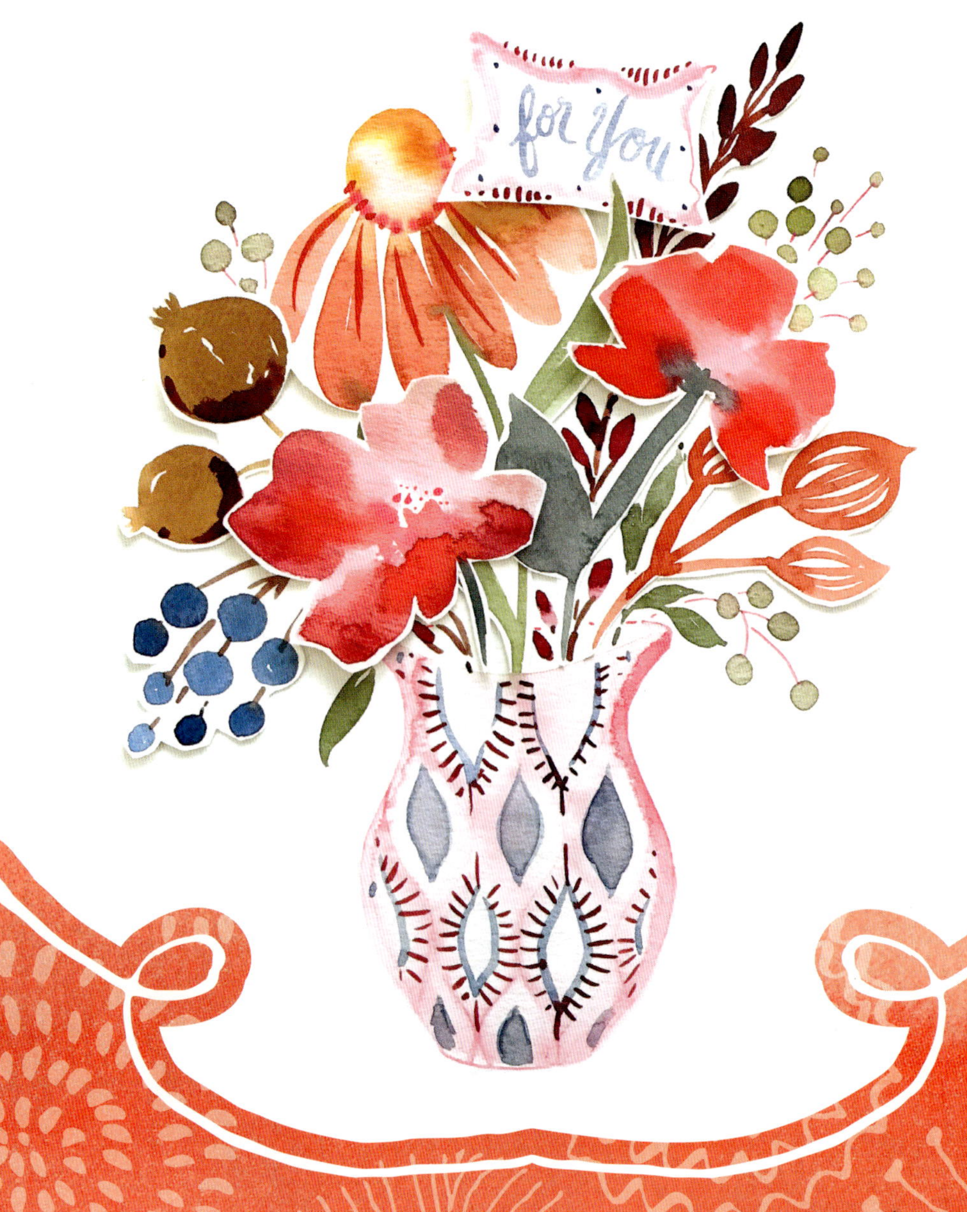

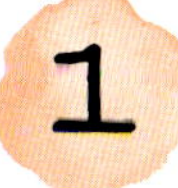

First, create a vase on a sheet of watercolor paper. A paint pen is a good tool, or use your brush like a pen to outline and add details to the vase. Let this dry.

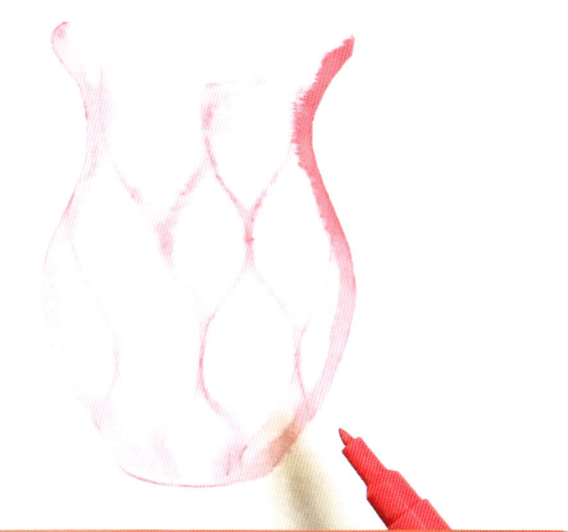

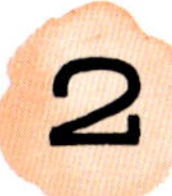

On a separate piece of paper, paint the flowers that will compose your bouquet. Coneflowers have an arching, droopy quality that looks pretty in a bouquet. Start by painting a wet wash for the seed head.

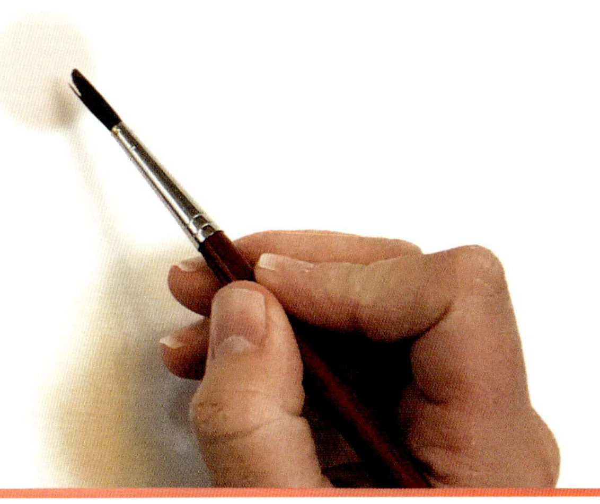

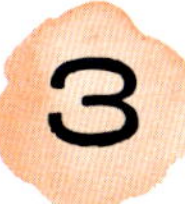

Then drop color into the center.

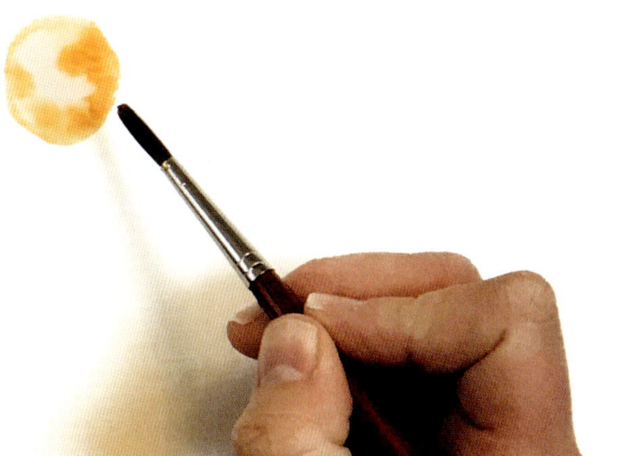

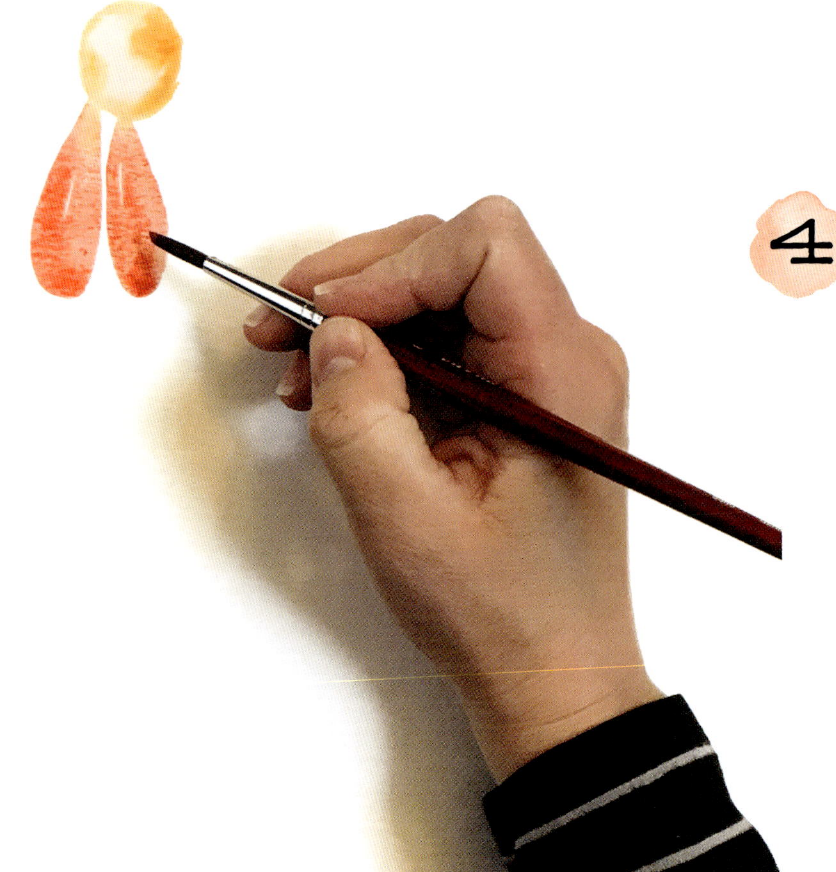

4 Using another color, paint petals around the bottom half of the seed head; this will create a flower shape as seen from the side.

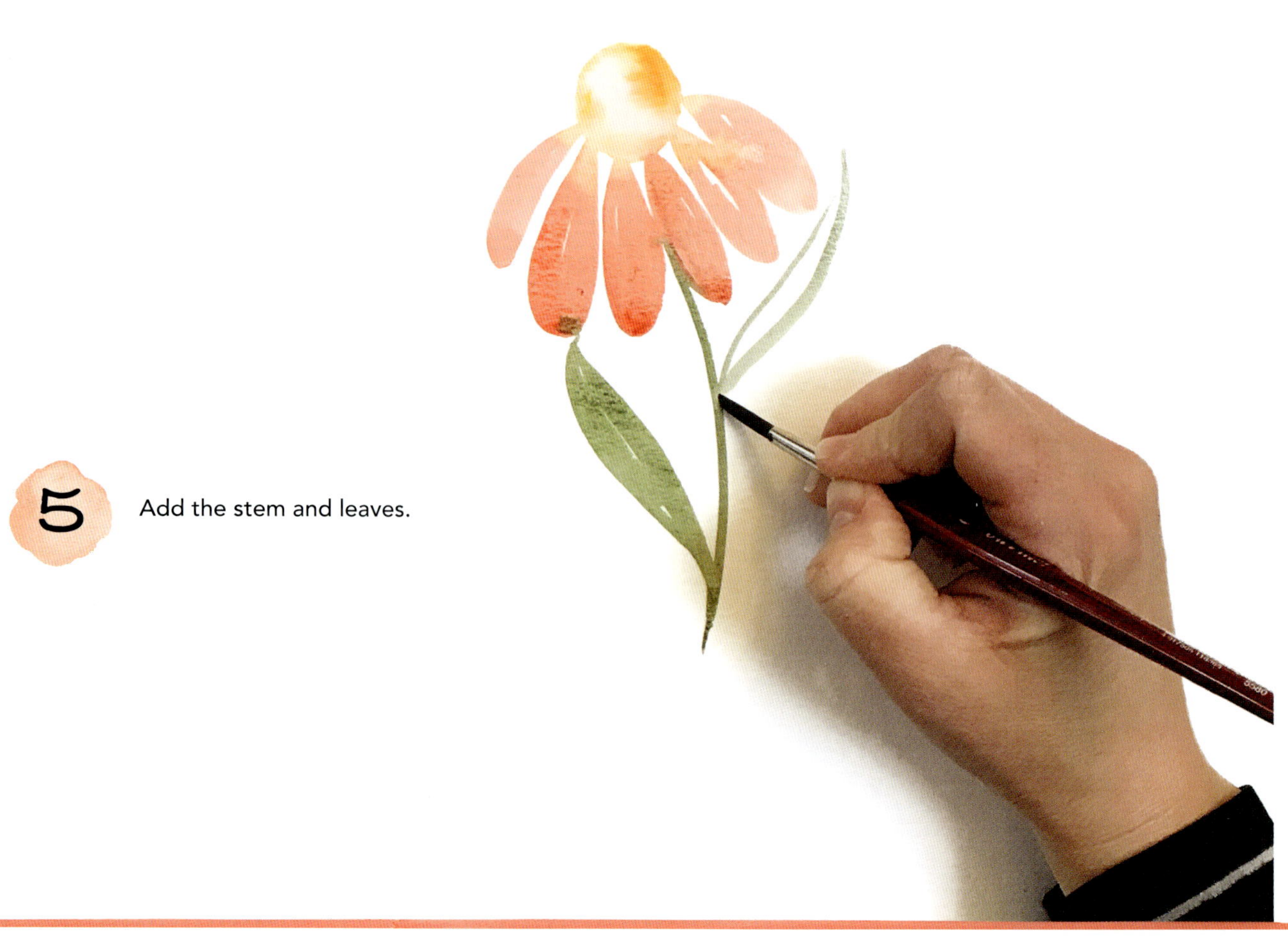

5 Add the stem and leaves.

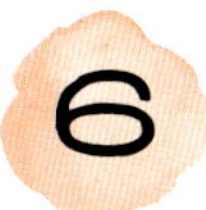

Fill the sheet of paper with various flowers. See "A Library of Flowers" on pages 30-41 for inspiration, and include different blooms, leaves, and buds.

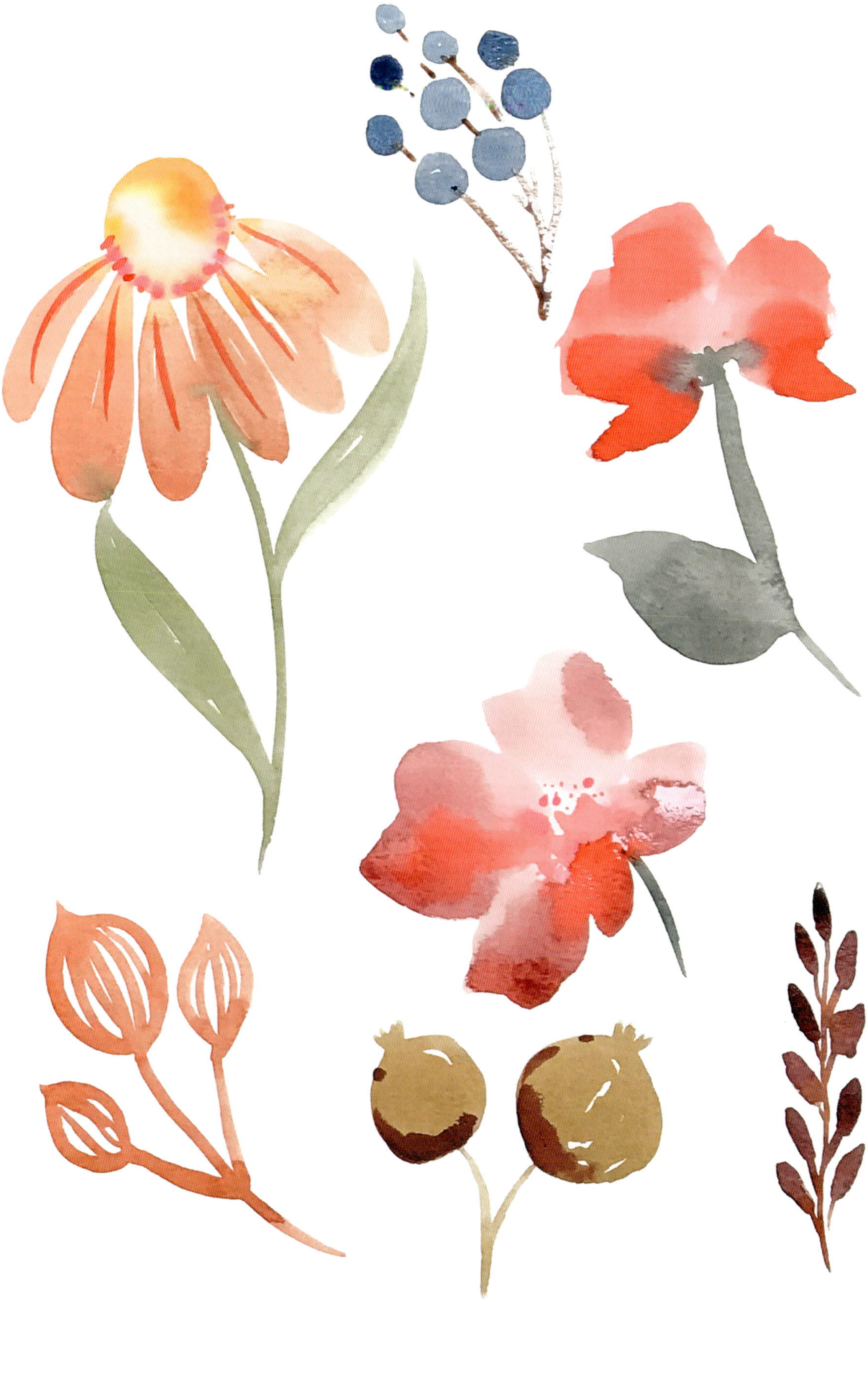

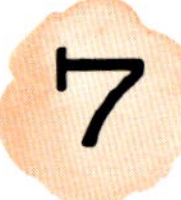

7

Return to the vase. With a contrast color, add a few more details to give it some additional interest.

Then cut out your flower shapes, and begin to "fill" the vase with your bouquet. Move your pieces around until you find an arrangement you like.

Carefully glue the flowers onto the sheet of paper. Leave some of the edges hanging off the paper to give your collage a three-dimensional look, and make sure to overlap the flowers.

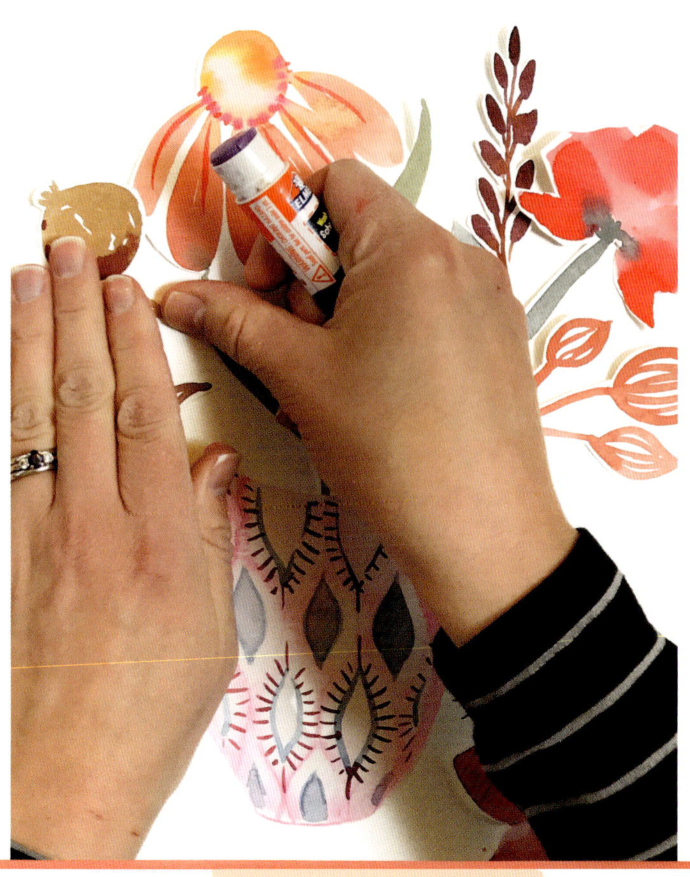

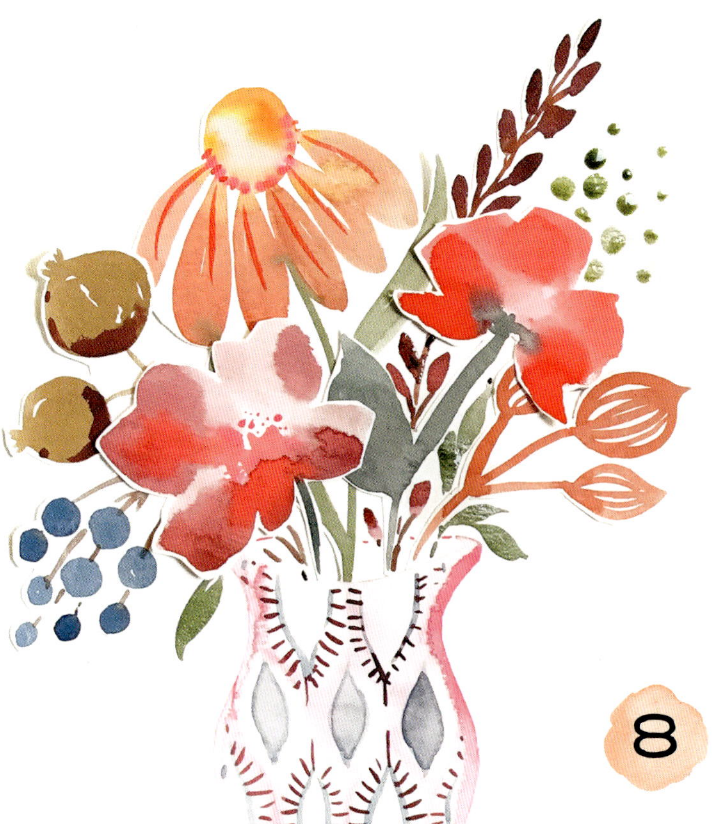

Layering pieces will add depth and realism to your collage.

8

Use a small brush to add the finishing touches: sprays of fowers to fill in any white areas and a few extra buds to introduce a pop of color.

9 Here is the finished floral collage. I painted a little gift tag to go with the vase and added it to my final painting. To go the extra mile, you could even mat and frame your piece and tie it up with a pretty bow!

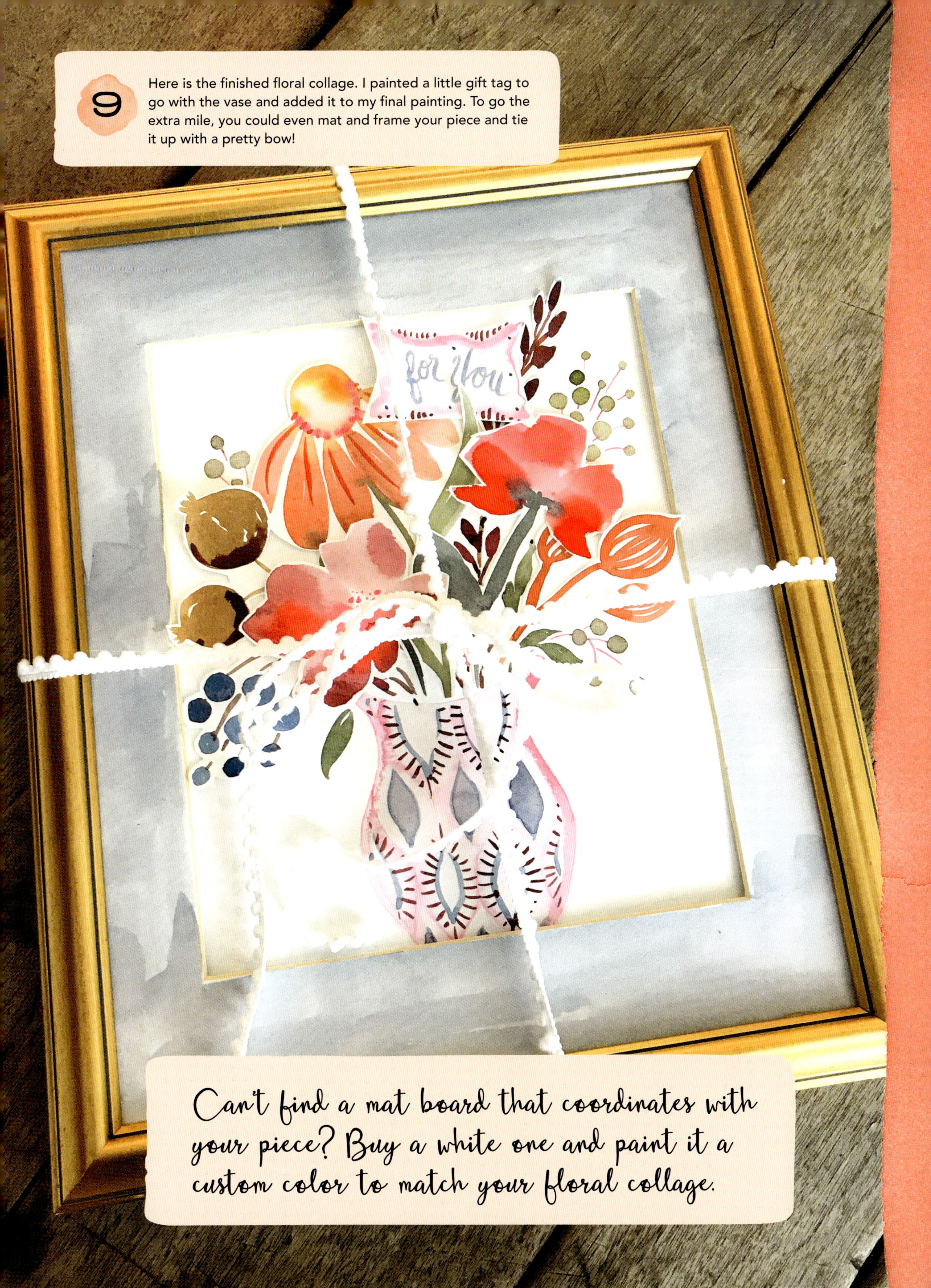

Can't find a mat board that coordinates with your piece? Buy a white one and paint it a custom color to match your floral collage.

Collage Concepts

Check out these floral collages for even more ideas and inspiration!

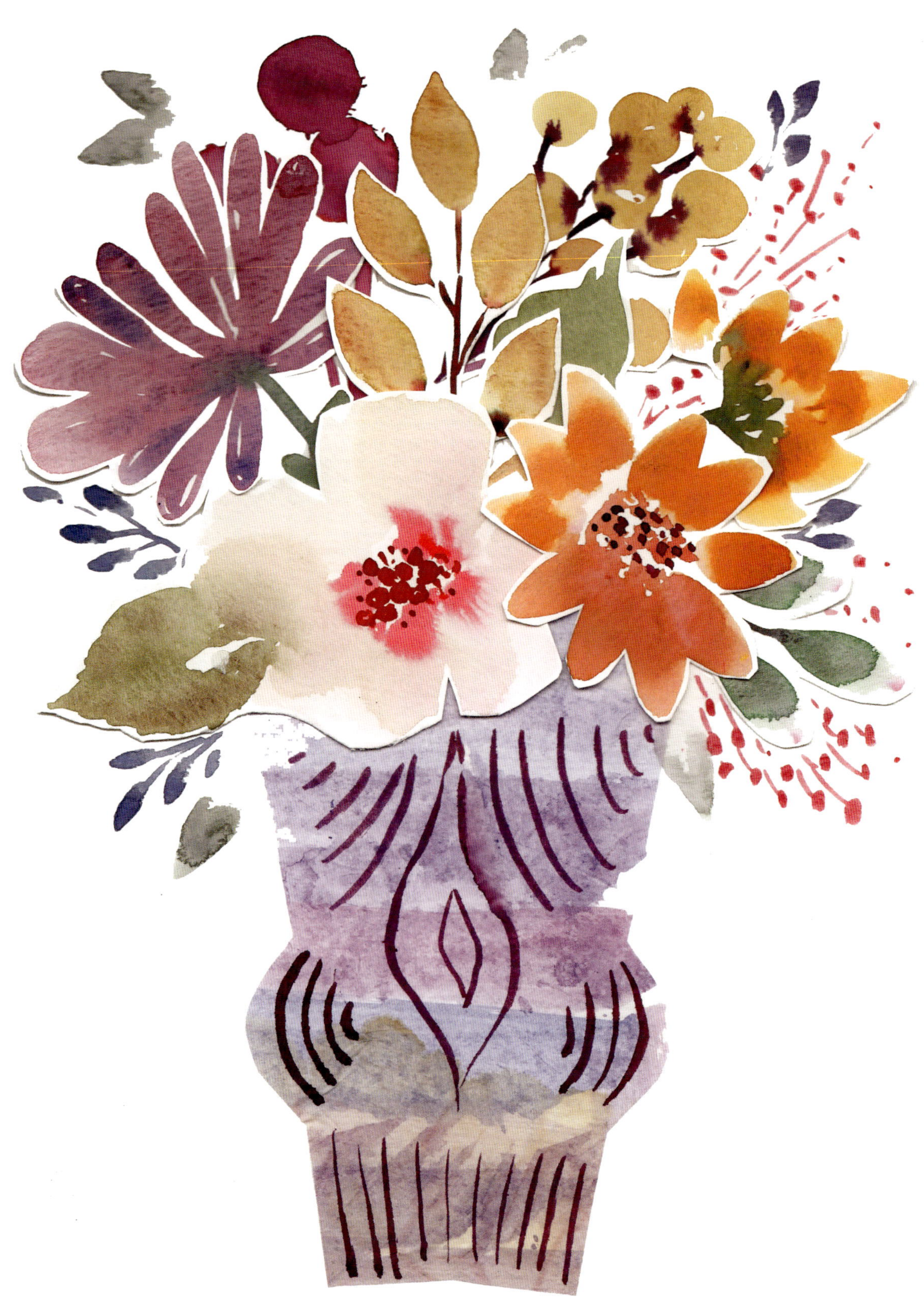

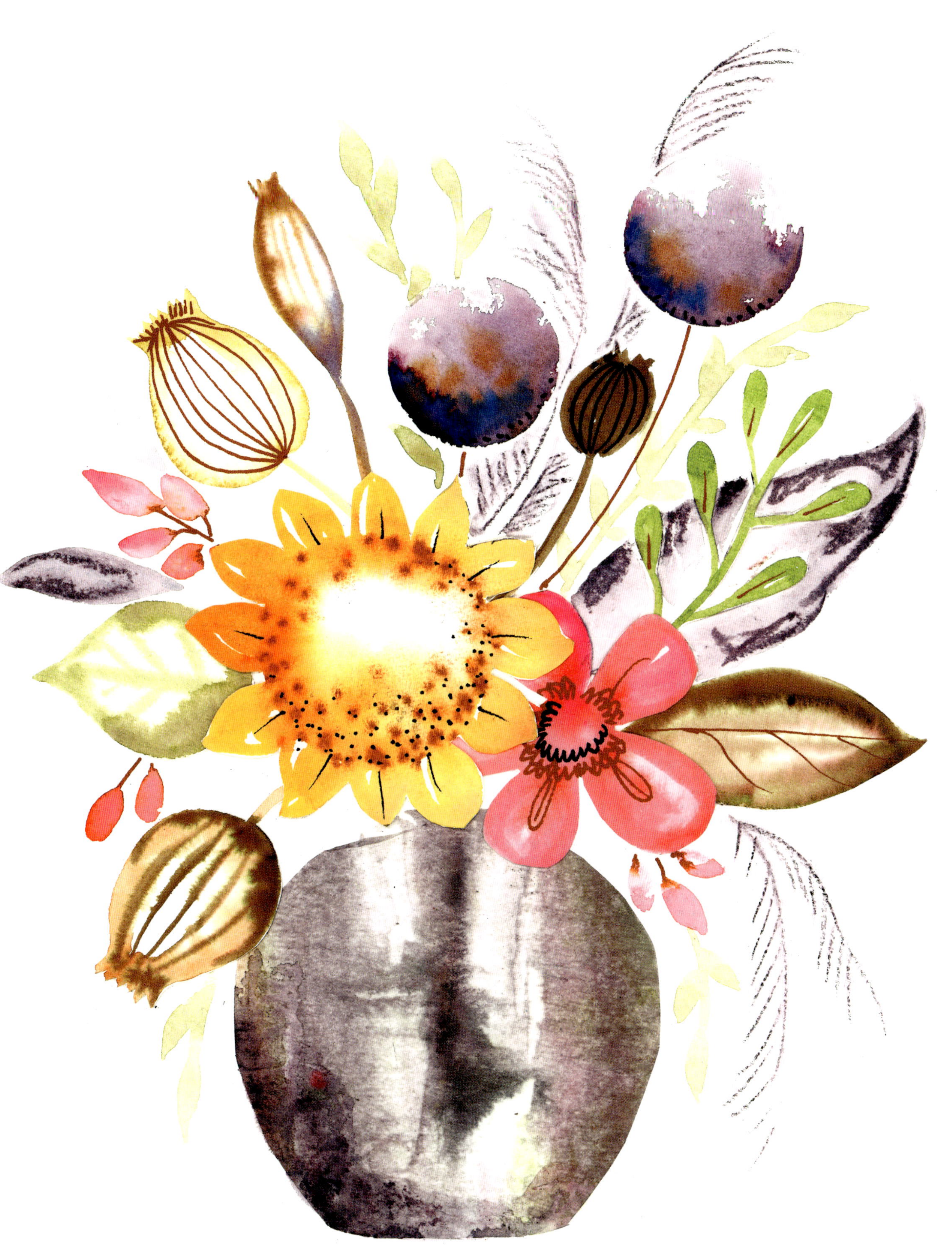

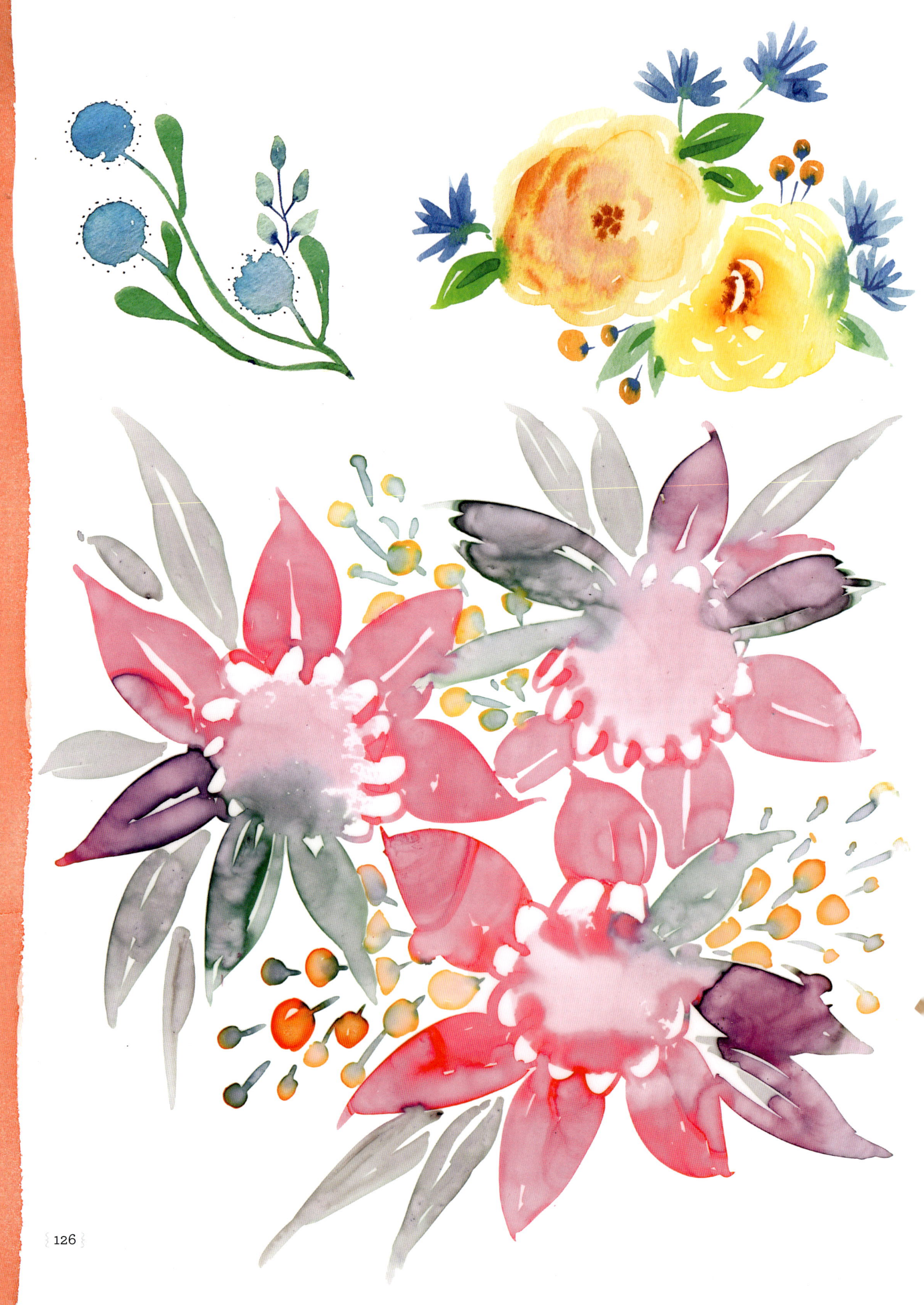

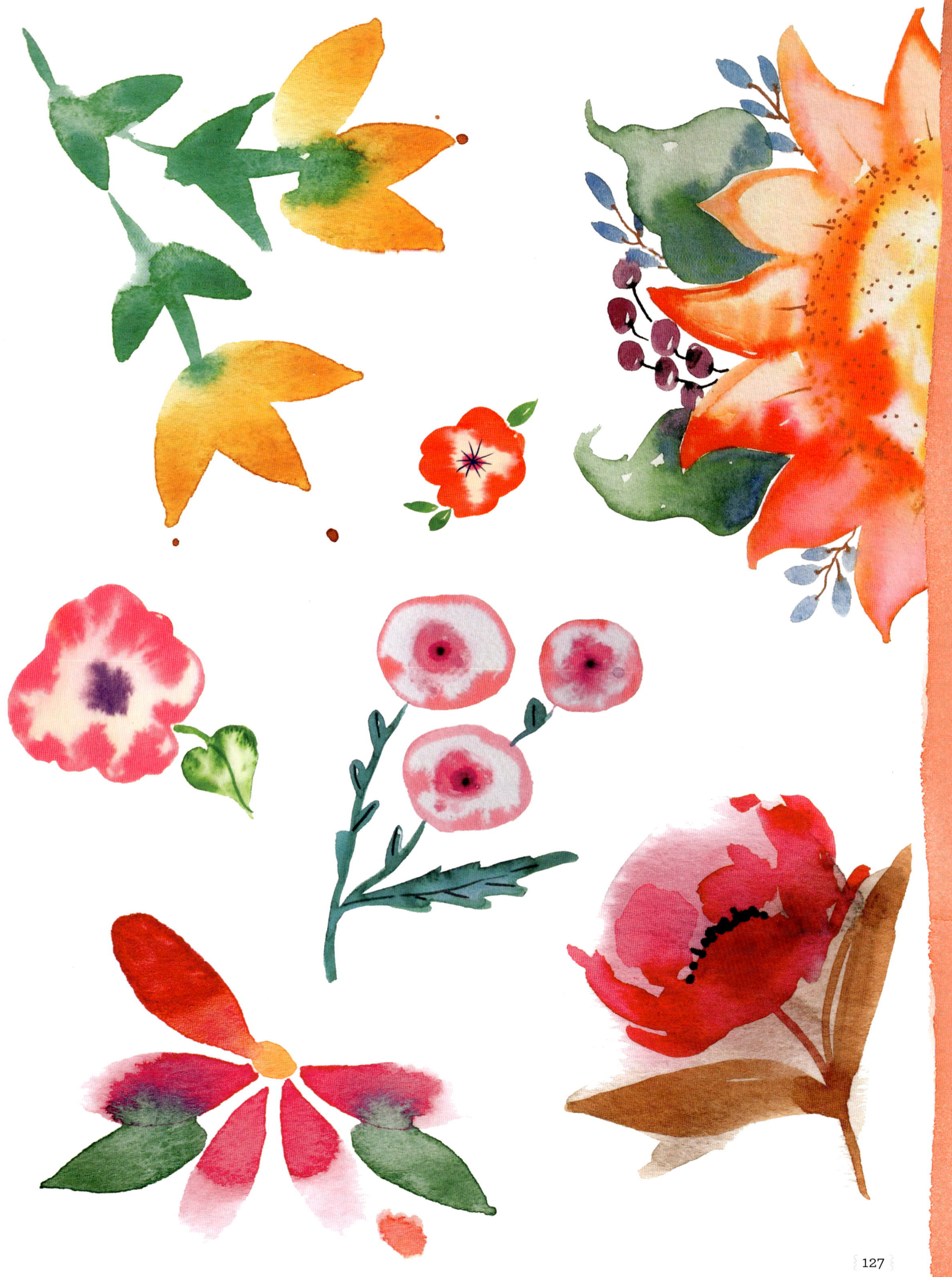

About the Artist

Bley Hack is a watercolor artist living on a farm in Ohio with her husband and their five children. Her paintings, designs, and surface patterns are inspired by the fresh florals and vintage charm she spies in daily life. Bley sells and licenses her work for products in retail markets. Learn more at estherbley.com.

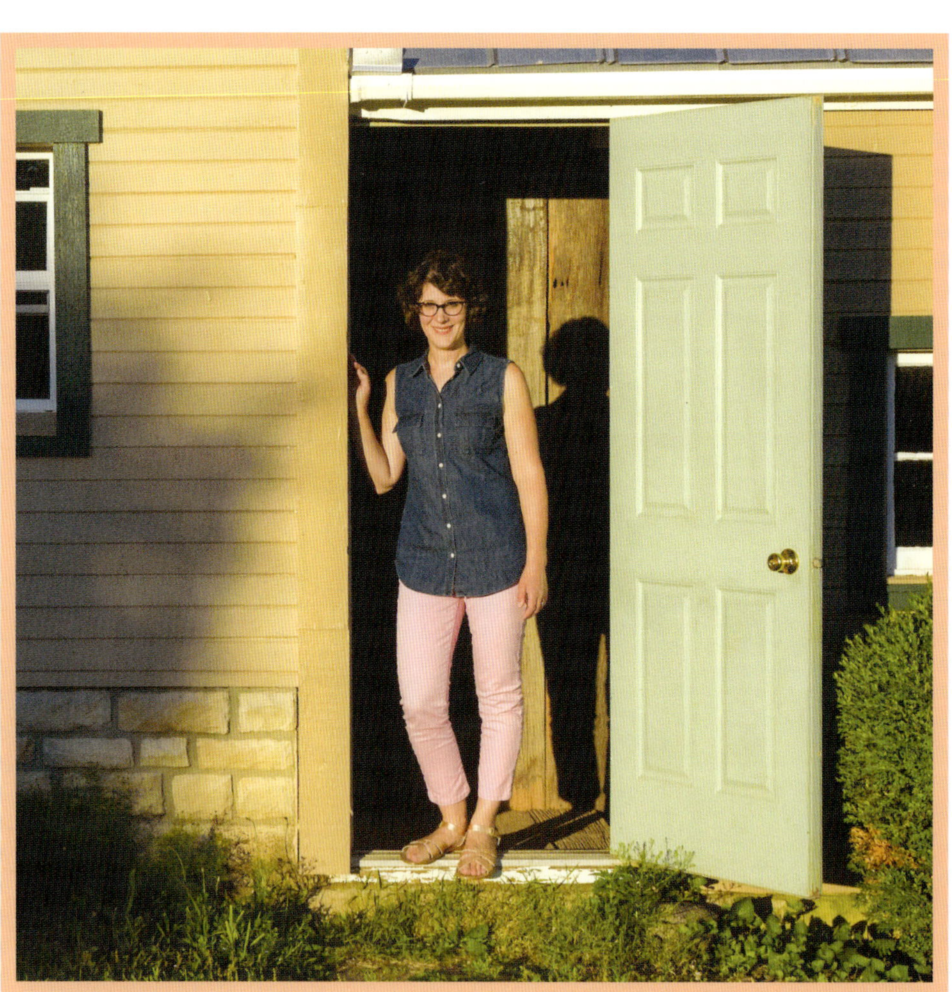